T0305113

Income, Inequality
and the Life Cycle

Income, Inequality and the Life Cycle

John Creedy
The Truby Williams Professor of Economics,
The University of Melbourne

Edward Elgar

Published by
Edward Elgar Publishing Limited
The Lypiatts
15 Lansdown Road
Cheltenham
Glos GL50 2JA
UK

Edward Elgar Publishing, Inc.
William Pratt House
9 Dewey Court
Northampton
Massachusetts 01060
USA

Reprinted 2015

A CIP catalogue record for this book is available from the British Library

Library of Congress Cataloguing-in-Publication Data
Creedy, John, 1949–
    Income, inequality, and the life cycle/by John Creedy.
        p. cm.
    Includes bibliographical references and index.
    1. Income distribution—Econometric models. 2. Income tax—
Econometric models. 3. Scientists—Salaries, etc.—Econometric
models. I. Title.
    HB523.C735 1992
    339.2—dc20   91–48334
                                                                            CIP

ISBN 978 1 85278 609 0

Printed and bound in Great Britain by T.J. International Ltd, Padstow

Contents

PART IV TAXATION

Figures

Tables

Preface

This book brings together a variety of analyses concerned with earnings and their distribution. The major unifying feature is the emphasis on the treatment of earnings in a life-cycle framework, rather than concentrating on a single period. The book may be described as a sequel to my earlier *Dynamics of Income Distribution* (1985) which was concerned largely with the development of statistical models for the analysis of earnings changes over the life cycle, and associated aggregation problems. The present book concentrates on applications in a variety of economic contexts.

Some of the material has been published in journal article form, but it has all been extensively revised for present purposes. I am grateful to the following journals for permission to use this work: *Economic Record*, *International Journal of Manpower*, *Journal of Economic Studies*, *Journal of Econometrics*, *Journal of Industrial Relations*, *Journal of Public Economics*, *Journal of the Royal Statistical Society*, *Manchester School* and *Metroeconomica*. I should again like to thank the anonymous referees whose suggestions were very helpful.

I should also like to thank several joint authors whose collaboration has been important. The work on Chapter 8 was carried out with Keith Whitfield; Chapter 9 is based on work with Margaret Morgan; and Chapter 14 was carried out with Patrick Francois. The heavy task of typing and retyping the many revisions has been carried out with considerable skill by Margaret Lochran, Sally Nolan, Julie Carter and Lynne Ki; their contribution is greatly appreciated.

Introduction

This book examines a variety of topics within the general subject area of personal earnings and their distribution. The major unifying feature is the emphasis on the treatment of earnings in a life-cycle framework, but the chapters divide naturally into four Parts. These are 'Lifetime Earnings', 'Earnings of Scientists', 'Demographic Effects' and 'Taxation'. This introduction provides a brief outline of the chapters.

Chapter 1, 'Lifetime Earnings and Inequality', reviews some of the difficulties and approaches used to extend the time period in measuring inequality. Despite the considerable interest in properties of inequality measures, problems of extending the time period have been relatively neglected. Many single-period comparisons are made when a longer period is really appropriate. A serious problem is that appropriate data are still scarce and in many contexts, for example where *ex ante* measures are relevant, would not even be observable.

It is seen that, using simple models of earnings dynamics, a limited number of explicit results have been obtained. These concern the coefficient of variation of the present value of earnings. However, it is suggested that simulations are particularly useful when evaluating the lifetime effects of alternative policies, such as tax and transfer scheme. Despite the association between mobility and the effects of extending the accounting period, several attempts have been made to examine the inequality of lifetime earnings without using assumptions about mobility. These attempts, involving decompositions of inequality measures or models of consumption behaviour, are discussed. The use of a so-called 'comprehensive' income measure, involving the conversion of net worth into an annuity, are then examined. Such a measure ignores the expected future earnings of individuals, leading to the use of measures based on consumption models.

Chapter 2 is concerned with 'Measuring Wealth in Imperfect Capital Markets'. Conventional present values overstate the lifetime wealth of borrowers if the lending rate is used and understate it if the borrowing rate is used. More seriously, the appropriate measure of wealth depends on all the parameters of the individual's optimization problem. This chapter uses a simple two-period model in which lending and borrowing rates differ. It argues that a nihilistic view of the possibility of measuring inequality using a longer time perspective would not be appropriate. The construction of any longer-term measure must inevitably involve the use of many assumptions that can only be regarded as useful descriptive approximations; the use of a single interest rate must be seen as a similar assumption whose limitations should be recognized.

Chapter 3 considers 'Earnings Comparisons between Generations', continuing the theme of the need to use longer-period measures of earnings. It examines alternative procedures for estimating the extent of 'regression towards the mean' in the earnings of fathers and sons. It is shown that a simple life-cycle adjustment of earnings based on an age profile of average log-earnings is not sufficient, because of the variation in ages and the fact that the dispersion varies with age. The use of standardized earnings is recommended. When sufficient information is available about earnings profiles for occupational groups, the use of earnings adjusted to a common age, and a measure of lifetime earnings, are also explored. Although information about earnings of fathers and sons during only a single period of the life cycle are usually available, the preferred estimate of the extent of mobility between generations is based on a measure of lifetime earnings, allowing for occupational differences in age-earnings profiles and adjusting for productivity growth over time. A second alternative involves the use of standardized earnings. If no information is available about the occupations of individuals, then at least it is useful to allow for the variation in the dispersion of earnings with age.

Chapter 4 estimates 'Lifetime Earnings of Men in Australia' using indirect evidence of the process of relative earnings mobility from cross-sectional data. Measures of the coefficient of variation of earnings over alternative accounting periods, and the extent to which the dispersion of earnings varies as the number of years is extended are obtained, and occupational comparisons are reported.

Chapter 5, 'Earnings Profiles and Compensation', explores the use of information about age-earnings profiles in the calculation of compensation to dependants of accident victims. The standard approach assumes a constant income stream, but the assumption is made in this chapter that relative (standardized) earnings remain constant. The proposed method would benefit the dependants of younger victims in occupations with steeply rising earnings profiles. However, the use of earnings profiles does not necessarily provide higher awards, particularly for dependants of older victims. The chapter also allows for interest income taxation using an iterative search procedure; this is necessary because no convenient analytical solution can be found for multi-rate tax structures. Adoption of the approach forces the user to be explicit, and therefore more consistent, about the various assumptions used in calculating awards.

Chapter 6 estimates 'Cohort and Cross-Sectional Earnings Profiles' for British and Australian scientists that allow for the rate of growth of earnings with experience to differ among cohorts (defined by the year of entry into the labour market). Earnings growth is assumed to be determined by quadratic 'experience' and 'time' effects. The model implies cross-sectional earnings profiles which have the same shape but shift their position over time, while cohort profiles can have different rates of earnings growth. It is found that for male scientists in Britain and Australia, more recent entrants into the labour market have experienced a slightly less rapid growth in earnings with experience. However, female scientists showed somewhat less conclusive results. The approach has the advantage that the nature of the specification can be examined more closely than is usual in the estimation of earnings equations.

Although pay is often thought to be related to responsibility, the problem of measuring responsibility has received relatively little attention in the economics literature. Chapter 7 examines 'Variations in Earnings and Responsibility' over the working lives of scientists, using a cardinal measure of responsibility devised and used by the Royal Society of Chemistry in Britain. The measure is based on the degree of autonomy that individuals have in carrying out their job duties. Variations in responsibility are then integrated into a life-cycle earnings model.

Chapter 8 is on the 'Earnings and Job Mobility' of professional scientists in Britain and Australia. The emphasis is on job mobility processes which involve movements within the same firm, and the analysis examines changes in job duties which take place within what is regarded by individuals as being the same 'job'. The association between earnings changes and the mobility process is also examined, both in the short run and over a longer period. The analysis was based on special job-history surveys carried out by the author and Keith Whitfield.

Chapter 9 considers the problem of 'Financing Pensions in an Ageing Population' using a wide range of policy options. Two types of scheme are examined: the first is similar in many respects to the Australian state pension and has a means-tested pension financed using only income taxation; the second scheme has an unconditional pension combined with a general consumption tax and national insurance contributions, in addition to an income tax. The second scheme is similar to the basic pension (the 'first tier') in the UK. In recent debates on pension finance, much emphasis has been placed on ageing populations. If the aim of a state pension policy is seen to be the transfer from the working population of a specified real amount to every retired person, then it is obvious that increased dependency will raise problems. However, the purpose of a state pension scheme is usually to ensure a basic minimum standard of living for pensioners. When pensions are taxable and when it is recognized that higher dependency ratios have been associated with higher average taxable incomes (from other sources) of pensioners, then the problems are no longer so severe. The relatively poorer pensioners are supported by transfers not only from the working population but also from the relatively richer pensioners. Although the schemes examined abstract from many complexities, an advantage of the approach is that it allows computations of a vast range of alternative policies to be carried out.

Chapter 10 considers in detail the process of obtaining 'Aggregate Consumption in a Life-Cycle Model' of consumption in which the utility function is expressed in terms of consumption per equivalent person. The model abstracts from problems of uncertainty about both the length of life of the household and the income stream, and does not include a bequest motive for saving, in order to concentrate on aggregation problems. The awkward process of aggregation has been neglected in work on the life-cycle hypothesis. This chapter shows how the ratio of aggregate consumption to aggregate income depends on the demographic characteristics of the population, in particular the profiles of the changing distribution of household size and income with age. In view of the skewness of the distributions involved, the average values of consumption and income over all households and age groups depend on the relative dispersion of those distributions. The results are useful for the examination of changes in consumption to income ratios over time, and for comparisons among countries.

Chapter 11 is concerned with 'Individual Choice and the Tax Structure'. It provides an analysis, based on Buchanan (1967), of the role of income tax progression as a mechanism for achieving intertemporal adjustments of earnings profiles. The individual preference for progression arises essentially from the existence of imperfect capital markets, whereby the government borrowing rate of interest is less than the rate that must be paid by individual borrowers, coupled with a rising income profile. For a given tax burden it is seen that each individual prefers maximum progression, with a unit marginal rate of tax and the threshold set as high as consistent with the tax obligation being met. Where each individual has to face a common tax structure, all individuals prefer some degree of income tax progression only so long as the first period income of the relatively richer person does not exceed that of the poorer, and the two lifetime incomes are sufficiently close. In this situation the richer individual is prepared to accept a slightly higher tax obligation in view of the intertemporal efficiency gains. However, in practice the difference between lifetime earnings of individuals would typically be too large for the trade-off to be viable so there is little scope for Pareto-efficient redistribution on the grounds of intertemporal allocation.

If income is independent of tax rates, the standard single-period indifference curve analysis shows that an individual will prefer to meet a specified tax liability with an income tax, or general consumption tax, rather than a specific tax on one of the goods. Buchanan and Forte (1964) have argued that this result must be modified in a multiperiod framework in which the tax liability is specified in present value terms, using the government's borrowing rate of interest, and there are capital market imperfections. A crucial feature of their analysis is the division of consumption into the two categories of 'basic needs' and 'residual needs'. They suggest that if basic needs differ between periods by more than income, the individual may prefer a specific tax levied on an item or set of items of residual needs. Chapter 11 also examines this proposition in detail.

Chapter 12 considers 'Revenue and Inequality Neutral Changes in the Tax Mix'. It examines the complex interaction among income taxation, a system of transfer payments and a general consumption tax where specified exemptions are used in order to make the tax progressive. It is found that, despite the systematic negative relationship between expenditure on exempt categories and total expenditure, there is little role for exemptions other than food. Changes in the tax mix are examined, with appropriate allowance being made for the effect of the consumption tax on the real value of transfer payments. It is found that a tax shift involving a cut in top income tax rates is regressive in its overall effect, however many exemptions exist. More comprehensive changes in the income tax structure, which lower rates and reduce the progressivity of income tax considered on its own, can be combined with a shift towards a consumption tax in order to achieve both revenue and progressivity neutrality.

Chapter 13 is concerned with 'Changing the Tax Mix and Unions' Wage Demands'. A shift fom direct to indirect taxation is achieved by eliminating the top marginal rate of income tax and simultaneously raising the consumption tax rate in order to leave total tax revenue unchanged. Unions are considered to maximize an objective function involving the real after-tax wage and the level of employment of members. The policy is expected to lead to an increase in the wage demands of all unions, thereby producing a once-and-for-all increase in nominal wages and unemployment. The intuition behind this result is as follows. The workers who were initially not paying the top marginal rate of income tax experience an increase in their average tax rate through the increase in the consumption tax, and therefore increase their wage demands. Those initially paying the high marginal tax rate experience a reduction in their overall effective marginal tax rate which, other things remaining unchanged, would raise wage demands by making wage increases relatively more attractive than employment increases, in terms of the union's objective function. This tendency is found to dominate the wage-reducing effect of the decrease in the average tax rate facing that group.

Chapter 14 examines the problem of 'Financing Higher Education and Majority Voting'. It considers the circumstances in which the majority of individuals in a cohort are prepared to subsidize a proportion of the costs of higher education through the income tax system. The median voter is assumed to choose the proportion of costs, to be financed through taxes and given in the form of a grant, in order to maximize the present value of net lifetime income. A two-period model is used in which investment in education not only leads to private returns, but also increases the rate of growth of all incomes through productivity increases. This public good effect increased the incomes of those without higher education, which has to be set against the extra taxation required. The implications of alternative assumptions are examined using numerical methods. It is suggested that a public choice approach is useful for the analysis of this kind of issue, and that the basic framework of analysis offers much potential for further development.

PART I

Lifetime Earnings

1. Lifetime Earnings and Inequality

A basic argument of this book is that measures of inequality that are based on observed incomes during a single year can be highly misleading. This argument applies to measures using cross-sectional data that include many age groups, and to measures based on a single year of a particular cohort. One society may experience a considerable amount of relative earnings mobility and may consequently have a lower degree of lifetime inequality (however measured) than another society; but a comparison based only on annual incomes could give the opposite impression. Only if all individuals' earnings remain constant from period to period will a measure of inequality give the same result irrespective of the length of the accounting period.

The need to consider a longer accounting period is particularly important when attempting to assess the redistributive effects of tax and transfer systems, especially when they contain elements of social insurance. The redistributive implications of unemployment or sickness benefits, or pensions, cannot be estimated in any meaningful way when the relevant flows are measured in a single year. This argument does not imply that *eligibility* for certain transfer payments should be based on a longer period measure of income, simply that redistribution involved does not take the form of only a current transfer between individuals but also involves a shifting of income between stages of the life cycle.

It still remains true that the majority of inequality comparisons are based on annual data, and a major reason for this limitation is the scarcity of appropriate longitudinal data. Nevertheless, a variety of attempts have been made to overcome this problem by constructing estimates based on more limited information. This chapter surveys the disparate literature and assesses the alternative approaches. It seems useful to begin by raising some basic problems that would remain even if extensive data were available.

3

Some Basic Problems

A first difficulty is that when the accounting period increases the
unit of analysis can also change through events such as household
formation, births and deaths; consequently the question of whose
income is relevant becomes rather complex; see Cowell (1984).
Furthermore, the use of intra-family income transfers introduces
features relevant to the inter-generational transmission of inequality. However, the following discussion abstracts from such
complications by assuming that the relevant unit is always a single
individual. Earnings comparisons between generations are
examined in Chapter 3. This chapter also abstracts from the
problems of dealing with household production and the valuation
of leisure.

Reference has already been made to data limitations, but the
problem is not simply that such data are expensive and time
consuming to collect; indeed the costs would be quite low compared with data collection in the natural sciences. A more basic
problem is that the concepts are often not even measurable in
principle. When it is argued that economic well-being depends in
some way on, for example, expected future income, or a planned
consumption stream, or some constant consumption stream that
gives the same utility as the actual stream, these *ex ante* concepts
cannot be observed.

It is also necessary to raise the fundamental problem of endo-
geneity. If an individual's income and its time stream are regarded
as resulting from a complex optimization problem, then it may be
argued that concern should not be with the *outcomes* but with the
processes involved. If this view is accepted, inequality cannot be
assessed using any measure of income or consumption, but
requires an investigation into the nature of the constraints imposed
on individuals through, for example, various types of discrimination or barriers to entry. While this argument must be accepted at
a general level, many investigators are nevertheless prepared to
take a more pragmatic view that the outcome, seen in terms of
some estimated distribution, is still relevant.

Finally, it is worth acknowledging that the search for an all-
purpose measure of economic welfare is perhaps chimerical. The
ultimate purpose of the analysis should always be made clear; it
cannot be taken as self-evident that a particular longer-term

measure is appropriate. Indeed, the choice of measure will itself involve a value judgement – a point that is too easily forgotten.

Outline of the Chapter

Section 1.1 discusses a number of descriptive studies which used limited longitudinal data for several years. The majority of these studies did not consider relative earnings mobility explicitly, but this was a serious limitation. Section 1.2 shows how attempts have been made to estimate the dispersion of the present value of lifetime earnings. While it has sometimes been argued that lifetime earnings will display less inequality than annual earnings, this type of statement is much too vague when the inequality of annual earnings itself varies over the life cycle. The approach taken by studies considered in section 1.2 has generally been to use fairly simple models of the process of earnings change over life, which can be estimated using limited available data. The models were used either to generate explicit solutions for a measure of inequality of the present value of lifetime earnings, or to simulate earnings profiles so that alternative measures of the resulting distributions could be compared.

Section 1.3 considers studies that have taken quite a different type of approach. The analyses discussed in this section explicitly avoid having to specify the process of earnings change, either by manipulating particular inequality measures, or by using extremely strong assumptions about consumption behaviour in order to derive indirect estimates of the dispersion of lifetime earnings.

The approaches considered so far convert the longer-period income stream into a present value. While this may seem to be a natural procedure, other investigators have attempted to convert the stock of non-human wealth into a flow measure so that it can be added to current income. This type of approach is examined in section 1.4. Section 1.5 goes on to consider the use of a flow measure of consumption rather than income, based on a model of life-cycle consumption. A major assumption made in the compilation and use of the types of long period measure of earnings discussed in this chapter is that all individuals can borrow and lend at a fixed rate of interest. Discussion of problems that arise when capital markets are imperfect is deferred until Chapter 2.

1.1 EARNINGS OVER SEVERAL YEARS

Basic Descriptions

As limited longitudinal data became available, covering incomes over two or three consecutive years, the effect of increasing the accounting period could easily be assessed. In the United States, early studies include Hanna (1948), Kuznets (1950) and Kravis (1962), and such descriptive exercises have often been repeated. While mentioning the use of a longer period for tax purposes, early studies also seemed to be moving towards a life-cycle consumption approach. It will be seen in later sections of this chapter that, following the extensive development of life-cycle and permanent income models of consumption behaviour, the later 'more comprehensive' measures of economic well-being relied explicitly on those models for their rationale.

In most cases the use of a longer accounting period was found to decrease substantially the measure of inequality used. Indeed the inequality (however measured) of two- and three-year distributions was found generally to be lower than in any of the component years taken separately. This type of finding prompted the Royal Commission on the Distribution of Income and Wealth (1975, p. 147) to suggest that it would also apply to complete life cycles. A second descriptive finding was that the proportionate reduction in the inequality measure decreased as the accounting period was extended. This led several authors, such as Hanna (1948, p. 214), Vandome (1958, p. 88) and Benus and Morgan (1974, p. 216), to suggest that the effect of lengthening the time period would become negligible after only a few years, so that the measure of inequality would become stable. This would be very convenient since it implies that relatively little information would be necessary to calculate inequality over periods as long as, say, the working life.

It is here that the limitations of the purely descriptive studies become apparent, since these issues require for their resolution an explicit model of the mobility process generating the earnings changes. Among the early descriptive studies, only that by Vandome (1958) can really be said to have examined the mobility process explicitly. He used the basic Markov model in a transition matrix framework, and compared the resulting equilibrium distribution with that of income in a single year. However, like many of the early studies, data were provided for all age groups combined rather than for separate cohorts. In the present context it is really necessary to distinguish cohorts. It is also argued that the concept of the equilibrium distribution is not appropriate here since the time period is much too short; aggregate stability is best seen as generated by birth and death processes.

Simple Analytics

It is possible to consider the two points mentioned above, concerning the ultimate stability of a longer-term inequality measure and its value relative to that of all individual years, using a reasonably basic approach. This at least is true of the coefficient of variation. It has not been possible to derive similar types of result for other measures of inequality, although for a general discussion in the context of constant mean incomes, see Shorrocks (1978).

Define the coefficient of variation of income of a constant group of individuals in period t as $\eta_t = s_t/\bar{y}_t$, that is, the standard deviation divided by the arithmetic mean. If $Y_i = \sum_{t=1}^{T} y_{it}$ for the ith individual, then $E(Y) = \sum_t \bar{y}_t$. Where s_{jk} is the covariance of earnings in periods j and k, then

$$V(Y) = \sum_{t=1}^{T} s_t^2 + 2 \sum_{j=1}^{T-1} \sum_{k=j+1}^{T} s_{jk} \qquad (1.1)$$

The analysis of the dispersion of the sum of earnings thus requires full details of the values of the s_{jk}, which depend on the mobility process.

Consider, however, just two periods and denote the correlation coefficient between earnings in the two periods by $\varrho = s_{12}/s_1 s_2$, which is a reasonable measure of relative earnings mobility in this context. Denote the coefficient of variation of the longer-term measure by $\eta_{(T)}$, and define the weighted average, η^*, as:

$$\eta^{*2} = (\bar{y}_1 \eta_1^2 + \bar{y}_2 \eta_2^2)/(\bar{y}_1 + \bar{y}_2) \qquad (1.2)$$

Then substitution into (1.2), and rearrangement gives:

$$\eta_{(2)}^2 - \eta^{*2} = -\{(\eta_1 - \eta_2)^2 + 2\eta_1\eta_2(1 - \varrho)\}\bar{y}_1\bar{y}_2/(\bar{y}_1 + \bar{y}_2)^2 \quad (1.3)$$

It can be seen that every term in (1.3) is non-negative, so that $\eta_{(2)}^2$ is always less than or equal to the weighted average η^{*2}. Hence $\eta_{(2)}$ cannot exceed the highest value of η_1 and η_2 (depending on the ratios η_1/η_2, $\bar{y}_1/\bar{y}_2$ and ϱ). The longer-term measure is therefore not necessarily lower than in all single years. By extension, the above argument shows that the coefficient of variation of lifetime earnings cannot be greater than the largest value for any single year, but *may* be lower than in every single year. However, estimates show that it is generally somewhere between the highest and lowest annual values.

Further analysis requires explicit treatment of the s_{jk}. It has been shown by Fase (1971) that if earnings in each year follow a two-parameter lognormal distribution and if the process of relative earnings change is the simple Gibrat process (whereby proportionate changes are serially independent and do not depend on the absolute value of earnings), then covariances take a very convenient form. Indeed, for $k > j$ it is found that:

$$s_{jk} = E(y_jy_k) - \bar{y}_j\bar{y}_k \quad (1.4)$$

$$= \bar{y}_j\bar{y}_k\,\eta_j^2 \quad (1.5)$$

This shows that the relative dispersion of the long period measure depends not only on the process of earnings change and dispersion within each period, but also on the average earnings in each period. It is instructive to consider the special case where $\bar{y}_j = \bar{y}$, for all j; that is, the arithmetic mean is constant. The above results can be used to show that:

$$\eta_{(T)}^2 = 2\sum_{t=1}^{T}(T + \tfrac{1}{2} - t)\eta_t^2/T^2 \quad (1.6)$$

The question of convergence can then be answered directly from equation (1.6). It can be seen that $\eta_{(T)}^2$ is a weighted sum of separate periods' η_t^2s, with the weights declining arithmetically as t increases. Clearly $\eta^2_{(T)}$ will not approach a stable value as η_t increases continually.

1.2 THE PRESENT VALUE OF LIFETIME EARNINGS

In estimating the inequality of the present value of lifetime income of a cohort, two approaches can be distinguished. The first involves the specification of a model of age-income profiles, which can be estimated using limited data, and the explicit derivation of formulae for inequality measures. The second approach involves the estimation of a model capable of generating a cohort's changing income distribution, and then using the model as a basis for simulations. These approaches are discussed briefly in this section.

Explicit Solutions

Explicit solutions for inequality measures are very difficult to obtain even for very simple models. However, solutions have been obtained for a model of age-income profiles originally developed by Aitchison and Brown (1957). This model, discussed in more detail in Chapter 4, used the simple Gibrat process described earlier, implying that the variance of the logarithms of annual income increases linearly with age. Using the result in equation (1.5) above, Cowell (1975) has shown that the variance $V(Y)$ of discounted earnings from period t to period T is given by:

$$V(Y) = \sum_{s=t}^{T-1} (\sum_{r=t}^{s} c_r \bar{y}_r \eta^2_r + \eta^2_s \sum_{r=s+1}^{T} c_r \bar{y}_r) c_s \bar{y}_s \qquad (1.7)$$

where c_r is the discount factor appropriate to year r. Equation (1.7) can thus be evaluated using the estimated parameters of the model of income profiles. This approach has been extended by Creedy (1985) to allow for first-order serial correlation in the process of year-to-year relative income changes. It was subsequently extended by Atoda and Tachibinaki (1980) to the assumption that the distribution of income in each year follows the

log-logistic form, and they obtained explicit results for the combination of serial correlation with 'regression towards the mean'.

This approach has yielded some interesting results. For
example, occupation comparisons show that many of those
occupations with relatively high average lifetime earnings have low
coefficients of variation of lifetime earnings and low variability in
year-to-year earnings. This may be interpreted as evidence of the
existence of 'non-competing' groups in the labour market.

Simulation Analyses

In view of the difficulty of obtaining explicit results it is natural to
turn to simulation methods, which have a considerable advantage
if the major purpose of the analysis is to examine the redistributive
effects of government policies. The use of earnings functions to
generate lifetime earnings distributions has not followed any set
pattern; examples include Stoikov (1975), Lillard (1977) and
Blomquist (1981a and b). A useful study of the inequality of
lifetime earnings using simulation methods is by Irvine (1981).
Simulation analyses of alternative pension schemes and the redistribution of lifetime earnings were reported in Creedy and Disney
(1985). One of the most extensive models that examined, *inter
alia*, the inequality of discounted lifetime income was produced by
Blinder (1974). Blinder argued that there are important questions
that, 'may not be amenable to empirical answers *even in principle*.
This is the strength of the simulation method, and, indeed, its
main justification' (1974, p. 88). A feature of his model is the
attempt to allow for variations in individual taste parameters.
Despite the admitted provisional nature of much of the model,
Blinder's contribution provides an excellent source for those
wishing to learn the issues involved in any attempt to simulate the
income distribution using an economic model.

There is no doubt that great care needs to be exercised in
carrying out simulations and in reporting their results, but the use
of sensitivity analyses combined with the need to specify all the
details of the generation process can make simulation a valuable
method. Indeed it is argued that the techniques have been under-
used in microeconomics.

1.3 ALTERNATIVE APPROACHES

The previous discussion has emphasized the process governing changes in income over the life cycle, and its role in affecting the inequality of discounted lifetime earnings. The relationship between lifetime and annual inequality has been examined in a number of alternative ways, usually involving very convenient simplifying assumptions. These are examined briefly in this section.

Inequality Measures

On the argument that differences in earnings that are attributable entirely to age differences should not be regarded as genuine inequalities, several authors have attempted to isolate such effects from inequality measures obtained using cross-sectional data. Weizsäcker (1978) has shown that this is easily achieved for a stationary economy, in which all individuals live until the same age, using the Atkinson (1971) inequality measure. Suppose individual i has incomes $y_{1i}, y_{2i}, ..., y_{mi}$ in periods $1, ..., m$; $i = 1, ..., n$. In the stationary economy, Atkinson's measure for the cross-section, A, is given by:

$$A = 1 - \hat{y}/\bar{y}$$

where

$$\bar{y} = \frac{1}{mn} \sum_{i=1}^{n} \sum_{t=1}^{m} y_{ti} \qquad (1.8)$$

and

$$U(\hat{y}) - \frac{1}{mn} \sum_{i=1}^{n} \sum_{t=1}^{m} U(y_{ti})$$

Here U is a social welfare function and $\hat{y}$ is the 'equally distributed equivalent' income; that is, $\hat{y}$ is the level of income which if equally distributed gives the same social welfare as the actual distribution. Weizsäcker then considered the constant income, $\hat{y}_i$, that, for the ith individual, gives the same utility as the actual stream. This is given by:

$$U(\hat{y}_i) - \frac{1}{mn} \sum_{t=1}^{m} U(y_{ti}) \qquad (1.9)$$

Hence if $\hat{y}^1$ is the arithmetic mean of the $\hat{y}_i$s, the corresponding inequality measure, A^1, is given by:

$$A^1 = 1 - \hat{y}/\bar{y}^1 \qquad (1.10)$$

since $\hat{y}$ is also the equally distributed equivalent of the $\hat{y}_i$s. Defining γ_i as individual i's share in total lifetime income and a_i as i's inequality measure of the fluctuating income stream ($a_i = 1 - \hat{y}_i/\bar{y}_i$), it can be shown that:

$$1 - A = (1 - A^1) \sum_{i=1}^{n} (1 - a_i)\gamma_i \qquad (1.11)$$

While the result in (1.11) has a straightforward interpretation, it is equally clear that the approach really begs the types of question that must be answered in empirical work. It does not offer a practical procedure for measuring inequality with extended accounting periods.

A more practically oriented approach to eliminating inequalities due to age differences was taken by Paglin (1975), using the Gini coefficient. Paglin attempted to eliminate both the systematic variation in earnings with age and the differences between cohorts that arise because of productivity changes, although his procedure, involving the rediscovery of a technique originally derived by Garvy (1952), gave rise to an almost unprecedented number of comments and criticisms. Notable among these is the production, by Friesen and Miller (1983) of a Gini coefficient of inequality in growth-adjusted lifetime incomes. This literature is too extensive to be reviewed here. A serious problem is that attempts to adjust cross-sectional distributions involve the use of rather strong assumptions that ignore relevant issues when the effect of extending the accounting periods is the primary focus. It is also argued that the analysis should concentrate on particular birth cohorts, rather than a broad cross-section.

Permanent Income

Another approach is the method used by Carlton and Hall (1978) to estimate a measure of permanent income. The model is based on the logarithmic version of Friedman's 'errors in variables'

model. Permanent income is essentially an *ex ante* measure and is
unobservable at the level of the individual, but Carlton and Hall
argue that 'stochastic assumptions about transitory income make
it possible to identify the distribution of permanent income within
a population on the basis of observations on actual income in two
years for each member of the population' (1978, p. 103).

In logarithmic terms y, u and v are measured income, permanent income and transitory income. It is assumed that $E(v) = 0$,
that successive transitory components are independent, as are
permanent and transitory components. Where subscripts denote
years, then:

$$y_1 = u + v_1$$
$$y_2 = u + v_2 \tag{1.12}$$

and the joint distribution $f(y_1, y_2)$ is available. Carlton and Hall
(1978, p. 105) show that, if the various distributions have moments
of all orders, the moments of the distribution of permanent income
can be obtained using a recursive relation. A linear programming
approach is then used to compute values of the cumulative
frequency distribution for specified values of u. They found, for
families with white male heads between 25 and 64 years, that the
variance of the logarithms of permanent income was well below
that of annual income. The authors stress however that their
'results to date are only at the borderline of usefulness' (1978,
p. 309). Furthermore, although they simply stated that 'most
economists agree' that well-being is better measured by permanent
income, this proposition needs further argument for its support.
In addition, it is not easy to relate the errors-in-variables concept
of permanent income to that of permanent income defined as the
constant flow of income (to be consumed in perpetuity) that is
obtainable from the stock of human and non-human wealth.

Reference may also be made to the method of estimating the
variance of discounted lifetime earnings devised by Eden and
Pakes (1981). This avoids using information about earnings
dynamics and instead uses a life-cycle consumption model with
specification of the relationship between realized and planned
consumption. Starting from the position that future earnings are
not known with certainty, the value of (appropriately discounted)

expected future income plus non-human assets, $Y(t)$, is conditional
on information available at time t. Greater uncertainty about the
income flow affects individuals' welfare through its effects on $Y(t)$
via a life-cycle consumption model.

The variance of $Y(t)$ changes over time as information is
acquired. Eden and Pakes define v_{t+1}^2 as 'the decrease in the
variance of the present value of future earnings that occurs as a
result of information that accumulates during period t' (1981,
p. 386). Then if r is the rate of interest,

$$v_{t+1}^2 = \text{Var } \{Y(t)\}(1 + r)^2 - \text{Var } \{Y(t + 1)\} \qquad (1.13)$$

for $t = 0, 1, ..., T - 1$.

Clearly Var $\{Y(T)\} = 0$, as the earnings path is known at the
end of the life cycle, whereas the variance of lifetime income, Var
$\{Y(0)\}$ is given by recursion as the discounted sum of the
'variances realized' over the life cycle; that is

$$\text{Var } \{Y(0)\} = \sum_{j=1}^{T} (1 + r)^{-2j} v_j^2 \qquad (1.14)$$

The time profile of $v_1^2, ... v_T^2$ is called the 'variance-age profile of
lifetime earnings' which is estimated using consumption data and
strong assumptions about adjustments in consumption.

In judging the alternative approaches discussed in this section,
it can be seen that they either involve manipulations of inequality
measures that beg some of the current issues of interest, or are
based on consumption models that use very strong assumptions in
order to obtain indirect estimates of lifetime inequality. It is
notable that none of these studies has formed part of a continuous
process of research.

1.4   COMBINING INCOME AND NET WORTH

Potential Income from Assets

In criticizing the use of current annual income as a measure of
economic well-being, several authors have concentrated on the

potential income derived from the ownership of assets or non-human wealth. Although such assets give rise to current income flows in the form of interest payments, net property income and imputed rents from owner-occupied housing, it has been argued that the potential to consume those assets over the remainder of the individual's life should be added to income. A stock cannot be added directly to an income flow so, following Murray (1964), the usual approach is to convert the stock to an annuity. The annuity is then added to income, suitably adjusted to avoid double counting of those items of net property income already included in current income. The use of an annuity provides a simple adjustment for differences in the length of time over which wealth is expected to be consumed.

This approach was extended by Weisbrod and Hansen (1968), who began with the value judgement that 'a unit's economic well-being should be thought of as a function of the flow of services over which it has command' (1968, p. 1315). However, their ambivalence about this is reflected in the later statement that, 'we are not implying either that people generally *do* purchase annuities . . . that they necessarily *should* do so, or that they *can* do so' (1968, p. 1317).

Using standard notation the term a_n denotes the present value of an 'annuity certain immediate', in which n payments of $1 are made, the first received at the end of the first year. Then if r is the rate of interest and $v = 1/(1 + r)$:

$$a_n = (1 - v^n)/r \qquad (1.15)$$

The conversion of net worth into an annuity is achieved by dividing net worth by a_n for given values of n and r. The value of n was chosen by Weisbrod and Hansen as the expected lifetime of the consumer unit using published mortality tables. However, depending on the use for which the measure is to be constructed, it might be argued that the income unit's own expectation of life is relevant; that this can differ widely from actuarial data is shown by Hamermesh (1985). A more appropriate adjustment would use the value of a 'whole life annuity' that gives an annuity as long as the unit survives. The present value of a whole life annuity, with payment at the end of each year, is denoted a_x, where

$$a_x = \{vl_{x+1} + v^2l_{x+2} + ... + v^{w-x}l_w\}/lx \qquad (1.16)$$

and l_x is the number of people alive at age x ($l_{w+1} = 0$).

The general implications of using this 'income-net worth' approach are fairly straightforward. Since net worth is more unequally distributed than income, and both are positively correlated, any measure of inequality is increased; since net worth increases systematically with age, the resulting increase in measured economic well-being will be greater for the aged units than for the young. Both effects are increased when the rate of interest is increased. It is not obvious that the new measure can be compared directly with standard 'poverty lines' but the temptation has been difficult to resist. It is worth noting that the approach is explicitly related to a life-cycle consumption model in which all wealth is consumed at death. A permanent income model would maintain wealth intact and would only imply consumption of the interest income; this is equivalent to an infinitely large value of n in equation (1.15).

Further Applications

Although the empirical illustrations of Weisbrod and Hansen were based on poor data and many arbitrary assumptions, the availability of micro-data sets giving information about the joint distribution of income and net worth has enabled the approach to be repeated and refined. Canadian data have been examined by Wolfson (1979) and Beach et al. (1981). For the US, studies include Taussig (1973) and Moon (1977), who looked at the economic status of the aged. More recent studies concentrating on the aged have been carried out by Burkhauser and Wilkinson (1983) and Burkhauser, Butler and Wilkinson (1986). However, these studies made no fundamental changes to the basic procedure of calculating a so-called 'comprehensive' income measure and provided little foundation for their approach. The last group of authors simply state that they use a 'theoretically superior measure of well-being' (1986, p. 70).

A criticism of the approach is that it treats human and non-human wealth in an asymmetric manner. The net worth of the elderly is annuitized and added to current income, whereas no allowance is made for the expected earnings of those at an earlier stage of the life cycle. One individual may have a much higher expected lifetime income than another, but a comparison of comprehensive income at different ages could easily provide a different ranking. The attempt to take a longer perspective by adding net worth but avoiding any examination of the dynamics of earnings is therefore judged to be too partial.

1.5   CONSUMPTION AND INEQUALITY

Although it has often been argued that a long accounting period is necessary for measuring economic inequality, there is still disagreement on whether some measure of income or consumption is appropriate. This disagreement is also reflected in debates about the tax base even though the difference between the two bases is reduced when a life-cycle perspective is taken. Longitudinal data on the consumption behaviour of a constant group of consuming units are even more scarce than such income data. However, this section discusses an approach to inequality measurement that is based not on measured consumption but on an explicit utility-maximizing life-cycle model.

Utility-Equivalent Annuities

The measurement of lifetime inequality in terms of consumption was pioneered by Nordhaus (1973) in the course of a simulation study of the effects of inflation on the distribution of economic welfare. Given a lifetime wealth constraint, it is possible to calculate the 'income annuity' of a consuming unit for a specified length of life and interest rate. This is a more general form of the annuity used in section 1.4. It can be interpreted as the maximum constant value of consumption that could be attained in each year of life. Nordhaus's measure of economic well-being was, however, defined as the constant consumption stream that would give the same utility as the optimal consumption plan; this is called the 'utility-equivalent annuity'. In this framework the difference between the income and utility-equivalent annuities will depend on the difference between the rate of interest and the time preference rate, and other characteristics of the utility function.

Nordhaus (1973, pp. 468–71) used a continuous time

framework, but the nature of the utility-equivalent measure may be seen using a discrete time model. Assume that the consumer aims to maximize utility, U_i, from period i to period L. Then for the isoelastic case:

$$U_i = \sum_{t=i}^{L} \xi^{-(t-i)} c_t^{-\beta} \tag{1.17}$$

where the time preference rate is $\xi - 1$ and $\beta = -(1 - 1/\eta)$, with η interpreted as the intertemporal elasticity of substitution. This must be maximized subject to the lifetime constraint:

$$\sum_{t=i}^{L} \delta^{-(t-i)} c_t = w_i + \sum_{t=1}^{L} \delta^{-(t-i)} y_t = v_i \tag{1.18}$$

where $\delta - 1$ is the rate of interest and w_i is net worth at time i. Maximization of (1.17) subject to (1.18) gives the log-linear time profile of consumption as:

$$c_t = \left(\frac{\delta}{\xi}\right)^{\eta(t-i)} k_i v_i$$

with
$$k_i - \{ \sum_{t=i}^{L} (\xi \delta^\beta)^{-\eta(t-1)} \}^{-1} \tag{1.19}$$

The utility-equivalent annuity, c_e, is then by definition given by:

$$\sum_{t=i}^{L} \xi^{-(t-i)} c_t^{-\beta} = c_e^{-\beta} \sum_{t=i}^{L} \xi^{-(t-i)} \tag{1.20}$$

where values of c_t in (1.20) are given from (1.19). After some manipulation it can be found that:

$$c_e = k_i v_i \left\{ \left(\frac{1 - \xi^{-1}}{1 - \alpha}\right) \left(\frac{1 - \alpha^{L+1-i}}{1 - \xi^{-(L+1-i)}}\right) \right\}^{-1/\beta}$$

with
$$\alpha = (\delta/\xi)^\eta / \delta \tag{1.21}$$

This is easier to apply than Nordhaus's formula. Computation of

c_e requires information about the lifetime budget constraint (from the earnings profile and non-human wealth) and the parameters of the utility function, along with the length of the planning period and the rate of interest. Even with the highly simplified assumptions underlying the model the calculation of the annuity measure requires a great deal of information. Nordhaus reported that inflation had an equalizing effect.

Few people have attempted to apply Nordhaus's method to other countries, although more information about the sensitivity of his results to some of the imposed values, and comparisons with alternative measures, would be useful. Irvine (1980) used the same methodology to investigate inequality in Canada and found the utility-equivalent annuity to be more equally distributed than other measures, including lifetime earnings. Irvine, like Nordhaus, used *ex post* earnings functions and lifespans. He carefully explains the many stages involved, although it is not always clear whether comparisons are being made with distributions taken over all cohorts combined or with separate cohorts. It also seems that more thought needs to be given to the problem of treating taxes and transfer payments in this type of framework.

Nordhaus's approach assumes that the intertemporal utility function is the same for all individuals. This is more than a convenient simplifying assumption, for without it the procedure would have very little to recommend it. A dispersion of taste parameters would give different values of the utility-equivalent annuity for individuals who face the same time profile of income and wealth. Nordhaus did not attempt to justify his measure, other than making the statement that consumption is usually regarded as the aim of economic activity.

In all the studies considered in this chapter, an individual's wealth has been regarded as a present value of a time stream, using the same rate of interest for all individuals. Hence capital markets have been assumed to be competitive. This assumption is relaxed in the next chapter.

NOTES AND FURTHER READING

Other studies using earnings over just a few years include Benus and Morgan (1974), Cohen et al. (1974), Hoffman and Podder (1976), Coe

(1976) and Steinberg (1977). In Britain, where data have been more scarce, early studies include Vandome (1958) and Prest and Stark (1967). Results for Sweden are reported in Creedy et al. (1981a). Soltow's (1965) study of Norway may also be mentioned, although the sampling procedure used by Soltow limits the value of the results. For further British examples see Creedy (1985). Grosse and Morgan (1981) looked at the question of whether there were compensating variations in the variability and levels of earnings.

An example of the use of the extent of the inequality reduction from combining time periods, in the measurement of mobility, is Shorrocks (1978). His index of mobility is one minus the ratio of the measure of inequality over several periods to a weighted average of the inequality measures for each period taken separately; the weight for each period is the proportion of total earnings that accrues in that period.

The comments on Paglin include Johnson (1977), Kurien (1977), Minarik (1977), Nelson (1977) and Wertz (1979), but this is by no means an exhaustive list. The later piece by Friesen (1986) may also be noted. A full treatment of aggregating over age groups is given in Creedy (1985). Also useful in this context is the type of decomposition developed in Mookherjee and Shorrocks (1982).

2. Measuring Wealth in Imperfect Capital Markets

The extremely convenient assumption that individuals can borrow and lend at a fixed rate of interest was made in all the analyses considered in Chapter 1. This has made it possible to define lifetime wealth as the present value of an income stream, using a common rate of interest for all individuals. The question of the choice of interest rate has usually been answered with reference to some average of market real rates, although sensitivity analyses have often been used. The most sensitive results are not surprisingly those using the 'comprehensive' income measure described in section 1.4. Layard (1977) has, however, argued that if individuals face different unknown rates of interest it is necessary to use a very low common rate in computing lifetime earnings distributions. Otherwise those who face favourable borrowing rates and have steep earnings profiles will have measured lifetime earnings that are much too low relative to others.

A more serious problem arises when there are imperfections in capital markets such that borrowing rates are higher than lending rates. In a standard life-cycle consumption model the timing of income flows is not important; only the present value matters. But when borrowing and lending rates differ not only is the time pattern important but the measure of wealth (used in solving the optimization problem) depends on subjective factors. This was examined in detail by Pissarides (1978), who defined lifetime wealth as the value of income that, if it were received in the first period, would give the same utility as the actual income stream. He showed that, 'wealth can be defined unambiguously only at the optimum point. Parameter changes that result in a change in behaviour also result in a change in lifetime wealth, although some of these, e.g., tastes, are traditionally not regarded as arguments in the determination of wealth' (1978, p. 285). Similar issues were treated extensively by Cowell (1979), who also allowed for income

21

uncertainty and uncertainty about length of life. A more recent analysis has been given by Le Grand (1987, pp. 56–61), who discusses the general problems for inequality measurement that are raised by non-linear budget constraints. Le Grand suggests alternative measures that depend on the nature of the constraint facing individuals, but it is very difficult to extend his treatment to more than two periods. The two-period case is, however, useful for clarifying some of the issues and is discussed in this chapter. The basic model is examined in section 2.1. The implications of the much-used isoelastic utility function are then discussed in section 2.2.

2.1 A BASIC TWO-PERIOD MODEL

The capital market imperfection considered by Le Grand (1987) is represented by a difference between borrowing and lending rates of interest. The approach can also be extended to allow for an upper limit on the amount each individual is allowed to borrow in the first period.

The Non-Linear Problem

Suppose an individual faces an exogenous income stream of y_0, y_1 and chooses the consumption stream c_0, c_1 in order to maximize utility $U(c_0, c_1)$. Gross amounts of lending and borrowing are denoted h and b respectively, with interest rates of $r - 1$ and $\varrho - 1$ (with $\varrho > r$). There are two equality constraints concerning consumption in each period. The first states that c_0 is equal to y_0 plus net borrowing, while the second states that c_1 is equal to y_1, plus interest received from loans made in the first period, less interest paid on the amount borrowed in the first period. Hence:

$$c_0 = y_0 + (b - h) \tag{2.1}$$

and
$$c_1 = y_1 + rh - \varrho b \tag{2.2}$$

There are also the non-negativity constraints

$$c_0, c_1, h, b \ 0 \tag{2.3}$$

With an upper limit on borrowing in the first period of b^*, then there is an additional inequality constraint

$$b \leq b^* \qquad (2.4)$$

Notice that for the borrowing constraint to be relevant, $b^* < y_1/\varrho$. The Lagrangian, L, for this non-linear problem is thus given by:

$$L = U(c_0, c_1) + \lambda_0(y_0 + b - h - c_0) + \lambda_1(y_1 + rh - \varrho b - c_1) +$$
$$\lambda_2(b^* - b) \qquad (2.5)$$

The Kuhn-Tucker conditions then give

$$\partial L/\partial c_0 = u_0 - \lambda_0 \leq 0; \ c_0 \geq 0; \ c_0(u_0 - \lambda_0) = 0 \qquad (2.6)$$

$$\partial L/\partial c_1 = u_1 - \lambda_1 \leq 0; \ c_1 \geq 0; \ c_1(u_1 - \lambda_1) = 0$$

$$\partial L/\partial h = -\lambda_0 + \lambda_1 r \leq 0; \ h \geq 0; \ h(-\lambda_0 + \lambda_1 r) = 0 \qquad (2.7)$$

$$\partial L/\partial b = \lambda_0 - \lambda_1\varrho - \lambda_2 \leq 0; \ b \geq 0; \ b(\lambda_0 - \lambda_1\varrho - \lambda_2) = 0 \qquad (2.8)$$

$\partial L/\partial \lambda_0 = 0$ and $\partial L/\partial \lambda_1 = 0$ give the equality constraints (2.1) and (2.2), so that the Lagrangian multipliers λ_0 and λ_1 are unrestricted in sign. Finally,

$$\partial L/\partial \lambda_2 = b^* - b \geq 0; \ \lambda_2 \geq 0; \ \lambda_2(b^* - b) = 0 \qquad (2.9)$$

The borrowing constraint ensures that $c_1 > 0$, and the following discussion concentrates on the case where also $c_0 > 0$; hence from (2.6), $u_i = \lambda_i$ for $i = 0, 1$. Consider first the case where the borrowing constraint is binding. The complementary slackness condition in (2.9) shows that $\lambda_2 > 0$, and from the complementary slackness condition in (2.8) it can then be seen that $\lambda_2 = \lambda_0 - \lambda_1\varrho$. Substitution for λ_0 and λ_1 from (2.6) gives

$$\lambda_2 = u_0 - u_1\varrho \qquad (2.10)$$

Since in this situation it is also known that $c_0 = y_0 + b^*$ and $c_1 =$

$y_1 - \varrho b^*$, appropriate substitution into equation (2.10) allows the 'cost' of the borrowing limit to be obtained; that is, λ_2 is the gain in utility that would be achieved from a marginal relaxation of the constraint. When the borrowing constraint in (2.4) is not binding, then of course $\lambda_2 = 0$.

The model also has the property that an individual will not simultaneously borrow and lend, so that a borrower for whom $0 < b < b^*$ will have, from (2.8).

$$\lambda_0/\lambda_1 = \varrho \qquad (2.11)$$

Similarly, when $h > 0$ the complementary slackness condition in (2.7) gives the result that

$$\lambda_0/\lambda_1 = r \qquad (2.12)$$

It is convenient to refer to Figure 2.1, which shows the situation for two individuals who face the same income profile but have sufficiently different preferences that one prefers to borrow in the first period while the other prefers to lend. The common budget constraint is shown as the line ADEF, where the coordinates of the kink at D are (y_1, y_0) and the kink E occurs at $(y_1 - \varrho b^*, y_0 + b^*)$. The lender reaches indifference curve I_L while the borrower reaches I_B.

Utility-Equivalent Wealth

There is no difficulty in obtaining the Pissarides measure of lifetime wealth for the lender, denoted W_L^P; it is the length OI given by $y_0 + y_1/r$ or, using the result in (2.12),

$$W_L^P = y_0 + y_1(\lambda_1/\lambda_0) \qquad (2.13)$$

The corresponding result for the borrower, obtained by using (2.11) in an expression similar to (2.13), would give $y_0 + y_1/\varrho$. This is the length OG in Figure 2.1. But if the borrower were given this value in the first period instead of the income stream y_0, y_1, he or she must become a lender at the interest rate $r - 1$. Hence it would not be possible to reach indifference curve I_B. Le Grand has pointed out that the appropriate value of utility-equivalent wealth

Figure 2.1   Wealth in a two-period model

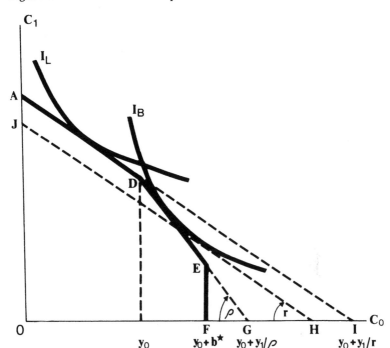

is the length OH. The borrower can reach I_B only if the budget constraint becomes the straight line JH, whose slope is r. Hence wealth cannot be written simply in terms of the present value of an income stream.

Essentially the same argument would apply to a borrower for whom the borrowing limit imposes a binding constraint and who would therefore be consuming at the corner solution E. The extra cost of the inequality constraint in (2.4) can clearly be seen in terms of the loss of utility.

The implication of all this for the measurement of inequality, when it is desired to use a longer-term measure of income than that received in single period, is that it would not be appropriate simply to construct present values for each individual based on a particular discount rate. When borrowing and lending rates differ, and when there is an upper limit on the extent of borrowing, the utility-equivalent measure of wealth is a simple present value only for those who are lenders in the first period. Le Grand's argument is that equity should be based on some measure of the constraint facing individuals rather than the outcomes of their diverse preferences. Hence both the conventional discounted values of income, evaluated using a common interest rate, and the Pissarides utility-equivalent measure of lifetime wealth are regarded by Le Grand as inappropriate.

2.2   THE ISOELASTIC UTILITY FUNCTION

In view of the fact that borrowing and lending rates of interest generally do differ, and that borrowing limits are often imposed on individuals, the argument of the previous section would suggest that little value should perhaps be placed on measures of inequality which use present values of income streams. However, it is difficult to assess the strength of this type of criticism without further information. It may, for example, be suggested that the typical life cycle involves borrowing in the early years and lending in later years. It may be useful to have some idea of the extent of heterogeneity in tastes that would produce variations in borrowing and lending behaviour among individuals with similar earnings profiles. Similarly, it is not clear what orders of magnitude are involved in comparing points like I and H in Figure 2.1. Appropriate information about tastes does not of course exist. The present section therefore examines the implications for a specific functional form of the utility function, the much-used isoelastic form.

The Optimal Consumption Stream

Suppose that the two-period utility function can be written as:

$$U(c_0, c_1) = c_0^{-\beta} + (1/\xi)c_1^{-\beta} \qquad (2.14)$$

where the time preference rate is $\xi - 1$ and $\beta = -(1 - 1/\eta)$, with η interpreted as the intertemporal elasticity of substitution. Hence each individual's preferences are described by two parameters and it is assumed that heterogeneity in tastes arises from the joint distribution of those parameters rather than variations in the functional form of the utility function. From (2.14) the marginal rate of substitution between consumption in the two periods is given by:

$$u_0/u_1 = -dc_1/dc_0 = \xi(c_0/c_1)^{-1/\eta} \qquad (2.15)$$

Consider the situation of the borrower for whom the upper limit b^* is not binding; this corresponds to the borrower depicted in Figure 2.1. Combining (2.6), (2.11) and (2.15) therefore gives, after rearrangement:

$$c_1 = c_0(\varrho/\xi)^\eta \qquad (2.16)$$

For the borrower, $h = 0$, and substitution into (2.1) and (2.2) above, followed by the elimination of b from the resulting simultaneous equations, gives

$$c_0 = y_0 + (y_1 - c_1)\varrho \qquad (2.17)$$
$$= W(\varrho) - c_1/\varrho$$

where
$$W(\varrho) = y_0 + y_1/\varrho \qquad (2.18)$$

$W(\varrho)$ is the standard form of the present value of the income stream y_0, y_1 evaluated using the interest rate $\varrho - 1$. The substitution of (2.17) into (2.16) gives, after rearrangement:

$$c_1 = W(\varrho)k(\varrho)\ (\varrho/\xi)^\eta \qquad (2.19)$$

where
$$k(\varrho) = \{1 + (\varrho/\xi)^\eta/\varrho\}^{-1} \qquad (2.20)$$

Then
$$c_0 = W(\varrho)k(\varrho). \qquad (2.21)$$

The circumstances in which the individual is indeed a borrower can be found by substituting for c_0 in the condition $c_0 > y_0$ (and using the expressions in 2.21, 2.20 and 2.18). Hence the individual borrows if:

$$\xi > \varrho(y_0/y_1)^{1/\eta} \qquad (2.22)$$

Similarly, the borrowing limit is not binding so long as

$$\xi < \varrho\{(y_0 + b^*)/(y_1 - \varrho b^*)\}^{1/\eta} \qquad (2.23)$$

Utility-Equivalent Wealth

The value of the utility-equivalent lifetime wealth for the borrower, W_B^P, can be obtained in two stages. First denote the coordinates of the point of tangency between the indifference curve I_B and the new linear budget constraint JH by (c_1^*, c_0^*). These must satisfy the condition that

$$U(c_0^*, c_1^*) = U(c_0, c_1) \qquad (2.24)$$

where the values of c_0 and c_1 in (2.24) are given by equations (2.19) and (2.21). It must also be true that $c_1^* = c_0^*(r/\xi)^\eta$ and $c_1 = c_0(\varrho/\xi)^\eta$. Substituting the latter two results into (2.24), with the form given in (2.14) gives, after some manipulation:

$$c_0^* = W(\varrho)k(\varrho)\{k(r)/k(\varrho)\}^{\eta/(\eta-1)} \qquad (2.25)$$

By definition:

$$W_B^P = c_0^* + c_1^*/r = c_0^* k(r)^{-1} \qquad (2.26)$$

so the substitution of (2.25) into (2.26) gives:

$$W_B^P = W(\varrho)\{k(r)/k(\varrho)\}^{1/(\varrho-1)} \qquad (2.27)$$

This contrasts with W_L^P given above as simply $W(r)$. Hence the ratio of utility equivalent lifetime wealth of the borrower to that of the lender depends on r, ϱ, ξ and π, and the income stream.

For a borrower whose time preference rate is so high that the borrowing limit is binding, the utility-equivalent wealth value can be obtained in a similar manner. However, since there is no tangency solution, equation (2.24) is replaced by:

$$u(c_0^*, c_1^*) = u(y_0 + b^*, y_1 - \varrho b^*) \qquad (2.28)$$

with the condition, as before, that $c_1^* = c_0^*(r/\xi)^\eta$. It can then be shown that

$$W_B^P = k(r)^{1/(\eta-1)}(y_0 + b^*)(1 + \psi/\xi)^{\eta/(\eta-)}$$

where $\quad\quad \psi = \{(y_1 - \varrho b^*)/(y_0 + b^*)\}^{(\eta-1)/\eta}$ $\quad\quad$ (2.29)

Utility-Equivalent Annuities

An alternative approach to measuring inequality, discussed in Chapter 1 above, was suggested by Nordhaus (1973) and used by Irvine (1980). Nordhaus assumed that capital markets are perfect and that all individuals have the same tastes. His measure of well-being is defined as the constant consumption stream that would give the same utility as the optimal consumption plan; this is called the 'utility-equivalent annuity'. Nordhaus provided very little rationale for his measure, other than to argue that consumption is more appropriate since it is usually regarded as the 'end' of all economic activity. The form of the measure may be seen using the present two-period model and the isoelastic utility function that was also used by Nordhaus. Let c_e denote the utility-equivalent annuity. Then:

$$U(c_e, c_e) = U(c_0, c_1) \quad\quad (2.30)$$

where c_0 and c_1 are the optimal values given, in the case of the borrower, by equations (2.19) and (2.21). For the borrower, substitution into (2.30) gives

$$(1 + 1/\xi)c_e^{-\beta} = \{W(\varrho)k(\varrho)\}^{-\beta}\{1 + (1/\xi)(\varrho/\xi)^{-\beta\eta}\} \quad (2.31)$$

and solving for c_e gives, after some simplification:

$$c_e = \{\xi/(1 + \xi)\}^{\eta/(\eta-1)}W(\varrho)k(\varrho)^{-1/(\eta-1)} \quad\quad (2.32)$$

For the lender, it is easily seen that r replaces ϱ in (2.32) and of course the taste parameters ξ and η will be different. Hence the ratio of the utility-equivalent annuities of borrower and lender is different from that of their values of utility-equivalent wealth. In particular, while the borrower will necessarily have $W_B^P < W(r) =$

W_L^P it is quite possible for the borrower to have a higher annuity value than that of the lender. This possibility can also be seen from Figure 2.1. The assumption by Nordhaus that the intertemporal utility function is the same for all individuals is thus more than a convenient simplifying assumption; without it the procedure would have very little to recommend it.

An alternative approach that does not depend on assumptions about consumers' tastes or consumption behaviour is that of Weisbrod and Hansen (1968), following Murray (1964). This calculates the constant maximum value of consumption in each period that could be financed with the available stock of wealth, and also requires perfect capital markets. In the two-period model this is given simply by the intersection of a 45° line drawn through the origin with a linear budget constraint, and is less than the corresponding Nordhaus measure. When applied in practice, the income annuity has been based only on non-human wealth, thereby treating the latter and expected income in an asymmetric manner.

Some Numerical Examples

It is useful to examine some orders of magnitude involved in comparing alternative measures. For convenience suppose that income units are such that $y_0 = 1$ and $y_1 = 1.1$; hence income is assumed to increase by 10 per cent from the first to the second period. If $\eta = 1.2$, the individual borrows in the first period if $(\xi/\varrho) > 0.924$. Only when $y_0/y_1 = 1$ is it necessary for $\xi > \varrho$ in order that the individual borrows. As y_0/y_1 decreases, the required ratio ξ/ϱ also decreases, and the same holds for variations in η. Suppose that the borrowing rate of interest is twice the lending rate and $r = 1.05$ with $\varrho = 1.10$. This means, from above, that ξ must exceed 1.016 if the individual is to borrow; suppose therefore that $\xi = 1.02$. With these simplifying assumptions it is seen that $W(\varrho) = 2$, $W(r) = 2.048$, $k(\varrho) = 0.501$ and $k(r) = 0.503$. Hence the measure of utility-equivalent wealth, W_B^P, is equal to 2.04. Thus the wealth value of the lender is less than one half of a percentage point greater than that of the borrower, although it is about 2.5 per cent greater than the present value of the income stream evaluated at the higher borrowing rate. An increase in ξ

to 1.04, with the other parameters unchanged, reduces W_B^P very slightly to 2.039; when $\xi = 1.15$, $W_B^P = 2.037$.

Now suppose that the time preference rate is very much higher, at $\xi = 2.6$. With an absolute limit on borrowing of $b^* = 0.5$, the individual would maximize utility at the corner solution, E, in Figure 2.1. With $\eta = 1.2$ and the other parameters the same as those used above, substitution into equation (2.29) gives the result that $W_B^P = 1.906$. The value of utility-equivalent wealth is thus (not surprisingly) lower than the present value of the income stream evaluated at the higher rate of interest. However, the very high value of ξ needed to achieve this result should be recognized. For a much higher value of η of 2.5, with the other parameters unchanged, the corner solution will be optimal when $\xi = 1.3$. With these tastes the utility equivalent wealth is found to be 2.005, which is slightly above the value of $W(\varrho) = 2.0$. The high values of either η or ξ required for the corner solution, E, to be optimal are of course reduced if the income profile is steeper and the borrowing limit is increased. For example, if there is a 50 per cent increase in income, so that $y_1 = 1.5$, a value of $\eta = 2.0$ gives a corner solution so long as $\xi > 1.38$.

These illustrations have shown that, for borrowers not affected by the upper limit, the utility-equivalent wealth value is very close to the present value of income evaluated using the (lower) lending rate of interest. Those individuals with a high elasticity of substitution and a high time preference rate, and who are thereby affected by the borrowing limit, are seen to have utility-equivalent wealth values closer to the present value obtained using the (higher) borrowing rate of interest.

In practice, any researcher attempting to measure inequality using a longer time period will not have information either about individuals' tastes or their capital market position. In using the present value of each individual's income stream as the measure of lifetime income, or wealth, the above results may perhaps be interpreted as suggesting that calculations will not be too misleading so long as a low interest rate is used, unless there is evidence to suggest that many individuals are affected by a borrowing constraint. The use of a low rate of interest was also suggested by Layard (1977), though for rather different reasons. A refusal to consider present values at all, on the argument that capital markets are not in fact perfect, would seem to be too nihilistic, at least until improved measures become available.

3. Earnings Comparisons between Generations

This chapter examines some of the basic problems which arise when attempting to measure the nature and extent of inter-generational earnings mobility. The classic statistical model for comparisons between fathers and sons is the basic regression model, first used by Galton (1889) to show that there was 'regression towards the mean' in the heights of fathers and sons. Thus, on average the sons of relatively tall fathers were found to be closer to the average height of the population, and the same applied to sons of relatively short fathers. This regression towards the mean has the effect of stabilizing the distribution of heights, so that the regression and correlation coefficients are equal. The comparison of heights is considerably simplified by the fact that, after a certain age, the variation in height with age can reasonably be ignored. But in attempting to apply the Galtonian model to inter-generational earnings differences, the existence of variations in earnings over the life cycle must be acknowledged. These variations include not only the more systematic changes associated with age, as shown by well-known age-earnings profiles, but also the relative changes from one period to the next made by individuals within an occupational and cohort group.

The ideal situation would be to have information about earnings (and other characteristics) for each year of the working life of a sample of fathers and sons, but such data are unlikely ever to be available. The usual situation is that an investigator has information about the earnings during only a particular year or week of a sample of fathers and sons, all of whom are fully employed during the relevant time period. Sometimes the earnings are measured over the same calendar time period or the sons' earnings are collected at a later date by tracing a proportion of the sons of a given sample of fathers. The differences in sampling procedures

32

are not, however, of importance in the present context; the main emphasis is on the need to allow for life-cycle factors.

This chapter shows how a number of adjustments to observed earnings may be made using a model of age-earnings profiles that can be estimated with the kind of data usually available. Strong simplifying assumptions must of course be made, but it is argued that this is preferable to ignoring these problems altogether. Any analysis of life-cycle variations raises the question of the difference between the unobserved cohort earnings profiles and the cross-sectional earnings profiles usually available. This issue is examined in section 3.1, which presents the basic model of earnings changes, enabling the different profiles to be obtained. Section 3.2 then considers some basic life-cycle adjustments where individuals' occupations are not known. The section also examines the problem arising from the fact that there is usually a large variation both in the fathers' and the sons' ages at the time when earnings are recorded, and the need to allow for the implications of an increasing relative dispersion of earnings with age. Section 3.3 then allows for occupational differences in age-earnings profiles, and considers the use of the estimated lifetime earnings of each individual rather than the short-term measure of earnings observed directly. Comparisons of alternative procedures are made in section 3.4 using information about the age, occupation and earnings of a sample of fathers and sons given by Bowley (1915). These data have a number of limitations, so the empirical results should only be seen as illustrations of differences between the various procedures. First, however, the following subsection briefly considers related literature and problems of interpretation.

Mobility and Inheritance

The basic Galtonian regression model has been used to examine inter-generational earnings mobility by Atkinson, Maynard and Trinder (1983). They did not distinguish between occupations, but life-cycle adjustments were based on the systematic variation in average earnings with age of a cross-sectional age-earnings profile obtained from extraneous data sources. Other relative earnings changes over the life cycle arising from short-term movements (within cohorts) were considered in terms of measurement errors in fathers' earnings. It is well known that measurement errors in the independent variable of a bivariate linear aggression model lead to a downward bias in the estimation of the regression coefficient. The simple life-cycle adjustment, using a cross-sectional profile, was obviously motivated by the fact that fathers and sons were not observed at the same age, although Atkinson et al. did not provide a detailed discussion of their procedure.

The difficult question of interpretation was, however, examined in more detail by Atkinson (1983), using a model in which individuals work for two periods and fathers and sons overlap for one of the periods. The logarithms of fathers' earnings in the first period are divided into permanent and stochastic components, while the second period's earnings depend on those of the first period, the permanent component and a serially correlated stochastic term. The son's permanent earnings are then assumed to be made up of a stochastic term and a weighted average of the father's permanent earnings and a permanent component not related to family background, with weights λ and $1 - \lambda$ respectively. Atkinson interpreted the parameter λ as reflecting the inheritance of economic opportunity, and examined the possible extent of bias in different regression coefficients, depending on the particular set of earnings available. Even in the simplified framework (with the parameters of the profiles being the same for fathers and sons), it was shown that inferences about inheritance from earnings regressions are far from straightforward. The model was subsequently used by Jenkins (1986) to examine the implications for lifetime utility, where utility is expressed as the product of earnings in the two periods. Jenkins interpreted the regression coefficient between sons' and fathers' (logarithmic) lifetime utilities as the appropriate measure of inter-generational inheritance, and showed that significant biases can arise when only earnings from a single period are available.

The specification of a joint model of earnings profiles and inter-generational inheritance that could be directly related to observable measures presents formidable difficulties. The work of Atkinson and Jenkins has demonstrated the difficulty of making inferences about inheritance from observations about different types of earnings mobility. It should thus be stressed that this chapter is limited to the construction of alternative measures of earnings *mobility* which may be obtained using only the sort of data that are typically available to researchers. It is however suggested that the types of adjustment proposed have advantages over the more straightforward regressions that have been carried out in previous empirical studies.

3.1 COHORT AND CROSS-SECTIONAL EARNINGS PROFILES

In examining changes it is usual to distinguish three different factors, called the 'age', 'time' and 'cohort' effects. Thus in principle the process of ageing can be distinguished from the effects arising simply from the passage of time, and in addition there may be cohort-specific influences on earnings changes, arising perhaps from the size of the cohort. However, it is recognized that these effects can only be identified if very strong restrictions are placed on the model being used, even when longitudinal earnings data are available for several cohorts. So progress can only be made if a highly simplified model is used; a possible approach is described in this section. The following basic model can be used irrespective of the type of data available, but for ease of presentation it is assumed that a single cross-section of individuals of different ages is used; this situation is relevant for the application in section 3.4.

A Simple Model

Suppose that there are no significant differences between separate cohorts, so that only age and time effects are relevant. Furthermore, assume as usual that the age effects are quadratic, but the time effects are linear. The latter may be taken to imply a constant rate of productivity growth, affecting all age groups and cohorts equally. If t, d and c represent age, calendar date (year), and year of birth respectively, and μ is arithmetic mean log-earnings, then the model is given by:

$$\mu_{td} = \alpha_0 + \alpha_1 t + \alpha_2 t^2 + \beta d \qquad (3.1)$$

where α_0, α_1, α_2 and β are parameters, and $\alpha_2 < 0$. If a set of cohorts is observed at the same date, say in year d_0, then the observed cross-sectional earnings profile is given by

$$\mu_{td_0} = (\alpha_0 + \beta d_0) + \alpha_1 t + \alpha_2 t^2$$
$$= \alpha_0' + \alpha_1 t + \alpha_2 t^2 \qquad (3.2)$$

With only one cross-section it is only possible to estimate α_0', α_1 and α_2, so that α_0 and β cannot be identified. Progress can however be made by making the strong assumption that β represents a constant rate of productivity growth, which may be estimated using extraneous information as, say, β^*. Hence an estimate of α_0, indicated by a 'hat', may be obtained as follows

$$\hat{\alpha}_0 = \hat{\alpha}_0' - \beta^* d_0 \qquad (3.3)$$

The Cohort Profiles

It is required to obtain the relationship between age and earnings for any particular cohort born in year c; the discussion is in terms of real earnings, measured in year d_0's prices. By definition, $c = d - t$, and substitution into equation (3.1) gives:

$$\mu_{t,t+c} = (\alpha_0 + \beta c) + (\alpha_1 + \beta)t + \alpha_2 t^2 \qquad (3.4)$$

Hence, given estimates of α_0, α_1, and α_2 from (3.2) and (3.3), and the extraneous estimate of β, equation (3.4) can be used to obtain the age-earnings profile for any birth cohort. The cohort profiles of mean log-earnings are seen to be parallel to each other, and are steeper than the cross-sectional profiles. The relationships among the various profiles can be seen in Figure 3.1, which shows two cross-sectional profiles and two cohort profiles. The above simple framework can be used to estimate a cohort (real) earnings profile of mean log-earnings for any birth cohort, given only one cross-sectional profile and an imposed value of the constant 'time effect'.

The above discussion has concerned only the general growth of earnings with age, but there is a widely observed tendency for the relative dispersion of earnings within each age group to increase steadily with age. In particular, for many occupations and other, more aggregative, groups the variance of logarithms has been found to increase linearly with age; see also the results shown in Chapter 4 below. The question therefore arises of whether it is

Figure 3.1   Cross-sectional and cohort earnings profiles

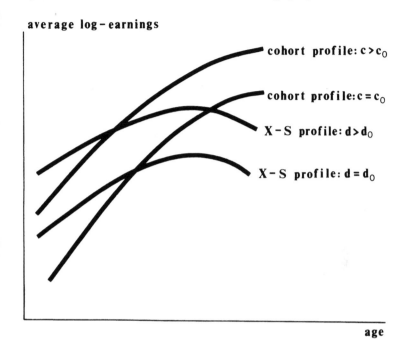

average log-earnings

cohort profile: $c > c_0$

cohort profile: $c = c_0$

X-S profile: $d > d_0$

X-S profile: $d = d_0$

age

necessary to distinguish between cohort and cross-sectional variations in dispersion with age. Here appeal may perhaps be made to
the fact that in lognormal distributions the mean and the variance
of the logarithms of earnings are independent. Furthermore,
available evidence does not suggest that cross-sectional and cohort
profiles of dispersion differ to any large extent.

3.2   ALL OCCUPATIONS COMBINED

The Basic Regression Model

In order to examine the possible extent of Galtonian regression
towards the (geometric) mean in the earnings of fathers and sons,
the basic approach may be written as follows:

$$(\log y - \mu)_S = \gamma + \delta(\log y - \mu)_F + u \qquad (3.5)$$

where individual subscripts have been omitted for convenience, S and F refer to sons and fathers respectively, and u is a stochastic term. The terms $(\log y - \mu)$ must be interpreted as the logarithm of an individual's earnings during a specified period, less the mean log-earnings of individuals in the same birth cohort. In the application of this type of approach to, say, the analysis of year-to-year changes in earnings it is of course only necessary to regress $\log y_t$ on $\log y_{t-1}$, since there are only two relevant means, μ_t and μ_{t-1}, which may be subsumed in the constant term. However, in the present context there is considerable variation in the ages of both sons and fathers. Notice that it is not appropriate to regress $(\log y)_S$ on $(\log y)_F$, because of the variation within both the groups of fathers and sons in their ages. Atkinson et al. (1983, p. 107) report a regression of this kind, but then use 'age-adjusted' data.

It is convenient to refer to Figure 3.2, which shows alternative profiles for a single pair of father and son, whose positions are F and S. The figure illustrates the case where information about fathers' and sons' earnings were recorded at the same calendar date, but no substantial difficulties arise where the observation dates differ. In compiling dependent and independent variables for a regression analysis based on equation (3.5), it is satisfactory to take values of μ from the cross-sectional age-earnings profile, since they coincide with the cohort profiles at the corresponding points, remembering that all values are expressed in real terms. No adjustment for the cohort profiles is therefore necessary.

Variations in Ages

The simple approach based on equation (3.5), and used by Atkinson et al. (1983), makes no allowance for the fact that there is considerable variation in the ages of both fathers and sons, other than ensuring the appropriate calculation of the μs. To examine whether or not this affects the results, consider using information about age-earnings profiles to adjust the earnings of all individuals to a common, or standard age. The most obvious way to do this would be to assume that each individual has a constant relative position in the earnings distribution of his cohort. From the earlier

Figure 3.2   Alternative profiles of fathers and sons

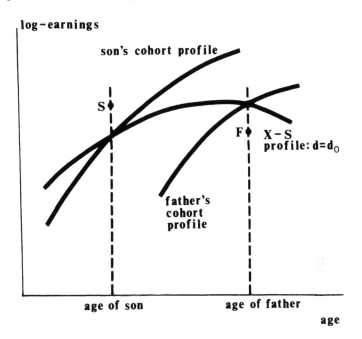

discussion of mobility within generations, this is tantamount to assuming that the observation on each individual does indeed reflect the true or permanent relative position. On the assumption, made earlier, that there are no significant differences between the cohort and cross-sectional profiles of the *dispersion* of earnings with age, the adjustment of all earnings to those corresponding to a standard age may be made with either the cross-sectional or cohort profiles of mean log-earnings. Furthermore, the assumption of constant relative position would mean that each individual's value of $\log y - \mu$ would remain unchanged, whatever the standard age. Hence the adjustment to a standard age would only affect the constant term in a regression analysis so that the straightforward use of equation (3.5) seems justified even after allowing for age differences.

Age and the Dispersion of Earnings

The conclusion reached in the preceding paragraph must, however, be qualified when it is realized that there is generally a systematic increase in the relative dispersion of earnings with age. When both generations are surveyed in the same year, the earnings of the sons will be relatively closer to the means of their age group than those of their fathers. Hence there is a systematic downward bias in the estimation of δ, thereby exaggerating the extent of regression towards the mean; this bias will depend on the extent to which relative dispersion increases with age. The implications are not straightforward when the sons are surveyed at a later date, but clearly an appropriate allowance must be made.

It is useful to consider the above problem directly. An individual of age t with earnings of y_t has a standardized value of earnings of $z = (\log y_t - \mu_t)/\sigma_t$, where σ_t^2 is the variance of logarithms of earnings in age group t. (As explained earlier, there is no need to distinguish between cohort and cross-sectional values at this stage.) If the same relative earnings position is retained at age t^*, say, then log-earnings at that age are given by

$$\log y_{t^*} = \mu_{t^*} + z\sigma_{t^*} \tag{3.6}$$

Hence $\log y_{t^*} - \mu_{t^*} = z\sigma_{t^*}$, and substitution into equation (3.5), with the addition of subscripts to denote fathers and sons, gives

$$z_S\sigma_{t^*} = z_F\sigma_{t^*} + u \tag{3.7}$$

so that division by the common σ_{t^*} gives the following specification:

$$\left(\frac{\log y - \mu}{\sigma}\right)_S = \gamma + \delta\left(\frac{\log y - \mu}{\sigma}\right)_F + v \tag{3.8}$$

where σ refers to the variance of the logarithms of earnings in the appropriate age group. The standard age, t^*, therefore turns out to be irrelevant so long as standardized values of earnings are used.

3.3 OCCUPATIONAL DIFFERENCES

If the data can be divided into a number of broad occupational groups, then it is desirable to attempt to allow for the fact that age-earnings profiles differ significantly among occupations. A son with relatively low earnings at the time of the survey may be in a more highly skilled occupation than his father, and may subsequently experience a more rapid growth of earnings over his remaining working life. One difficulty of assigning individuals to occupations on the basis of one observation is the possibility that there may be mobility among occupations over the life cycle, but this problem is reduced with the type of broad classification generally used.

A Basic Adjustment

It has been shown in section 3.2 that an attempt to allow for the variation in the ages of fathers and sons, by adjusting all individuals' earnings to a common age, actually results in the use of a simple regression of the standardized value of sons' earnings on that of fathers' earnings at the time of the survey. Perhaps surprisingly, no adjustment to a different age needs to be made for any individual, so there is no difficult choice to be made about the common age to be used. However, this convenient result no longer holds when allowance is made for differences in occupations, as shown below.

Consider adjusting all individuals to the common age t^*, making the assumption, as before, that each individual remains in the same relative position in the distribution of his cohort and occupation. Denote the mean and variance of log-earnings at age t for occupation i by $_i\mu_t$ and $_i\sigma_t^2$ respectively. Then the standardized value of an individual's log-earnings at the time of the survey, at age t, is given by

$$z = (\log y_t - {_i\mu_t})/({_i\sigma_t}) \tag{3.9}$$

Hence the individual's adjusted earnings at age t^*, $\log y_{t^*}$, are

$$\log y_{t^*} = {_i\mu_{t^*}} + z({_i\sigma_{t^*}}) \tag{3.10}$$

Lifetime Earnings

The specification required to examine the extent of regression towards the overall mean is then

$$(\log y_{t^*} - \mu_{t^*})_S = \gamma + \delta(\log y_{t^*} - \mu_{t^*})_F + u \qquad (3.11)$$

where μ_{t^*} denotes the mean log-earnings in age group t^*, for all occupations combined.

The discussion leading to equation (3.11) ignored the question of whether the cross-sectional or cohort profile should be used in obtaining the value of log y_{t^*}, for each individual, and the value of μ_{t^*}. Using the model of section 3.1 it can be seen that, as in section 3.2, the use of cross-sectional profiles gives precisely the same results as with the cohort profiles. When taking log $y_{t^*} - \mu_{t^*}$, the crucial terms in the cohort profiles, such as βc in the constant and β in the coefficient on t^*, can be seen to cancel, giving the same expression as when cross-sectional profiles are used. The need to specify a value of β is therefore again avoided. Furthermore, when using the cross-sectional profiles, the value of μ_{t^*}, in equation (3.11) will be the same as both left- and right-hand sides. Hence it is perhaps more convenient to estimate

$$(\log y_{t^*})S = \text{constant} + \delta(\log y_{t^*})_F + u \qquad (3.12)$$

This simplification cannot be used if the cohort profiles are used, since μ_{t^*} will depend crucially on the year of birth, as well as the age, of fathers and sons. The important implication of the above results is that the calculated value of δ will depend to some extent on the common age, t^*, used.

Estimated Lifetime Earnings

The fact that measured regression depends on the standard age used suggests that it may be useful to construct a measure of lifetime earnings, even though, following the earlier approach, an assumption of 'constant relative position' must be used to generate a lifetime earnings profile for each individual. Discounted lifetime earnings, Y, can then be calculated using

$$Y = \sum_{t=t_1}^{t_2} (1 + r)^{-(t-t_1)} \exp \{_i\mu_t + z(_i\sigma_t)\} \qquad (3.13)$$

where, as before, $_i\mu_t$ and $_i\sigma_t$ give the profiles of the mean and standard deviation of log-earnings in the ith occupational group, and r is the constant discount rate. It would also be possible to allow for differential mortality, by for example allowing t_2 to vary according to the individual's occupation and relative earnings position, but this complication will not be explored here.

If the cross-sectional profiles are used then it is not necessary to use the average value of lifetime earnings; it can be shown, as before, that this will only affect the constant term in the regression. The specification is therefore

$$(\log Y)_S = \text{constant} + \delta(\log Y)_F + u \qquad (3.14)$$

Unlike the earlier approach of equation (3.11), the use of variables based on a measure of lifetime earnings would not give the same result for both cross-sectional and cohort profiles, even with the simple model developed in section 3.1

3.4 AN APPLICATION

Bowley's Measurement of Social Phenomena

Bowley's book on *The Measurement of Social Phenomena* (1915) seems to have been neglected in more recent studies. In a section on 'the very troublesome problem' of classification by social position, Bowley (1915, p. 81) summarized the results of a study of the status (based on current occupation) of children compared with that of their fathers. The data were obtained from sample surveys of working-class households in Northampton, Warrington and Reading. In an appendix (1915, pp. 227–41), Bowley gave details of 193 households in which at least one child was found to be placed in a different grade from that of the father. This information, including the age, occupation and weekly earnings of each working member of the household, is used in the comparisons given below. In 128 households at least one child was in a higher grade than the father, and in 65 households at least one child was in a lower grade. There were 472 households where there was no change in status, and in 1 076 households no children were in employment. The advantages of using earnings rather than occupation to study inter-generational mobility are discussed in Atkinson et al. (1983).

It must be stressed immediately that these data are seriously limited, and are used mainly to illustrate the different point estimates of 'regression towards the mean' which may be obtained using alternative procedures, rather than to provide a serious measure of regression. The primary purpose of this chapter is to discuss alternative techniques of analysis which could be applied to better data. Bowley's data do not include information about children who may have left the parent's household, or about other non-working members of the household. Furthermore, they do not include details of the 472 households in which no change of occupation status was observed. The results therefore measure regression within a rather restricted group.

Earnings Profiles for Bowley's Data

The first stage of the analysis requires the estimation of earnings profiles. Not all the information about occupation, age and earnings was complete, although full details were available for 109 families. In these families there was a total of 72 second or later sons, and regressions can be obtained for 181 father–son pairs by creating an 'additional' father for each extra son. In addition to these 290 (= 2(109) + 72) individuals, full information was given for a further 70 individuals where details for the rest of the family were incomplete. The age-earnings profiles used were therefore based on a sample of 360 (= 290 + 70) individuals. Using the classification given by Bowley, the individuals could be grouped into the following occupational classes: labourer (85); unskilled (6); skilled (215) (this category also includes the small number classified as clerical).

The profiles of mean-log-earnings, μ_t, with age, t, were obtained by carrying out ordinary least squares regressions on the individual observations. The results are given in Table 3.1. Individuals in each category were then placed in seven age groups, within each of which the variance of log-earnings was calculated. Regressions were carried out of the variance of log-earnings on the average age in each age group, giving the results in Table 3.2. For the labourers and unskilled workers there was no systematic increase

Table 3.1   Earnings profiles

All occupations combined	$\hat{\mu}_t = 0.657$ (0.125)	$+ 0.129t$ (0.008)	$- 0.00148t^2$ (0.0012)	$R^2 = 0.560$
Labourer	$\hat{\mu}_t = 1.238$ (0.191)	$+ 0.0896t$ (0.0113)	$- 0.001t^2$ (0.0001)	$R^2 = 0.536$
Unskilled	$\hat{\mu}_t = 0.908$ (0.234)	$+ 0.0935t$ (0.0150)	$- 0.001t^2$ (0.0002)	$R^2 = 0.643$
Skilled	$\hat{\mu}_t = 0.125$ (0.189)	$+ 0.172t$ (0.013)	$- 0.002t^2$ (0.0002)	$R^2 = 0.611$

in the variance of the logarithms of weekly earnings with age; these were taken as being constant at 0.015 and 0.07 respectively.

Empirical Results on Mobility

In estimating the specification in equation (3.5) the values of μ at appropriate ages may be taken from the estimated age-earnings profiles given above. The estimated value of δ using this approach was found to be 0.065 ($\pm$ 0.0775), with $R^2 = 0.004$. This was based on a regression using 183 observations and including information about all sons. Results obtained when the sample was restricted to oldest sons were very similar, but gave slightly lower estimates of δ. Bowley's data therefore indicate considerable mobility and regression towards the mean. It may be added that the same basic results are produced when a transition matrix framework is used. Thus if all individuals are placed in quartiles, relative to the distribution of earnings of those in the same age group, a four-by-four transition matrix can be produced showing age-adjusted relative earnings movements between fathers and sons. Using this approach it was found that about one third of father–son 'pairs'

Table 3.2   Variance profiles

All occupations combined	$\sigma_t^2 = 0.657$ (0.0362)	$+ 0.0011t$ (0.0008)	$R^2 = 0.238$
Skilled	$\sigma_t^2 = 0.0056$ (0.00755)	$+ 0.00364t$ (0.00185)	$R^2 = 0.436$

were on the leading diagonal, one third were above the leading diagonal, and the remaining third were below the diagonal.

Estimation of equation (3.8), for all occupations combined, produced an estimate of δ of 0.079 ($\pm$ 0.0926) with $R^2 = 0.004$. This approach therefore yields a higher value of δ than that obtained when the variation in the dispersion of earnings with age is ignored. This result occurs even though the systematic increase in relative dispersion with age is quite low. When allowing for occupational differences, as in section 3.3, the Bowley data were divided into only three groups: labourer, unskilled and skilled. In this context it was seen that the calculated value of δ will depend on the common age, t^*, used. For example, estimates of δ based on the specification in (3.12) ranged from 0.141 ($\pm$ 0.2697) for t^* = 25, to 0.132 ($\pm$ 0.2506) for t^* = 35, and 0.121 ($\pm$ 0.2901) when t^* = 50 years. In each case the value of R^2 was only 0.0015. The differences between the various values of t^* are nevertheless very small. More interesting is the result that these estimates are all somewhat larger than when the specifications in (3.5) and (3.8) were used. Hence the appropriate allowance for differences between the age-earnings profiles of broad occupational groups has increased the estimate of δ and thus reduced the extent of measured regression towards the mean. This result arises because the sons were all younger than their fathers at the time of the survey (all members of the household were interviewed at the same date), and because the higher-earning occupations have relatively steeper profiles. Atkinson et al. (1983) did not allow for occupational differences in age-earnings profiles, but because of the indifferent sampling procedure it cannot be said, without having further details, that their results are unambiguously biased downwards.

Estimated lifetime earnings were calculated using equation (3.13) and allowing for the use of weekly earnings, in order to carry out the estimation of equation (3.14). It was found that with t_1 and t_2 of 15 and 65 respectively, and for discount rates of 0 and 0.10, the estimated values of δ using Bowley's data are 0.121 ($\pm$ 0.2901) and 0.117 ($\pm$ 0.2829) respectively (in both cases $R^2 = 0.001$). These are slightly lower than when a standard age is used, but still higher than the value of δ obtained when no allowance is made for occupational differences in age-earnings profiles. If, however, all earnings values are calculated using cohort profiles, with β = 0.03, estimates of δ are 0.125 ($\pm$ 0.3006) and 0.117 ($\pm$ 0.2812) for rates of interest of 0 and 0.10 respectively. With β increased to 0.05, the values change to 0.123 ($\pm$ 0.3083) and 0.118 ($\pm$ 0.2819). Hence, using Bowley's data the use of cohort profiles makes very little difference to the results. Thus, the various modifications, especially the allowances for occupational differences in earnings profiles, showed less regression towards the mean than when a very simple life-cycle adjustment was made. It is therefore suggested that results which use only simple life-cycle adjustment should be treated with caution.

NOTES AND FURTHER READING

In the sample used by Atkinson et al. (1983) the distribution of fathers' wages is truncated, although this does not lead to bias. Where sampling involves tracing the fathers of a (truncated) sample of sons (as in Harbury and McMahon, 1973), a bias is introduced, as shown by Prais (1977). Atkinson et al. (1983) use weekly earnings for fathers and hourly earnings for sons, assuming that the difference affects only the constant term. This seems reasonable in view of the fact that little is known about the relationship among the different measures. The problems of using simultaneous equation models of inter-generational inequality, involving the role of education, have also been examined by Jenkins (1982), and Atkinson and Jenkins (1984).

Bowley later returned to the subject of occupational mobility between generations in Bowley (1935), when he reported on findings from the New Survey of London Life and Labour.

In consulting the results of section 3.4, it is worth noting that when only weekly earnings are available the extent of increasing dispersion tends to be understated compared with that of annual earnings. If the variance of the logarithms of earnings is assumed to increase by 0.002 units per year (compared with the 0.0011 units used above), then a slightly higher value of δ is obtained. Estimation of equation (3.8) gives a regression coefficient of 0.0842 ($\pm$ 0.0995). However, the opposite applies for the approaches which allow for occupational differences, when the age profiles of σ_t^2 are assumed to be steeper for each occupation.

4. Lifetime Earnings of Men in Australia

The majority of occupational earnings comparisons and attempts to measure inequality are based on the use of annual data even though, as argued in Chapter 1, a concept of income which is based on a much longer period is usually more appropriate. It is also unusual for commentators to disaggregate by age groups, despite the usefulness of such a basic decomposition. The single most important reason for the concentration on annual aggregative measures is without doubt the paucity of data covering a longer period, particularly in Australia, where official sources of information about incomes are weak and where longitudinal data are scarce by comparison with many European countries and the United States of America.

The collection of longitudinal information over an extended period is of course expensive and time consuming. But it is often possible to gain very useful information from quite short time periods. This is because in considering inequality over a longer period there is a fundamental connection between relative earnings mobility and the extent to which any measure of inequality changes as the accounting period is extended. Only in the extreme situation where there is no relative mobility, so that everyone receives the same percentage change from one year to the next, will inequality be unaffected by the time period over which incomes are measured. Information about the mobility process itself can therefore be used to provide insights into the effects on inequality of measuring incomes over longer periods. Fortunately, such information can often be obtained from relatively short longitudinal surveys, covering as little as three years. Knowledge of the mobility process, assuming it to be stable, can therefore be combined with data relating to the distribution of income in different age groups to provide estimates of the inequality of income over a much longer period.

Unfortunately, researchers in Australia do not have access to even such limited information. The attempt to consider longer periods may therefore appear to be hopeless. This raises the question of whether it is possible to gain some insight into the mobility process using only cross-sectional data giving information about the distribution of income within different age groups. The question concerns the possibility that simple assumptions about the mobility process, operating on a cohort of ageing individuals, have convenient implications for the income distributions of different age groups so that the parameters of the mobility process can be identified and estimated from cross-sectional data. It turns out that it is possible, in certain circumstances, to obtain such indirect estimates.

This chapter considers indirect estimates of the process of relative earnings mobility from one year to the next, using only cross-sectional data. These estimates are then used to provide measures of the distribution of earnings over longer accounting periods. The basic approach is described in section 4.1. Measures of inequality are examined in section 4.2, while section 4.3 provides a limited number of occupational comparisons.

4.1   AGE-EARNINGS PROFILES

Dispersion and Mobility

Consider first the implications for annual inequality of relative earnings mobility, that is, the extent to which individuals move relative to each other within the distribution of income from year to year. Concern is therefore with the way in which relative earnings, defined as the ratio of earnings to geometric mean earnings in the individual's age group, change over time (and thus over age). The proportional change in the ratio can be approximated by the difference between the logarithms of the ratio from one period to the next. Hence if for individual i at time t, z_{it} denotes the logarithm of the ratio of income to geometric mean income in the age group, the proportional change in relative income from period $t - 1$ to period t is $z_{it} - z_{i,t-1}$. The simplest kind of mobility process to envisage is one in which at any time the proportional change in relative income is independent of both the level of income and of previous proportional changes. This implies that there are no *systematic* movements of individuals within the income distribution of their contemporaries. The changes may for present purposes be regarded as 'random'. In a more detailed analysis it would of course be necessary to relate these movements to particular factors such as sickness or unemployment experience, but this is not the concern of the present chapter, which simply requires a broad description of the process. If u_{it} is a random variable distributed independently of z and previous values, relative earnings are generated by the simple first-order Markov process whereby:

$$z_{it} = z_{i,t-1} + u_{it} \qquad (4.1)$$

This type of Markov process is, in the contexts of earnings changes and the growth of firms, generally referred to as Gibrat's 'Law of proportionate effect'. If, further, the variance of the u's is the same in each period and is denoted σ_u^2, and the variance of z_{it} is denoted σ_t^2, then taking variances of equation (4.1) gives:

$$\sigma_t^2 = \sigma_{t-1}^2 + \sigma_u^2 \qquad (4.2)$$

Equation (4.2) is a simple first-order difference equation, and continual substitution (using $\sigma_{t-1}^2 = \sigma_{t-2}^2 + \sigma_u^2$ and so on) gives:

$$\sigma_t^2 = \sigma_o^2 + t\sigma_u^2 \qquad (4.3)$$

Equation (4.3) implies that the variance of the logarithms of income in each year grows linearly with the number of years in the labour market. If σ_t^2 is plotted against time, the result is a straight line with intercept σ_o^2 and slope σ_u^2. An implication of the above argument is that, if σ_u^2 remains constant over time and there are no other independent factors acting over calendar time to influence the dispersion of earnings in different age groups, an estimate of σ_u^2 can be obtained using cross-sectional data. These assumptions are of course rather strong and cannot be expected to hold precisely, but in many cases they are found to provide a good approximation.

A frequency distribution of income for men in five age groups in the year 1985–86 is given in the Australian Bureau of Statistics'

Income Distribution Survey (1988, p. 18, Table 10). Gross annual earned income is given for men who were full-time, full-year workers during the period. These data were used to calculate the variance of the logarithms of income in each age group shown in the second column of Table 4.1. In the absence of further information about the age distribution within each age group, it is reasonable to take the midpoints of each group in assigning the values of t. It is convenient to measure t from the midpoint of the lowest age group (20 years); the age groups therefore correspond to values of t of 0, 9.5, 19.5, 29.5 and 40.

These data can be used to estimate the parameters in equation (4.3). Instead of estimating the profile of σ_t^2 separately, the approach involved the joint estimation of (4.3) along with the profile of geometric mean income with age, discussed below. A non-linear (iterative) maximum likelihood procedure was used that makes full use of all the information contained in the joint distribution of age and income. The process is equivalent to a series of weighted regressions. All the parameters are highly significantly different from zero. The point estimates of σ_o^2 and σ_u^2 were found to be 0.1817 and 0.00575 respectively.

Hence the variance of the distribution of proportional changes in relative earnings from one year to the next is estimated to be 0.00575. It would of course be possible to obtain highly significant parameter estimates even if the specification of linearity were inappropriate. Useful information is therefore provided by the estimated values of σ_t^2 corresponding to these parameters, which are shown in the last column of Table 4.1.

Table 4.1   Earnings in various age groups: Australian men 1985–86

Age group	Geometric mean income ($s)	Variance of logarithms of income	
		Actual	Estimated
15–24	14 580.57	0.192	0.182
25–34	20 585.43	0.234	0.236
35–44	22 861.70	0.265	0.294
45–54	20 570.04	0.361	0.351
55 and over	18 848.73	0.454	0.412

Despite the fact that this linear specification provides a very good approximation, it is necessary to consider whether such a linear relationship could be generated by a different process of relative earnings mobility. It can be shown that a process in which relative changes are correlated with previous changes, but which is otherwise similar to that described above, produces a profile of σ_t^2 that is almost linear. The deviation from a straight line is too small to allow discrimination by the data, using the method of maximum likelihood. For example, if instead of assuming the independence of u_{it} from earlier values, it is assumed that:

$$u_{it} = \varrho u_{it-1} + \varepsilon_{it} \tag{4.4}$$

with ε_{it} having a constant variance of σ_ε^2, the profile of σ_t^2 is a very complex, but almost linear, function of t. Experiments with alternative parameter values show that values of $\varrho = 0.3$ and $\sigma_\varepsilon^2 = 0.0029$, combined with $\sigma_o^2 = 0.1817$ from above, can be found to give a profile of σ_t^2 which is hard to distinguish from the last column of Table 4.1. For present purposes, however, this potentially awkward problem turns out to be unimportant. This is because calculations have shown that combinations of ϱ and σ_ε^2 giving the same profile for σ_t^2 as the simple model of equation (4.1) also turn out to give the same inequality measures for earnings measured over longer periods than a single year.

Geometric Mean Earnings and Age

The analysis has so far concerned the estimation of the extent of relative earnings mobility using information about the increasing dispersion of earnings with age in a cross-sectional sample. The first column of Table 4.1 gives the geometric mean income in each of the five age groups, showing the typical parabolic pattern observed in so many cross-sectional samples. If μ_t denotes the logarithm of the geometric mean in age group t, the parabolic function is given by:

$$\mu_t = \mu_o + \theta t - \delta t^2 \tag{4.5}$$

where μ_o is the value when $t = 0$ and θ and δ are parameters controlling the variation in μ_t with age. It is well known that this type of profile is consistent with a simple human capital approach to earnings profiles, but the present analysis concentrates on producing a statistical description. Estimation of these parameters using the information in the *Income Distribution Survey* gives values of 9.612, 0.0385 and 0.00086 for μ_o, θ and δ respectively. As mentioned above, these were estimated jointly with the other two parameters using maximum likelihood, and are highly significantly different from zero. The observed and expected values (in parentheses) of μ_t are: 9.587 (9.612); 9.932 (9.901); 10.037 (10.038); 9.932 (10.003); 9.844 (9.782). This shows the close fit of the quadratic in (4.5) to the data.

Productivity Growth

In the present context it is necessary to ask how reliable the variation in earnings with age in a cross-section is likely to be as a guide to the growth of earnings within a particular cohort of individuals, for example those aged 20 years in 1985–86. The variation in average earnings of the cohort will in general depend on factors associated with calendar time (the special circumstances of the period), and factors related to the cohort itself (such as the size of the cohort), in addition to those associated purely with the process of ageing. It is extremely difficult, even with detailed longitudinal data, to separate the three sets of effects. The cross-section profile will provide a reliable guide only when effects other than those associated with ageing are absent. In the present circumstances the most suitable adjustment to the cross-section profile of μ_t is to impose an appropriate rate of productivity growth over the working life of a cohort. If all individuals benefit equally from growth, then it is necessary simply to add the proportional rate to the term θ in (4.5). The rate of growth chosen has a negligible effect on inequality measurement even though it affects the absolute values of lifetime earnings. The following results are obtained on the assumption that growth is 3 per cent, so that θ is increased from 0.0385 to 0.0685. The main implication of this is that average earnings reach a maximum much later than is shown in Table 4.1.

Earnings Profiles

The parameters of equations (4.3) and (4.5) estimated from the cross-sectional data, together with the growth parameter, can be used to generate prospective age-earnings profiles. In addition to the variation in mean earnings with age it is also useful to examine the profiles of various deciles of the distribution in each age group. Hence an assumption about the form of the distribution is necessary, and it is assumed here that the distribution in each age group can be described by the lognormal form which is defined by the mean and variance of the logarithms. Figure 4.1 shows profiles of arithmetic mean income, $\bar{y}$, together with the first and ninth deciles D_1 and D_9, and the median D_5. In the lognormal distribution the median is equal to the geometric mean, the logarithm of which is the arithmetic mean of the logarithms of earnings, while the value of $\bar{y}_t$ can be shown to be equal to $\exp(\mu_t + \sigma_t^2/2)$. The increasing spread of the deciles in Figure 4.1 reflects the increasing

Figure 4.1   Projected age-earnings profiles: Australian men aged 20 in 1985/86, with 3% growth

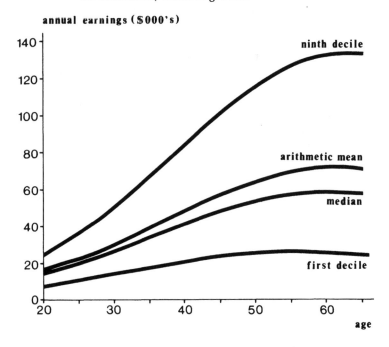

dispersion with age, as measured by σ_t^2, and it can be seen that the lower deciles reach a maximum earlier than the higher deciles.

A number of investigators have calculated the present value of earnings obtained by individuals who follow the profile of arithmetic mean income, $\bar{y}$. This is also equal to the arithmetic mean value of discounted earnings. But it is also of interest to consider the present value of earnings which result from other deciles, particularly when comparing occupations. It should of course be remembered that individuals do not move along such profiles in practice, because of the relative earnings mobility reflected by the term σ_u^2. Some examples are given in Table 4.2, for the periods 20–40 years and 20–65 years, using two different discount rates of 6 per cent and 10 per cent.

4.2 INEQUALITY AND THE TIME PERIOD

For the dynamic process described in the previous section it is possible to derive an explicit expression for the coefficient of variation of income measured over any specified period as mentioned in Chapter 1, but it does not seem possible to derive useful expressions for other measures of inequality. Denote the coefficient of variation of income in year t by η_t and that of the discounted value of income measured from period 1 to period t by

Table 4.2   Discounted earnings: Australian men aged 20 in 1985–86

Decile	Age 20–40		Age 20–65	
	6%	10%	6%	10%
1	168 315	123 273	271 576	159 057
3	242 529	176 682	404 181	232 370
5	312 463	226 786	533 031	302 456
Mean	351 446	254 211	614 592	344 060
7	402 689	291 190	703 737	394 039
9	581 156	417 989	1 053 143	578 259

Note
Assumed growth rate = 3%.

$\eta_{(t)}$. If $\bar{y}_t$ is arithmetic mean income of the cohort is year t and if c_t is the appropriate discount factor $(c_t = 1/(1 + r)^t)$, it can be shown that:

$$\eta_{(t)}^2 = \sum_{s=1}^{t} \left\{ \sum_{r=1}^{s} c_r \bar{y}_r \eta_r^2 + \eta_s^2 \sum_{r=s+1}^{t} c_r \bar{y}_r \right\} c_s \bar{y}_s \Bigg/ \left\{ \sum_{r=1}^{t} \bar{y}_r c_r \right\}^2 \quad (4.6)$$

The values of $\bar{y}_t$ and η_t^2 are obtained from the values of μ_t and σ_t^2 (using equations 4.3 and 4.5) and the fact that for the lognormal distribution:

$$\eta_t^2 = \exp(\sigma_t^2) - 1 \quad (4.7)$$

Table 4.3 gives the coefficient of variation measured over a variety of time periods using discount rates of 6 per cent and 10 per cent. The value of the coefficient of variation of annual income in the last year of the period is also given. The first row of the table shows that η_2 is 0.454 while the values of $\eta_{(2)}$ for discount rates of 6 per cent and 10 per cent are respectively 0.315 and 0.318. It can be seen that for relatively shorter periods, up to ten years, the value of $\eta_{(t)}$ is lower than for *any* single period and significantly lower than the value of η_t. For longer time periods the value of $\eta_{(t)}$ exceeds those of η_t in the earlier years.

Table 4.3 also shows that the value of $\eta_{(t)}$ increases with the discount rate for the relatively shorter time periods, but falls for higher values of t. This result may at first seem a little surprising, but in the notes to this chapter it is shown that a sufficient condition for $\eta_{(t)}$ to increase with the discount rate is that it is lower than for any single year. The complete profiles of $\eta_{(t)}$ and η_t are shown in Figure 4.2, which shows clearly the difference between the annual dispersion of earnings and that of the long period measure. This figure gives the profile for a discount rate of zero, for comparisons.

It is of interest to consider the extent to which relative earnings mobility contributes to inequality, both within a single period and for earnings measured over a longer period. It is of course obvious that mobility will have a larger effect, the longer the time period. The effect of mobility only can be examined by repeating the above calculations with σ_o^2, the initial variance of logarithms of annual earnings, set equal to zero. This corresponds to the

*Figure 4.2   Dispersion of annual and long period earnings:
Australian men aged 20 in 1985/86*

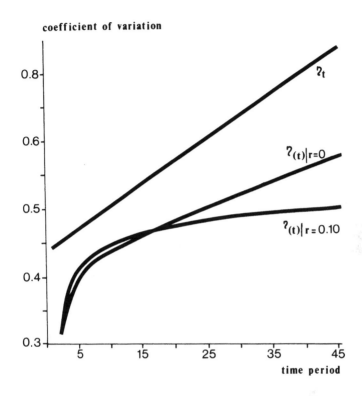

*Table 4.3   Coefficient of variation of annual and long period
income: Australian men aged 20 in 1985–86*

Income measured from year 1 to year –	Annual income in year –	Total income over period	
		6%	10%
2	0.454	0.315	0.318
4	0.469	0.390	0.394
8	0.499	0.432	0.434
10	0.513	0.443	0.445
20	0.581	0.480	0.476
30	0.646	0.504	0.492
45	0.738	0.528	0.502

situation in which all members of the cohort have an 'equal start' at the beginning of the working life. Results are shown in Table 4.4, which gives the ratio of the coefficient of variation when $\sigma_o^2 = 0$ to that obtained with the actual value of σ_o^2 of 0.1817; this ratio is denoted $\eta_{(t)}^0/\eta(t)$ for the long period measure, and $\eta_t^0/\eta(t)$ for the annual measure. The final column shows that when all individuals start with the same income, annual inequality gradually increases to about 73 per cent of its actual value from being zero in the first year, reflecting the importance of mobility in causing earnings to become more widely dispersed. In the extreme case where the discount rate is zero, the coefficient of variation of earnings measured over the longer period increases to about 60 per cent of its value when allowance is made for the unequal start. For a discount rate of 10 per cent, mobility contributes to 42 per cent of the coefficient of variation when earnings are measured over a 45-year period. It is not surprising that the contribution of mobility to long period inequality falls as the discount rate increases, and the initial extent of inequality is given more prominence.

4.3 OCCUPATIONAL COMPARISONS

It has been stressed that there are few data in Australia relating

Table 4.4 Contribution of mobility to inequality

Income measured from year 1 to year –	$\eta_{(t)}^0/\eta_t$		η_t^0/η'
	0%	10%	
4	0.143	0.132	0.281
8	0.248	0.225	0.407
10	0.287	0.256	0.448
20	0.425	0.349	0.585
30	0.514	0.394	0.659
45	0.590	0.420	0.728

to the distribution of income in various age groups, for different occupational or industrial groups. Some information is, however, available from the data collected as part of the 1985–86 income distribution survey carried out by the Australian Bureau of Statistics. The magnetic tapes contain information about 17 714 individuals, of whom fewer than 5 000 men can be included in an analysis of age-earnings profiles. When the sample is further divided into occupations and/or industries, there are often insufficient numbers for further disaggregation into age groups. In some cases the profile of σ_t^2 is too irregular so that, even where the estimated values of σ_u^2 are significantly different from zero, there is too much doubt about either the sample or the applicability of the simple process of relative earnings mobility described above.

Reliable estimates were, however, obtained for several occupations and industries. The parameters of the earnings profiles are reported in Table 4.5. It can be seen that in all cases the coefficient δ is not significantly different from zero, but it is clear from profiles of μ_t that omission of the term involving the square of t would not be appropriate. Only for construction workers is the estimated parameter σ_u^2 not significantly different from zero; the variation in σ_t^2, despite being quite systematic, is very small. This suggests that earnings mobility within the distribution of contemporaries is

Table 4.5   Age-earnings profiles

Group	μ_o	θ	δ	σ_o^2	σ_u^2
Tradespersons	9.627	0.0197	0.00052	0.179	0.01148
	(0.038)	(0.00014)	(0.00517)	(0.013)	(0.00096)
Clerks	9.650	0.0356	0.00074	0.070	0.00387
	(0.078)	(0.00019)	(0.00863)	(0.0137)	(0.00081)
Manufacturing	9.531	0.0436	0.0009	0.127	0.0076
	(0.035)	(0.00012)	(0.0047)	(0.0105)	(0.00071)
Construction	9.477	0.0280	0.00069	0.520	0.0012
	(0.094)	(0.00026)	(0.0108)	(0.0426)	(0.0021)
Wholesale/	9.513	0.0291	0.00065	0.311	0.0159
Retail Trade	(0.059)	(0.0002)	(0.00784)	(0.0266)	(0.0018)

Note
Standard errors are given in parentheses.

limited in the construction industry, although the initial level of
dispersion is very high. Thus tradespersons and wholesale/retail
male workers, who display much more earnings mobility, have a
higher dispersion of income in older age groups than construction
workers, despite the fact that the initial level of inequality is much
lower.

It can be seen that construction and wholesale/retail workers
have very similar profiles of μ_t, although their inequality and
mobility characteristics are different. The implications for earnings
measured over a longer period are shown in Table 4.6, for a rate
of interest of 10 per cent and earnings measured from age 20 to
age 55. As before, real earnings growth of 3 per cent has been
assumed. The limitation of calculating only the present value of
mean earnings is clearly shown in this table.

Table 4.6   Earnings from age 20 to age 55
(Rate of interest = 10%)

Group	D_1	Mean	D_9	Coefficient of variation
Tradespersons	124 999	292 334	508 118	0.538
Clerks	192 123	314 880	460 098	0.322
Manufacturing	155 941	313 522	510 124	0.446
Construction	90 050	300 051	586 108	0.831
Wholesale/Retail	100 762	313 231	600 371	0.726

For clerks and those in manufacturing and wholesale/retail work
the present values along the arithmetic mean profiles are similar.
However, earnings along the first and ninth deciles are different,
because of the differences in mobility and inequality characteristics. Decisions concerning occupational choice would be
different, depending on the anticipated relative position in the
distribution. It is also noticeable that tradespersons, who have the
second highest value of σ_u^2 have the lowest average present value
of earnings. If mobility, as reflected by σ_u^2, is thought to measure
the riskiness of the earnings profiles, then there is little evidence
in Table 4.6 to suggest that higher risk is compensated by higher
earnings measured over the longer period. This contradicts a

common argument that high earnings provide a compensating variation for risk.

NOTES AND FURTHER READING

It was shown in Table 4.3 and Figure 4.2 that, for a small number of years, the coefficient of variation of the present value of income is higher when the discount rate is higher. The condition required for this result to hold is obtained here for the simplest case of aggregation over two periods. If y_{it} denotes individual i's income in period t and Y_i denotes the present value over two periods, with discount rate r, then

$$Y_i = y_{i1} + y_{i2}/(1 + r) \tag{4.8}$$

If $E(Y)$ and $V(Y)$ denote the mean and variance respectively of y, then:

$$E(Y) = \bar{y}_1 + \bar{y}_2/(1 + r) \tag{4.9}$$

$$\begin{aligned} V(Y) &= E(Y^2) - E(Y)^2 \\ &= s_1^2 + s_2^2/(1 + r) + 2s_{12}/(1 + r) \end{aligned} \tag{4.10}$$

where s_1^2 and s_2^2 are variances of y_1 and y_2, and s_{12} is the covariance between y_1 and y_2. If the correlation coefficient is ϱ, then $s_{12} = \varrho s_1 s_2$. The coefficient of variation of earnings in each year is given by $\eta_t^2 = V(y)/E(y)^2$, while the coefficient of variation of earnings measured over t periods is given by $\eta_{(t)}^2 = V(Y)/E(Y)^2$. Then:

$$\eta_{(2)}^2 = \frac{(1 + r)^2 s_1^2 + s_2^2 + 2(1 + r)\varrho s_1 s_2}{(1 + r)^2 \bar{y}_1^2 + \bar{y}_2^2 + 2(1 + r)\bar{y}_1 \bar{y}_2} \tag{4.11}$$

Differentiating (4.11) with respect to r, gives after some tedious manipulation:

$$\frac{d\eta_{(2)}^2}{dr} = 2\{(1 + r)\bar{y}_1^2(\eta_1^2 - \eta_{(2)}^2) + \varrho\bar{y}_1\bar{y}_2(\eta_1\eta_2 - \eta_{(2)}^2)\}/E(Y)^2 \tag{4.12}$$

Hence (4.12) shows that a *sufficient* condition for $\eta_{(2)}$ to increase when r increases is that $\eta_{(1)}^2 > \eta_{(2)}^2$ and $\eta_1\eta_2 > \eta_{(2)}^2$. In the present context the dispersion of earnings rises with age so that $\eta_2 > \eta_1$ and only the first condition in the previous sentence is required for sufficiency.

Hancock and Richardson (1985) used the 1976 Australian Census to make inferences from cross-sectional data about arithmetic mean lifetime earnings in various occupations. Their paper considers the relationship between the discount rate and the coefficient of variation of average lifetime earnings (the latter is the 'between group' component of overall lifetime inequality).

The estimation procedure used to obtain age-earnings profiles is explained in Creedy (1985, pp. 68–70). The precise equation for σ_t^2 is derived in Creedy (1985, p. 39). The values of ϱ and σ_ε^2 cannot be identified by cross-sectional data, but require genuine longitudinal data for a sample of individuals over at least three years. Geometric mean income reaches a maximum for the value of t given by $\theta/2\delta$, so that the increase in θ to allow for productivity of, say g, increases the value of t by $g/2\delta$.

5. Earnings Profiles and Compensation

This chapter considers the use of information about age-earnings profiles in the calculation of the lump sum to be awarded to the dependants of an accident victim. The usual assumption is that real earnings remain constant at their annual value at the time of the accident unless there is specific evidence relating to a pay rise or promotion. No allowance is made for the general growth of real earnings in the economy which may be anticipated over the period of the dependency. More importantly, the assumption of constant earnings ignores the fact that the distribution of earnings within each age group varies systematically over the life cycle. There is clearly an asymmetry in the standard treatment of earnings, since probabilities of sickness and unemployment, along with information from life tables, are often used to reduce prospective future earnings.

Dependants of young accident victims who are in occupations with relatively steeply rising earnings profiles will receive significantly less than anticipated. The use of data on age-earnings profiles to produce a projected earnings profile of the deceased is examined. An important additional element in the calculation of an award is the appropriate allowance for the taxation of interest income arising from the investment of the lump sum. This potentially important factor is often treated in a very cursory manner by the courts. The following therefore concentrates on earnings profiles and the allowance for income taxation, and neglects other considerations which have been given more attention in the literature.

Section 5.1 presents the basic calculation required under the assumption of constant earnings and discusses the allowance for interest income taxation. The use of a model of age-earnings profiles is then examined in section 5.2. Further comparisons are reported in section 5.3.

5.1   CONSTANT EARNINGS

Suppose an individual dies aged t_1 with an annual income of y. The period of the dependency may be taken to extend from t_1 to the date of retirement, at t_2. First it is necessary to deduct income taxation from y, to arrive at net earnings of w. The use of a constant value of w over the period of the dependency thus requires an assumption, usually quite implicit, that the tax structure remains unchanged and is indexed appropriately. The present value of the fixed stream of w, evaluated at the real interest rate, r_r, must then be multiplied by a dependency proportion, d, in order to obtain the lump sum, V_1. Consistent with the use of a fixed income stream, it is typically assumed that d is also constant, though a more general treatment may wish to allow it to vary. The value of V_1 is given by:

$$V_1 = dw \sum_{t=t_1}^{t_2} \left(\frac{1}{1 + r_r} \right)^{t - t_1} \qquad (5.1)$$

The real interest rate used is often specified by law, giving the courts no degree of freedom over its value. In terms of the nominal rate of interest, r_n, and the inflation rate, p, the real rate is given by:

$$r_r = \frac{1 + r_n}{1 + p} - 1 \qquad (5.2)$$

For example, suppose $r_n = 0.13$ and $p = 0.08$, so that the real interest rate is equal to 0.0463. Consider an individual earning \$30 000 at age 40 years, in 1986 (the choice of 1986 will be clear in section 5.3). The income tax structure in that year is given in Table 5.1.

Table 5.1 shows that no tax is paid below \$4 595, and that income above this threshold and below \$12 500 is taxed at the

Table 5.1   Income tax structure: Australia 1986

Threshold	1	2	3	4	5
Income (\$s)	4 595	12 500	19 500	28 000	35 000
Tax rate	0.25	0.30	0.46	0.48	0.60

constant marginal rate of 0.25. Hence the income of $30 000 would be liable to taxation of $8 946.25, leaving a net income of $21 053.75. With a dependency proportion, d, of say 0.7, it is required to find the present value of the constant consumption stream of $14 737.63 (equal to 21 053.75 multiplied by 0.7) from age 40 to 65, that is, over a 26-year period. At the above real rate of interest of 0.0463, the present value, V_1, is found to be $230 383.80.

Allowing for Taxation

The amount V_1 does not give the appropriate value of the award because of the fact that the interest income arising from the award, which will be quite significant during the early years of the dependency, is subject to income taxation. Only when the income tax structure is proportional is it possible to make a simple adjustment; with a proportional rate of t the calculations could simply be made using a net-of-tax real interest rate of $r_r(1 - t)$. But with a multi-step tax function no analytical solution is available, as shown in the notes to this chapter. The typical approach is to make a very *ad hoc* adjustment to V_1, with very little explanation. It must, however, be recognized that the appropriate adjustment requires an explicit assumption about the *nominal* rate of interest over the period of the dependency, along with an assumption about the way in which the tax thresholds are adjusted. This is because nominal, rather than real interest, income is taxable.

Suppose that interest and inflation rates are as specified above, but that tax thresholds are adjusted at the rate of 0.09 per year (this allows for some real income growth and the adjustment of thresholds in relation to incomes rather than prices). The lump sum of $230 383.80 would yield interest income of $29 949.89 in the first year, which would attract income tax of $8 837.20. After the consumption of the dependency of $14 737.63 this would leave $236 758.90. The second year's interest income is thus higher, at $30 778.65, attracting tax of $8 736.51; this is lower than the first year because of the threshold indexation. But to keep real consumption constant, an amount equal to $15 916.64 must be withdrawn from the fund, leaving $242 884.40 for the next year. Thus the lump sum increases in the early years, but the effect of inflation on the nominal consumption (while real consumption is constant) eventually dominates. By the 18th year the lump sum is reduced to $174 407.50, interest income taxation is only $696.87 but consumption increases to $54 529.54. It can be found that the original lump sum will last only 20.7 years rather than the 26 required. If tax thresholds are not adjusted, the lump sum lasts only 18.5 years (in the 18th year interest income tax is $1 527.80).

The appropriate adjustment of the lump sum to allow for interest income taxation can be found numerically using a process of iteration. It can be found that, with indexation of 0.09 and the other assumptions made earlier, the present value of $230 383.80 needs to be increased to $286 998 in order to finance a real consumption flow of $14 737.63 for 26 years. This 'tax adjusted' lump sum may be denoted V_2 in order to distinguish it from V_1 of equation (5.1). It would be helpful if the courts were to use such numerical procedures (using microcomputers) and at the same time make their assumptions explicit.

5.2   THE USE OF EARNINGS PROFILES

An Alternative Approach

The assumption of constant earnings from t_1 to t_2 is unrealistic. In exceptional cases, for example where a promotion was imminent, the courts will make an adjustment. But they ignore the well-established pattern of age-earnings profiles and the evidence showing that profiles differ between occupations. Consider Figure 5.1, which shows the estimated profiles of the median income, and several deciles. These were obtained using cross-sectional data for males in Australia 1985–86 for all occupations combined; see Chapter 4. These profiles reflect the typical shape of age-earnings profiles, showing the systematic increase, until a maximum is reached, and the increasing 'spread' of the deciles in the higher age groups. The latter phenomenon reflects the increasing relative dispersion of incomes with age that has been found in many samples.

The individual considered in section 5.1, who dies aged 40 earning $30 000, is at point D in Figure 5.1. The standard approach assumes that real earnings continue along the horizontal

Figure 5.1 Earnings profiles and compensation

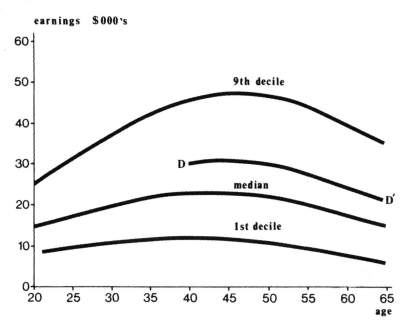

line through D. In view of the fact that it is obviously not possible to know what the individual would have earned between the ages of 40 and 65, the question arises of whether an alternative to the standard approach is reasonable. The dashed line DD' is the earnings profile of the percentile passing through D; that is, along DD' the relative income is exactly the same as at D. Now in practice an individual's relative income position would be expected to fluctuate somewhat, in a manner that cannot be predicted with any certainty. But it seems useful to consider the alternative approach of calculating future income *as if* the individual's relative income position remained unchanged. This is really a less extreme assumption than the view that real income remains unchanged.

It should also be remembered that the profiles in Figure 5.1 are obtained using cross-sectional data; such data are likely to remain the main source of information about earnings profiles. But as individuals age over calendar time, they will also benefit from the growth of real incomes in addition to that associated with ageing. Although the courts have not allowed for real earnings growth in calculating 'lost' earnings, it has been seen that an *implicit* assumption has been made concerning real growth and the indexation of tax thresholds in relation to earnings. It would seem most sensible to be consistent in the treatment of growth, by allowing for it *explicitly* in all stages of the calculations. Because of the obvious uncertainty about future trends, such calculations should also be accompanied by sensitivity analyses. Despite the usual practice of the courts, a consistent treatment of these issues cannot avoid being explicit about absolute values of interest and inflation rates (rather than simply taking an assumed real rate), because it is the *nominal* rather than the real interest income which is liable to taxation.

The alternative approach suggested here is therefore that the award should be based on the present value of earnings, after allowing for income taxation, along a profile such as DD', after allowing for nominal wage growth (combining inflation and real growth) over the period. This present value, multiplied by the proportion d, may be denoted V_3 to distinguish it from the previous lump sums considered. But it is then necessary to adjust V_3 for interest income taxation, using the same assumptions about inflation and indexation as used in the calculation of V_3. This calculation requires the specification of a profile of real consumption over the period. There is clearly an additional arbitrary element introduced here, but the approach suggested here is to use that constant real value of consumption that could be financed over the dependency period using the lump sum V_3, if there were no interest income taxation. The iterative procedure mentioned in section 5.1 could then be used to calculate the tax-adjusted lump sum, which is denoted V_4.

A More Formal Statement

The procedure described above requires the specification and estimation of a model of age-earnings profiles. Define the mean of the logarithms of earnings and the variance of the logarithms of earnings in age group t as μ_t and σ_t^2 respectively. As argued in Chapter 4, the following specification has been found to provide a very good fit to a wide range of data:

$$\mu_t = \mu_0 + \theta t - \delta t^2 \tag{5.3}$$

$$\sigma_t^2 = \sigma_0^2 + \sigma_u^2 t \tag{5.4}$$

The terms μ_0, θ, δ, σ_0^2 and σ_u^2 are parameters which can be estimated using information about the distribution of income in selected age groups. Equation (5.3) shows that μ_t is a quadratic function of age while (5.4) shows that σ_t^2, a measure of relative dispersion, increases linearly with age. It is this growth of σ_t^2 with t which is responsible for the increasing spread of the deciles in Figure 5.1.

As before, the individual dies aged t_1 years with income y. The first stage of the process of calculating the lump sum to be awarded requires the standardized value of y, denoted by q and given by:

$$q = \frac{\log y - \mu_{t_1}}{\sigma_{t_1}} \tag{5.5}$$

A basic assumption is that q remains constant between t_1 and t_2. Hence earnings y_t are generated using:

$$\log y_t = \mu_t + q\sigma_t \qquad t = t_1, \dots, t_2 \tag{5.6}$$

so that
$$y_t = \exp(\mu_t + q\sigma_t) \tag{5.7}$$

Values of σ_t are obtained using equation (5.4), but (5.3) has to be modified to allow for nominal earnings growth (allowing for both inflation and real growth). Suppose that nominal earnings over time are expected to grow at the rate g. This must be added to the growth expected from ageing, so that:

$$\mu_t = \mu_0 + \theta t + g(t - t_1) - \delta t^2 \tag{5.8}$$

for
$$t = t_1, \dots, t_2$$

It should be recognized that the use of (5.5), that is an assumption that the standardized value of log-income remains constant, does not imply that the ratio of income to arithmetic mean income is constant. This may be seen as follows. This may be seen by using the further assumption, again a good approximation to reality, that the distribution of income in each age group can be described by the lognormal distribution. It is known that the arithmetic mean income of age group t, $\bar{y}_t$, is given by:

$$\bar{y}_t = \exp\left(\mu_t + \sigma_t^2/2\right) \tag{5.9}$$

Dividing (5.7) by (5.9) therefore gives:

$$y_t/\bar{y}_t = \exp\left\{\sigma_t(q - \sigma_t/2)\right\} \tag{5.10}$$

which varies with t since σ_t is not constant.

Having obtained the profile of y_t, it is then necessary to convert this to a profile of after-tax incomes, w_t, for $t = t_1, \ldots, t_2$. This requires an explicit assumption about tax threshold indexation. The present value of the dependency, V_3, is then given by:

$$V_3 = d \sum_{t=t_1}^{t_2} w_t \left(\frac{1}{1 + r_n}\right)^{t-t_1} \tag{5.11}$$

Notice that equation (5.11) uses the nominal rate of interest r_n in view of the fact that w_t measures nominal post-tax earnings. This is required in order to maintain consistency with assumptions regarding the indexation of tax thresholds. There is no need to adjust each w_t to a real value in terms of period t_1's prices and then use a real rate of interest. This is because the value of w_t would be adjusted using $w_t/(1 + p)^{t-t_1}$, which would then be discounted using a real interest rate, giving $w_t/\{(1 + r_r)(1 + p)\}^{t-t_1}$. This would give the same as (5.11) given the relationship between real and nominal rates in equation (5.2).

Having obtained V_3 it is then necessary to make the appropriate adjustment to allow for interest income taxation. First, calculate the constant real consumption, c, that could be financed from V_3 if all the previous assumptions hold but there is no taxation. This is given by:

$$c = V_3 r_r v/(1 - v^N) \tag{5.12}$$

with $v = 1/(1 + r_r)$ and $N = t_2 - t_1 + 1$.

The value of c from (5.12) is then used in the iterative procedure which calculates the value of the award, allowing for interest income taxation. This final value gives the award V_4.

An Example

Consider, as above, an individual who dies aged 40 earning an annual income of \$30 000. Using the data from the 1985–86 income distribution survey discussed in Chapter 4, the parameters of the profiles in equations (5.3) and (5.4) are given in section 4.1 with $\tau = t - 20$ as:

$$\mu_\tau = 9.612 + 0.0385\tau - 0.00086\tau^2 \qquad (5.13)$$

$$\sigma_\tau^2 = 0.1817 + 0.00575\tau \qquad (5.14)$$

On the assumption that nominal income grows by 0.09 per year, and that the 1986 income tax thresholds are fully adjusted at the same rate, the various profiles shown in Table 5.2 can be calculated. This table gives information about before and after tax nominal income of the deceased, assuming a constant relative income, along with information about the distribution of income among contemporaries, for five-year intervals (where equation 5.8 is used to calculate μ_t).

At age 40, an individual earning \$30 000 has a standardized log-income, using equation (5.5), of 0.50. It can be found that the

Table 5.2   Income profiles from age 40: 1986 +

Age	Geometric mean income exp (μ_t)	Variance of logarithms σ_t^2	Individual's income before tax	Income tax	Individual's income after tax
40	22 880	0.297	30 000	8 946	21 054
45	35 846	0.331	47 609	14 461	33 148
50	53 798	0.354	72 334	21 809	50 525
55	77 343	0.389	105 222	30 641	74 581
60	106 511	0.412	146 557	39 990	106 566
65	140 505	0.440	195 464	47 714	147 750

Notes
Values have been rounded to the nearest \$. The income tax structure is given in Table 5.1, with thresholds adjusted annually at the rate 0.09.

present value, V_3, of equation (5.11) is equal to $247 747, assuming again a dependency proportion of 0.7 and a nominal rate of interest of 0.13. Without interest income taxation, this lump sum would finance a constant *real* consumption of $15 848.35 per year, on the assumption that inflation is constant at 0.08 and using equation (5.12). It is of interest to compare this annual value with the consumption stream of $14 737.63 that would be used following the standard procedure examined in section 5.1. Hence the allowance for the systematic increase in earnings reflected in the age-income profiles, along with a little real growth in incomes, gives just over $1 000 per year extra for the dependency.

If, however, the lump sum of $247 747 were invested at the constant nominal interest rate of 0.13, where the inflation rate is 0.08, the taxation of interest income means that the attempt to consume a constant real consumption of $15 848.35 would exhaust the lump sum after 20.5 years, rather than the 26 years required. (This assumes that thresholds are adjusted at the same rate as nominal incomes, that is 0.09.) Using the iterative procedure to adjust for taxation, it can be found that the award would need to be increased to $315 920.00; this is the value V_4 discussed above. The method of assessment suggested here would therefore produce an award that is significantly higher than the standard method.

This example has been based on earnings profiles for all males in Australia, but it would be desirable to use information relating to particular occupational or professional groups, where this is available. Further comparisons using such data are presented in the next section. The above approach has taken the annual income at the time of death as the value on which to base the relative position (the value of q). But if evidence (such as data for previous years) suggests that this value is not representative, then a further adjustment may be made.

It should be stressed that this method, using information about age-income profiles, does not necessarily produce a higher award than the standard method. For example, suppose that an individual is earning $30 000 per year at age 50. The corresponding income profiles are shown in Table 5.3. The shape of the age-earnings profiles, illustrated in Figure 5.1, shows that in a cross-sectional comparison the geometric mean in the 40-year age group is slightly higher than that in the 50-year age group. This is also shown by the first row of Table 5.3, compared with the first row of Table 5.2. An individual aged 50 in 1986 has a higher relative income position, given by $q = 0.53$, than a 40-year-old with the same income. The projected nominal earnings of the 50-year-old, as shown in Table 5.3, continually rise until retirement at age 65. But they rise much more slowly than those of the 40-year-old because of the effect of the age-earnings profile.

Table 5.3 Income profiles from age 50: 1986 +

Age	Geometric mean income exp (μ_t)	Variance of logarithms σ_t^2	Individual's income before tax	Income tax	Individual's income after tax
50	21 873	0.354	30 000	8 946	21 054
55	31 445	0.383	43 675	12 573	31 102
60	43 304	0.412	60 878	16 419	44 460
65	57 125	0.440	81 253	19 551	61 702

Notes
See Table 5.2.

It can be found that the present value of after-tax income from age 50 to 65, adjusted for the dependency proportion of 0.70, is equal to $169 462.80 (using the same assumptions as earlier). This would finance a constant real consumption of $14 553.06 per year for 16 years, if there were no interest income taxation. Allowance for taxation gives an award (V_4) of $175 373.10. But the conventional method would be based on a constant dependency of $14 737.63 (as discussed in section 5.1), which can be financed with a lump sum (V_2) of $177 947. Hence in this situation the method suggested here would give an award that is approximately $2 500 *below* the conventional value (provided of course that the correct allowance for interest income taxation is made).

There is another situation in which the present approach (using V_4) gives a lower award than the conventional method (using V_2). It was stressed in section 5.1 that the standard approach makes the *implicit* assumption that the tax thresholds are fully adjusted in line with earnings growth (by the simple application of an assumed real interest rate to a fixed real dependency). A merit of the approach suggested here is that it forces those involved to make their assumptions explicit; such assumptions will usually be the subject of some debate. The calculations reported here have also assumed full indexation of tax thresholds, but it is of interest to consider the implications of partial indexation.

If tax thresholds are not adjusted in line with earnings then the first implication is that a constant real before-tax income stream will be subject to higher tax rates. This is the standard 'built-in flexibility' of a progressive tax structure used by governments to increase tax revenue without appearing to do anything. Thus even if it is assumed that real income remains the same as at death, allowance should be made for the fact that post-tax income will fall. However, in the case considered above of the 40-year-old who dies earning $30 000, the conventional award would be based on a fixed dependency (in real terms) of $14 737.63. The adjustment for interest income taxation, with thresholds adjusted at the annual rate of 0.06, would give an award of $315 223. This involves an asymmetric treatment of tax indexation. The approach suggested here would give a slightly lower real consumption of $14 557 per year, leading to a value of V_4 of $309 874.

5.3 SOME FURTHER COMPARISONS

The examples used in the previous section have been based on the estimated age-earnings profiles for all occupations combined, but of course in practice it would be useful to obtain information about the profiles of particular occupational groups. It is well known that the shapes of earnings profiles differ between occupations. Some further comparisons are shown in Table 5.4, for all males combined and for five occupational/industrial groups. The parameters of the earnings profiles are given in Chapter 4. Results are given for two incomes at death, $30 000 and $40 000, and two ages at death, 30 and 50 years. For the younger age and higher income, the importance of allowing for interest income taxation is clearly very important. The values V_1 to V_4 are those defined earlier. Hence the significance of allowing for age-earnings profiles is reflected in comparisons between V_2 and V_4, for each group.

The biggest differences arise, not surprisingly, for the younger age for those in occupations with the more steeply rising profiles. However, the differences between occupational and industrial

Table 5.4   Some comparisons

	\$30 000		\$40 000	
	30	50	30	50
Constant real income				
Consumption	14 738	14 738	17 958	19 958
V_1	267 762	171 612	326 265	209 107
V_2	413 253	177 947	555 195	223 954
Age-Income Profiles				
ALL OCCUPATIONS				
Consumption	18 663	14 553	23 151	18 071
V_3	339 089	169 463	420 622	210 426
V_4	587 766	175 373	803 252	225 576
TRADESPERSONS				
Consumption	18 637	15 142	23 495	18 784
V_3	338 608	176 325	426 870	218 727
V_4	586 578	183 610	820 516	236 108
CLERKS				
Consumption	19 265	14 943	24 275	18 562
V_3	350 012	174 006	441 044	216 147
V_4	615 807	180 820	859 007	232 836
MANUFACTURING				
Consumption	19 720	14 741	24 964	18 340
V_3	358 282	171 652	453 561	213 562
V_4	637 097	177 995	893 795	229 515
CONSTRUCTION				
Consumption	17 426	14 519	21 141	17 882
V_3	316 560	169 072	384 111	208 225
V_4	530 890	174 915	705 081	222 870
WHOLESALE/RETAIL TRADE				
Consumption	19 224	15 098	24 178	18 720
V_3	349 280	175 806	439 281	217 988
V_4	613 787	182 996	854 308	235 128

Notes
(a) All calculations assume: dependency proportion = 0.7; Inflation rate = 0.08; nominal interest rate = 0.13; nominal wage growth = 0.09; tax threshold indexation = 0.09.
(b) For parameters of age-earnings profiles see Chapter 4.
(c) All values are for the period from the age of death to age 65 inclusive.
(d) All values are rounded to the nearest \$.

groups are relatively small compared with the difference between the basic approaches. If suitable data for particular groups cannot be obtained, it is therefore suggested that the use of earnings profiles for all occupations combined would be more appropriate than the extreme assumption underlying the current procedure, that real earnings remain unchanged. In view of the *ad hoc* way in which adjustments for interest income taxation are made, it is most unlikely that adequate adjustments are applied, particularly for young accident victims.

One result that is perhaps worth noting relates to comparisons between tradespersons on the one hand and clerks and those in manufacturing. The award, allowing for earnings profiles, for tradespersons is higher than for the other two groups where the age at death is 50 years. But this ranking is reversed when the age at death is 30 years. This comparison reflects the difference in the concavity of the age-earnings profiles of the groups.

It is argued that the approach suggested here forces the user to be explicit, and therefore more consistent, about the various assumptions used in calculating awards. In particular, the taxation of nominal interest income means that assumptions must be made about various nominal rates, such as interest rates and threshold indexation. The calculations required are of course more complex but may easily be carried out using a microcomputer.

NOTES AND FURTHER READING

First consider the case where there is no interest income taxation. Denote the lump sum and dependency by A and c respectively. After one year the capital sum remaining is equal to $A(1 + r) - c$; after two years it is $\{A(1 + r)-c\}(1 + r) - c(1 + p)$, since now $(1 + p)c$ must be withdrawn for consumption; after N years it can be found to be:

$$A(1 + r)^N - \sum_{j=i}^{N} (1 + p)^{j-1}(1 + r)^{N-j} \qquad (5.15)$$

For the lump sum to be exhausted after N years, the expression in (5.15) is zero and:

$$\frac{A}{c} = \left(\frac{1}{1 + p}\right) \sum_{j=i}^{N} \left(\frac{1 + p}{1 + r}\right)^{j} \qquad (5.16)$$

With interest income taxation, denote by W_j the capital value remaining at the end of the jth year, so that the interest income accruing in the $j + 1$ th year is $W_j r$. If $T_j(y)$ represents the amount of tax paid on an income of y in period j then, ignoring other sources of income, the tax paid in period j is given by $T_j(W_{j-1}r)$. The tax structure can change over time as a result of policy changes to the marginal rates or income thresholds, and of course the latter may change depending on the extent to which thresholds are indexed to prices.

Following the procedure adopted above it can be found that if the lump sum, A, is to be exhaustive at the end of N years, then:

$$A(1 + r)^N = c \sum_{j=p}^{N} (1 + p)^{j-1}(1 + v)^{N-j} + \sum_{j=i}^{N} T_j(W_{j-1}r)(1 + r)^{N-j} \quad (5.17)$$

with
$$W_j = (1 + r)W_{j-1} - T_j(W_{j-1}r) - c(1 + p)^{j-1} \quad (5.18)$$

and
$$W_0 = A \quad (5.19)$$

For any realistic tax structure the expression in (5.17) is extremely awkward to deal with. Only in the very simple case where the tax structure is proportional does the expression simplify conveniently. If $T_j(y) = ty$ for all j, then W_j simplifies to:

$$W_j = W_{j-1}\{1 + r(1 - t)\} - c(1 + p)^{j-1} \quad (5.20)$$

and (5.17) can be found to reduce to precisely the same as equation (5.16) above, but with r replaced by the 'after-tax' nominal interest rate $r(1 - t)$.

For comprehensive treatments of compensation, see Luntz (1990) and Atiyah (1984). On the use of worklife expectancies, see Alter and Becker (1985), Nieswiadomy and Slottje (1987a, 1987b), Nieswiadomy and Silberberg (1985), and the references therein. The prescribed interest rate precludes further adjustment for tax changes. The assumed rate may of course under- or over-compensate, depending on the actual rates over the dependency period; see Mukatis and Widicus (1986).

The calculations reported here assume for convenience that the dependant has no other income. However, this assumption may easily be relaxed. For discussion of the case where the overall growth of earnings varies see Harris (1977). Such growth is relatively more important for older victims, where the earnings profile is flatter; see also Larsen and Martin (1981). In practice, the short-term interest rate on riskless securities is often used. Alternative approaches which take into account the slope of the yield curve and risk aversion are discussed in Harris (1977), and Carpenter et al. (1986).

PART II

Earnings of Scientists

6. Cohort and Cross-Sectional Earnings Profiles

It has long been recognized that cohort and cross-sectional age-earnings profiles differ. A standard procedure, which is quite reasonable in the absence of more information, is to obtain a cohort profile by simply adding the general rate of growth of real earnings to the growth of earnings associated with age, as shown by cross-sectional data. Indeed, this would seem to be supported by the observation that cross-sectional earnings profiles for a number of different years show a great deal of stability in their general shape. This approach was used in Chapter 3 when examining inter-generational mobility. The main question considered in the present chapter is whether cohort profiles can in fact be estimated in this simple way. A basic statistical model of age-earnings profiles is described in section 6.1. The model is then applied to several groups of professional scientists, chemists and physicists in Britain and Australia, in section 6.2. The data were obtained from special surveys of career histories and sufficient data were collected to enable separate analyses of male and female scientists to be carried out.

6.1 THE BASIC MODEL

Components of Earnings Changes

It is convenient to distinguish three elements in the determination of systematic year-to-year earnings changes. An individual's earnings may change because of age effects, time effects and cohort effects. These effects were also distinguished in Chapters 3 and 4. The age effects refer to factors associated with ageing alone; these may be attributed to the increase in productivity arising from increased experience, the use of incremental payment systems or other features of structured labour markets designed to reduce labour turnover and increase incentives. The time effects refer to factors relating to the passage of calendar time; these may include a general increase in productivity arising, say, from technical progress, or other factors leading to changes in real earnings over time. The cohort effects refer to cohort-specific factors, such as the size of the cohort or particular influences that apply only to those individuals belonging to a certain group, distinguished here by the date of entry into the labour market. The cohort may be defined by date of birth, but in the present context it is preferable to use year of entry to distinguish cohorts; hence the term 'experience effects' should be substituted for age effects.

A fundamental problem is that it is not possible, without very strong restrictions, to identify the three sets of effects, even with longitudinal data. For discussion of the general issues involved in the analysis of longitudinal data see, for example, Glenn (1977) and Heckman and Robb (1983). The approach taken here is thus to consider a model which assumes that there are no cohort effects, so that only experience and time effects operate. Some justification for this strong assumption will be given below. Following Creedy et al. (1981b) it is also assumed that both effects, when considered to operate on the logarithms of earnings, are quadratic. The use of a quadratic specification is indeed ubiquitous in the literature on earnings profiles. Hence the starting point of the analysis is the following equation:

$$y_{td} = \alpha_0 + \alpha_1 t + \alpha_2 t^2 + \beta_1 d + \beta_2 d^2 + u \qquad (6.1)$$

where y_{td} is the logarithm of earnings of an individual with experience t, at calendar date d, and where u is a stochastic term governing the non-systematic components of earnings.

If all individuals are observed at the same date, say d_0, then

$$y_{td_0} = \alpha_0 + \beta_1 d_0 + \beta_2 d_0^2 + \alpha_1 t + \alpha_2 t^2 + u \qquad (6.2)$$

Hence equation (6.2) gives the cross-sectional relationship between log-earnings and experience that applies at time d_0. The assumed absence of cohort-specific effects implies that different cross-sectional profiles will have the same shape, but their position will change. There is a certain amount of evidence to support this assumption; it has been a feature of the series of cross-sectional profiles produced by the British Royal Society of Chemistry. These have resulted from remuneration surveys dating from 1919 (and on a regular basis from 1953); the stability in the shape of these cross-sectional profiles is demonstrated by estimates given in Creedy (1974, p. 53). But the important question remains of whether different *cohorts* will necessarily have similar-shaped profiles. The implications of the above specification for the cohort profiles are examined in the following subsection.

The Cohort Profiles

If c denotes the year in which an individual enters the labour market, then by definition $c = d - t$. Substitution for $d = c + t$ in equation (6.1) gives, after collecting terms:

$$y_{t,t+c} = \alpha_0 + (\alpha_1 + \beta_1)t + (\alpha_2 + \beta_2)t^2 + \beta_1 c$$
$$+ \beta_2 c^2 + 2\beta_2(ct) + u \qquad (6.3)$$

Thus for individuals in cohort c_0, say, the relationship between log-earnings and experience is given by:

$$y_{t,t-c_0} = (\alpha_0 + \beta_1 c_0 + \beta_2 c_0^2) + (\alpha_1\beta_1 + 2\beta_2 c_0)t + (\alpha_2 + \beta_2)t^2 + u \qquad (6.4)$$

Hence the cohort profile, just like the cross-sectional profile of equation (6.2), is a quadratic function of experience. But it can be seen from equation (6.4) that the *shape*, as well as the position, of the experience-earnings profile varies among cohorts. This is reflected by the presence of the term $2\beta_2 c_0$ in the coefficient on t. This result arises essentially because the time effect is assumed to be quadratic, producing the interaction term in equation (6.3). A specification in which the time effects were assumed to be linear (that is, $\beta_2 = 0$) would imply cohort profiles that, like the cross-sectional profiles, simply shifted between groups. Equations (6.2) and (6.4) compare particular cross-sectional and cohort profiles. While the cross-sectional profiles simply have a different position, the average rate of increase in log-earnings will not be the same for every cohort.

Of particular interest is the sign of β_2. If this is negative, it means that the rate of growth of real earnings with experience is slower for the more recent entrants into the labour force; remember that the absolute value of $\beta_2 c$ increases for more recent entrants (with higher c). Consequently maximum real earnings are on average reached at an earlier stage in the career. This important kind of information is not revealed by the apparently stable cross-sectional profiles. The experience, t_m, at which maximum real earnings are attained is given by differentiating equation (6.4) with respect to t and setting the result equal to zero, from which it can be seen that:

$$t_m = -(2\beta_2 c_0 + \alpha_1 + \beta_1)/\{2(\alpha_2 + \beta_2)\} \qquad (6.5)$$

Differentiating t_m with respect to c_0 then gives

$$\partial t_m/\partial c_0 = -\beta_2/(\alpha_2 + \beta_2) \qquad (6.6)$$

and as α_2 is generally negative an increase in c_0 must reduce t_m if β_2 is also negative. If, however, β_2 is positive (implying a higher rate of growth of real earnings with experience for the more recent entrants), the direction of change in t_m depends on the relative sizes of α_2 and β_2.

6.2   EMPIRICAL RESULTS

The Data

The data were obtained from special surveys of members of several profession institutes; these are the Royal Society of Chemistry in Britain, the Royal Australian Chemical Institute and the Australian Institute of Physics. In September 1985 a questionnaire was sent to 6 000 members of the Royal Society of Chemistry (RSC); this included all 1 721 females and a random sample of 4 279 males. The purpose of the survey was to obtain information about the job mobility of individuals from the beginning of the first job up to the date of the survey. The response rates were 50.5 per cent and 48.3 per cent respectively for males and females, which is considered good in view of the complex nature of the questionnaire and the fact that many would have been sent to members who were retired, unemployed, students, or not working for family reasons. Each individual was asked to give his or her annual earnings at the beginning and end of each job held, and this information forms the basis of the results below. The earnings were converted to 1985 values, using a retail price index, so the profiles are in terms of real earnings. Not all individuals gave complete information about the earnings at each relevant point in the career. In view of the retrospective nature of the survey it is worth stressing that the members of the RSC are generally very experienced and conscientious in responding to the frequent remuneration surveys carried out by the professional activities department. They recognize the value of the information for the ability of the Society to represent its members over matters of pay and conditions of employment, and they clearly appreciate the ability to compare themselves with others in similar conditions. Without the valuable experience of the RSC, this kind of survey would not have been worth while.

Somewhat earlier in 1985 very similar surveys were sent to 1 957 members of the Royal Australian Chemical Institute and 1 000 members of the Australian Institute of Physics. The effective response rates for the surveys were 61 and 62 per cent respectively. The slightly higher response rate for the Australian surveys reflects the use of a follow-up letter sent to all members of the survey population one month after the questionnaire was distributed.

For each sample a data file was produced, where each data point related to a particular observation of annual earnings. Each line in the data file contains details of the earnings in 1985 values, the experience of the individual at the time, and the year of entry of the individual into the labour market. Clearly the year of entry is the same for all observations on the same person. The number of observations on each individual differs according to the number of jobs held. In addition, dummy variables for holding a PhD and whether or not the individual was in a managerial or administrative job at the time were generated, but it is not known when the individual obtained the doctorate.

An advantage of the model set out in the previous section and the data used here is that it is possible to carry out the estimation in several ways and thereby examine the specification more closely. Such an examination is rather unusual; researchers usually just write down an earnings function to be estimated and then carry out only basic tests of significance of individual coefficients. Consider equation (6.3) above. It is clear that the coefficients could be estimated by running a regression containing just the four variables t, t^2, c and $c(c + 2t)$. But if the variables t, t^2, c, c^2 and ct are used, it is possible to examine whether or not the coefficient on the interaction term ct is in fact twice the coefficient on c^2. In addition, it is possible to estimate equation (6.1) directly, giving an alternative set of estimated coefficients which may be compared with the first set. The main interest of the present analysis of course is the value of β_2, since it is this term alone which influences any variation in the shape of earnings profiles among cohorts. The results of each approach are described in turn below.

British Chemists

The results for British males and females are shown in Table 6.1. For the men it can be seen that all the coefficients are significantly different from zero, at any reasonable level of significance. In particular, the coefficients on the square of 'year of entry into labour market' and the interaction term between experience and year of entry are both significant, indicating that there is a significant difference between the profiles of different cohorts. As β_2 is negative, the more recent entrants into the labour market have a slightly lower rate of growth of earnings with experience. As shown above, this result is compatible with the shape of the cross-sectional profiles remaining stable over time.

As noted earlier, the specification requires that the coefficient on the interaction term should be double that on the square of 'year of entry'. This condition does not hold for either the British males or females, although it will be seen below that it is much closer for Australian males. These results for British chemists cannot therefore be regarded as fully satisfactory, although they do show aspects of the changing relationship between earnings and experience which have not previously been revealed.

For the women, the coefficient on 'year of entry' is not significantly different from zero, but that on its square is significant and positive. Hence in contrast to male chemists, the growth of earnings with experience appears to have been slightly *higher* for more recent female entrants to the labour market.

The cross-sectional earnings profiles generally show average

Table 6.1 Earnings profiles: members of the RSC

Variable	Males		Females
	With PhD	Without PhD	
Constant	3.1734	5.1313	7.722
	(8.063)	(20.429)	(18.301)
Experience	0.2299	0.2236	0.1391
	(18.557)	(31.401)	(8.451)
Experience^2	−0.0019	−0.0021	−0.0017
	(−15.605)	(−31.967)	(−9.818)
Year of entry to	0.1401	0.0611	−0.0074
labour market	(12.008)	(7.962)	(−0.602)
(Year of entry)^2	−0.008	−0.0002	0.00026
	(−9.838)	(−3.624)	(2.549)
(experience) ×	−0.0023	−0.0019	−0.8458
(year of entry)	(−14.079)	(−19.147)	(−4.088)
Management	0.2152	0.1999	0.1705
(=1 if in man;	(11.127)	(16.620)	(7.669)
0 otherwise)			
PhD	NA	NA	0.2554
(=1 if PhD;			(12.971)
0 otherwise)			
R^2	0.4115	0.550	0.356
N	3 808	8 499	2 782

Notes
Dependent variable: logarithm of annual earnings expressed in 1985 prices.
'*t*-values' are given in parentheses underneath parameter estimates.

earnings reaching a maximum at about 55 years of age, but for the cohort profiles average real earnings continually increase, though at a decreasing rate. Maximum earnings are, on average, reached in the year of retirement, though of course some individuals may experience decreases in real earnings in their later years.

Australian Chemists and Physicists

The results for male and female chemists and physicists in

Australia are shown in Table 6.2; the number of observations for females is much smaller than for the British survey. For the males all coefficients are highly significantly different from zero, but for female chemists the majority of coefficients are not significant. The results for female physicists are better, but not as strong as for the males, and the coefficients on the dummy variables are not significantly different from zero. But the relationship between the coefficients on the interaction term and the square of 'year of entry' are more satisfactory (except for the female chemists). Thus, the increase in earnings with experience can be seen to have been slightly less rapid for the more recent entrants into the labour

Table 6.2   Earnings profiles: Australian scientists

Variable	Chemists		Physicists	
	Males	Females	Males	Females
Constant	0.8849	6.5364	−1.3038	−6.596
	(3.280)	(4.516)	(−2.626)	(−1.711)
Experience	0.2648	0.0829	0.2922	0.4317
	(29.869)	(1.689)	(17.620)	(2.887)
Experience^2	−0.0020	−0.0008	−0.0023	−0.0030
	(−23.331)	(−1.666)	(−14.287)	(−1.870)
Year of entry to	0.2144	0.0590	0.2902	0.4609
labour market	(26.401)	(1.446)	(19.778)	(4.109)
(Year of entry)^2	−0.0013	−0.0002	0.0019	−0.0032
	(−21.537)	(−0.893)	(−18.031)	(−3.997)
(experience) ×	−0.0027	−0.0003	−0.0030	−0.0056
(year of entry)	(−22.111)	(−0.465)	(−13.645)	(−2.999)
Management	0.1690	0.0656	0.1455	0.5058
(=1 if in man;	(11.599)	(1.218)	(5.063)	(1.622)
0 otherwise)				
PhD	0.1805	0.2233	0.2318	−0.1220
(=1 if Ph.D.;	(13.143)	(4.268)	(11.498)	(−0.846)
0 otherwise)				
R^2	0.504	0.275	0.452	0.139
N	6 937	490	2 847	158

Notes
Dependent variable: logarithm of annual earnings expressed in 1985 prices.
't-values' are given in parentheses underneath parameter estimates.

market. As with the British cohorts, real earnings increase continually up to the time of retirement, unlike the cross-sectional profiles.

Alternative Regressions

It was suggested above that equation (6.1) may be estimated directly, thereby providing an alternative set of parameter estimates and giving more information about the basic specification. Regression results are given in Table 6.3 for equation (6.1), except that age has been used instead of experience. However, as argued earlier, in the present context the crucial questions concern the parameter β_2. As with the previous results, the Australian female chemists have a number of coefficients which are not significantly different from zero. Whereas the earlier results showed that the British female chemists experienced a relatively steeper earnings profile if they entered the labour market more recently, the corresponding coefficient (on the square of calendar date) in Table 6.3 is not significantly different from zero. For each of the groups of males, the general result that earnings have grown less rapidly for more recent cohorts continues to hold. However, despite the

Table 6.3   Regressions using age and calendar date

Sample	Constant	Age	Age^2	Date	Date^2	R^2
British males (with PhD)	1.5470 (4.639)	0.1478 (27.674)	−0.0015 (−21.060)	0.1266 (12.975)	−0.00085 (−12.291)	0.498
British males (no PhD)	1.9720 (9.646)	0.1561 (51.723)	−0.0016 (−38.833)	0.1030 (17.090)	−0.00065 (−15.021)	0.609
British females	5.0915 (12.312)	0.1166 (19.757)	−0.0013 (−14.932)	0.0327 (2.873)	−0.0001 (−1.734)	0.378
Aus. male chemists	0.1689 (0.679)	0.0859 (21.215)	−0.0008 (−14.115)	0.2027 (27.299)	−0.0013 (−23.584)	0.501
Aus. female chemists	5.1244 (3.756)	0.0918 (5.260)	−0.0010 (−3.868)	0.0621 (1.651)	−0.0003 (−1.145)	0.269
Aus. male physicists	−1.621 (−3.567)	0.1175 (16.461)	−0.0011 (−11.229)	0.2450 (18.389)	−0.0016 (−17.169)	0.451
Aus. female physicists	−5.2386 (−1.443)	0.0896 (1.729)	−0.00095 (−1.336)	0.378 (3.751)	−0.0027 (−3.721)	0.121

Notes
Dependent variable: annual earnings expressed in 1985 prices. '*t*-values' are given in parentheses underneath parameter estimates.

robustness of the latter result it must be acknowledged that the basic specification cannot be regarded as fully satisfactory. In view of the simplifications used it would indeed be surprising if the basic model passed all the tests required. It is again worth stressing that the majority of earnings equations in the literature are reported with no attempt to provide anything more than tests of the significance of coefficients.

One possible extension might be to attempt to allow for cohort-specific effects by introducing variables such as the size of each cohort, although this would present considerable difficulties for single occupations.

NOTES AND FURTHER READING

Appropriate longitudinal data for particular occupations are still rare, especially in Britain and Australia. However, cohort profiles of several occupations in Sweden have been estimated in Creedy et al. (1981b), while Weiss and Lillard (1978) have examined the experience of scientists in the United States. Cohort profiles for all occupations combined in Britain were estimated by Creedy and Hart (1979), who found no evidence of differences among cohorts in the slopes of the earnings profiles.

In the present context it was decided not to use both age and experience as independent variables. However, Klevmarken and Quigley (1976) distinguished both age and experience effects, and using the human capital interpretation argued that those who were youngest with more experience were more efficient at producing human capital. Weiss and Lillard (1978) found a significant interaction between the year at which a PhD was obtained and experience. With the present data it is not known precisely when the PhD or other qualifications were actually obtained. In estimating cohort profiles Berger (1985) used only experience.

For an analysis of the effects of labour force growth on *inequality*, using a human capital approach, see Dooley and Gottschalk (1984). For a useful analysis of the impact of cohort size on education and earnings see Connolly (1986); see also Dooley (1985).

The results may briefly be compared with those obtained using more aggregative data in other countries. Weiss and Lillard (1978) found that more recent cohorts of American scientists experienced a relatively more rapid rise in earnings. In an examination of cohort-specific effects on earnings profiles, Welch (1979) replaced year of entry with cohort size and found that the large cohort size of the baby boom depressed earnings on entry, but that subsequent earnings grew at a faster rate. Berger (1985) found, however, that earnings growth rates did not approach 'normal' levels after a brief period in the labour force.

7. Variations in Earnings and Responsibility

It is widely thought that high earnings are associated with high levels of responsibility, and that a component of the systematic variation in earnings with age is the tendency for responsibility to increase with age. However, there is very little detailed information available about these relationships. Several 'hierarchical' models of the distribution of earnings have been produced, in which earnings are related to the number of subordinates (a cardinal measure of responsibility) have been produced, such as those by Simon (1957) and Lydall (1968). These may seem to offer a method of relating the personal distribution of earnings to the size and growth of firms, and thereby perhaps to the 'functional' distribution of income, but developments along these lines have not been made. An alternative, less well known, hierarchical model is by Tuck (1954), which generates a lognormal distribution of earnings in contrast with the Pareto upper tail of Lydall's model. Studies have also been made of the probability of promotion, and its relationship with various individual characteristics, but these have not been directly concerned with the variation in earnings with responsibility.

A difficulty arises because of the problem of defining responsibility in a practically useful manner. Rather than using the number of individuals over which a person has authority, it may seem natural to think of responsibility in terms of job titles; indeed many job titles are explicitly designed to reflect levels of status or seniority within an occupation or organization. It is therefore not surprising that official statistics provide little help in this context, since they would have to deal with thousands of job titles. However, the use of titles is not unambiguous, and makes comparisons very difficult.

Even among the professional bodies, covering for example scientists and engineers, little information is gathered about remuneration in relation to responsibility. This is perhaps surprising in view of the fact that one of their roles is to provide detailed information about the conditions of employment of their members, not only for individual use but to monitor the 'status' of the profession in society, and to help discussions with employing organizations. The Royal Society of Chemistry is the most advanced in this respect, and since 1971 their regular surveys have requested information about each individual's level of responsibility. Between 1971 and 1978 the responsibility level was defined according to a sixfold classification depending on the job title of the individual's immediate superior, using titles such as 'works chemist', 'senior chemist', 'chief chemist', and 'works manager'.

The use of job titles produces a set of levels which is unambiguously ordinal in nature. A chief chemist is recognized as having more responsibility than a works chemist, and having less responsibility than a member of the Board, or managing director. Any attempt statistically to relate earnings to a number of explanatory variables must necessarily specify responsibility using one or more dummy variables. Similiarly, any attempt to examine variations in responsibility over individuals' careers must use statistical techniques which have been specifically developed for such dichotomous variables.

In 1978 the RSC's survey contained a major innovation, in the form of a question designed to produce a 'responsibility score' for each individual. Henman (1978) has described the use of the responsibility assessment schedule. Instead of relying on the use of job titles the question examined the extent of an individual's autonomy within his or her employing organization, and produced scores ranging from 4 to 20. This question is described in more detail in the following subsection, but the essential feature of the approach is that it produces a cardinal measure of responsibility. This chapter examines the characteristics of the RSC's responsibility scale, and considers its possible use in further analyses of earnings. The scale does not rely on specific job titles and may easily be used for other professional groups of employees. Serious consideration of its properties therefore seems warranted. Section 7.2 considers the relationship between earnings and the responsibility score, and then section 7.3 goes on to examine the use of such scores in a model of age-earnings profiles. First, however, the nature of the scale is described.

7.1   MEASURING RESPONSIBILITY

The RSC Responsibility Score

The principle of the RSC's cardinal measure of responsibility is the assessment of an individual's level of autonomy exercised in four areas of work. These four areas are 'job duties', 'technical decisions and recommendations', 'supervision exercised' and 'supervision received'. Within each of these headings are five separate statements describing the extent of autonomy, and these are given scores from 1 to 5. The full assessment schedule is shown in Table 7.1. Each individual has to work out his or her appropriate score for each aspect of work, and then add the four separate scores together. Thus the full range of possible scores runs from 4 to 20. If scores for each aspect of work were recorded separately on the questionnaire, the addition of the separate scores to produce a total responsibility score immediately introduces an element of cardinality into the assessment. The assumptions used to obtain the responsibility score are therefore very strong. For example, a reduction in the score for 'supervision received' of unity (irrespective of whether the change is from 5 to 4 or, say, 2 to 1) is regarded as being exactly balanced by an increase of unity in the score for 'technical decisions and recommendations' (or any of the other three areas of responsibility), irrespective of the initial position. Not only are the four areas regarded as directly comparable according to the numbers given, but the use of simple addition (that is, a linear scale) is also thought to be appropriate.

It is worth noting some features of a scale based on multiplication, rather than addition. If the responsibility score were obtained by multiplying together the four numbers obtained, then the scores would run from 1 to 625. The scale is therefore very much longer, but not all the integers would be relevant. For example 625 is the score of someone with 5 points for each of the four areas, but an individual with three values of 5 and one value of 4 achieves a score of 500; the next value in the series is 400. Furthermore, a reduction of one point in any area of responsibility has different implications according to the values in the three other areas. For example, 4 points in each of the four areas gives a total score of 256, and a fall from 4 to 3 in one area would reduce the

Table 7.1   Responsibility assessment schedule

Duties

I receive on the job training working on simple projects or assisting more senior staff. 1

I perform responsible and varied assignments within projects. 2

I plan, conduct and co-ordinate projects of some complexity. 3

I undertake long term and short term planning and supervision of projects plus decisions on work programmes, together with budgetary control of projects. 4

I have full managerial responsibility for a function with full responsibility for the operation of a budget and long term planning. 5

Supervision received

My work is assigned with detailed instructions, guidance being always available. My results are subject to close scrutiny. 1

My work is assigned in terms of detailed objective and priorities, guidance being available on problems and unusual features. 2

My work is assigned in terms of general objectives and priorities, guidance being available on policy or unusually complex problems. My work is reviewed for effectiveness only. 3

My work is such that I receive executive instruction on broad overall objectives and it is reviewed only for its general effectiveness and adherence to policy. 4

My work is unsupervised, other than that I comply with the policy decided with the governing body. 5

Technical decisions and recommendations

I am responsible for minor technical details only, all other matters being checked. 1

I am responsible for technical detail which is reviewed overall. 2

I am responsible for technical matters but am subject to occasional review. 3

I have full technical responsibility for projects. 4

I am responsible for all technical matters, including the delegation of responsibility. 5

Supervision exercised

I have no authority but may give technical guidance to juniors working on the same project. 1

I have no managerial responsibilities for qualified staff but may be assigned graduates, technicians or other juniors as assistants from time to time. 2

I supervise a group of qualified staff, technicians and other employees; I assign and review their work; I can recommend on the selection, discipline, rating, training and perhaps rates of pay. 3

I am responsible for leaders of groups containing qualified staff, technicians and other employees, I give guidance on policy and complex technical matters delegating responsibility for discipline, rating training and rates of pay. 4

I have full control over senior staff who are in turn responsible for groups of qualified staff and other employees. 5

Source
Royal Society of Chemistry.

score by 64 to 192. But from the previous discussion a drop from
5 to 4 points in one area, when all the other areas have 5 points,
would cause a drop of 125. While the linear scale involves strong
assumptions, and since the early training of economists inculcates
a scepticism towards any type of cardinal scale, the present chapter
investigates as far as possible the properties of the scale used by
the RSC. From the point of view of the applied economist it would
be extremely useful to have a cardinal scale which allows
individual measurement in a wide variety of occupations and
organizations.

The precise meaning of responsibility has received surprisingly
little attention by economists; those using the number of subordinates as a cardinal measure have not seriously examined the
nature of the concept. However, reference may usefully be made
to the work by Jaques (1956), based on an extensive study of the
Glacier Metal Company. Jaques found that the simple measures
of responsibility were inadequate and developed a measure based
on the 'time-span' of work. This was defined as the maximum
length of time during which an individual was allowed to exercise
discretion before being subject to direct supervision. He then
discovered that pay scales were systematically related to the time-
span of jobs, and that dissatisfaction with pay could generally be
resolved into anomalies between individuals with similar time-
spans. Jaques argued that the firm

> had been applying, without knowing it, a systematic pattern of salaries
> and of ranks – a pattern that could be observed once level of work was
> measured by time-span. But because this pattern was unrecognised, it
> could not be used as a conscious aid to planning; and divergences from
> the pattern, although intuitively felt as such, could not be readily
> pinpointed. (1956, p. 48)

Jaques (1956, pp. 50, 74) suggested that changes in responsibility
can take place gradually over time although an individual retains
the same job title and that where a person's skill or experience
was greater than the level of work performed, he or she was paid
according to the work. Both these points are now part of the
alternative theories of pay, such as 'osmotic' labour mobility, and
'job competition' models.

The measurement of the time-span of each individual's job
required extensive investigations and lengthy discussions;

individuals had some difficulty assessing their own time-span. This experience contrasts with the self-assessment score used by the RSC, the introduction of which was generally welcomed by members. The similarity is, however, that Jaques's cardinal measure was based fundamentally on discretion or autonomy allowed to each individual in performing his or her duties. Although it is argued here that the extent of autonomy is basic to the concept of responsibility, the following discussion is entirely objective. Although the chapter concentrates on the observed relationship between measured responsibility and earnings, and their variation over age, no normative judgement is attempted. This contrasts with Jaques's approach. His finding, that people thought it 'fair' that those with the same time-span are paid the same, soon developed into the argument that a complete pay structure, if based on an observed relationship between pay and time-spans, was itself 'fair'. He also speculated that pay was based on a percentage (based on the rate of interest) of the possible loss from exercising discretion during the time-span (or the value of resources entrusted to the discretionary control of each person). Jaques later expanded his views, along with arguments about people's ability to exercise discretion over their expenditure, into a grand normative view of pay; see Jaques (1961).

7.2   EARNINGS AND RESPONSIBILITY

Following the first survey in which the responsibility scores were used, the general results were described further by Henman, who stated that, 'high responsibility showed a marked degree of linearity with high earnings' (1978, p. 157). The sample responses were in fact divided into age groups, and linear regressions of annual earnings against responsibility score were run, showing high correlation coefficients. However, it was reported that a relatively small number of individuals with very high earnings had responsibility scores as low as 4 and 5. It was believed that these observations may have resulted from certain senior employees working alone on one-person projects, or from some self-employed members in one-person businesses. Thus it was recognized at an early stage that the assessment schedule does not work very well for the very low scores, and those with scores of 4 or 5 were omitted from later regressions. (In 1983 this involved dropping only 155 observations from the total sample of 12 386.)

In the 1983 *Remuneration Survey* (RSC, 1983, p. 16, Table 21) information is given, for eight separate age groups, about the median and lower and upper quartile earnings within each responsibility score. The RSC presents results for what are described as the 'coefficient of correlation' and the 'equation of line' (no standard errors are reported). Two points can be made about these results; the first concerns the method of estimation, and the second concerns the form of the fitted equation. These points are examined below.

Although the RSC survey report is not explicit about the statistical approach used, it can be found (using the published data) that the results were obtained by carrying out an ordinary least squares regression analysis for each age group using median earnings as the dependent variable, and responsibility score as the independent variable (omitting information about scores 4 and 5). For example in the lowest age group (25–29) median earnings are given for responsibility scores 6–17 inclusive (that is, 12 classes). The method used was unweighted least squares, since no allowance was made for the fact that there is a considerable variation in the number of observations within each responsibility score. Furthermore, the 'coefficient of correlation' is not, as may be thought, the linear correlation coefficient between earnings and responsibility score, but is the conventional R^2 for the regression based on medians. After rerunning the regressions, the full results are given for comparison purposes on the left-hand side of Table 7.2 below.

It is, however, more appropriate in this context to use the method of weighted least squares in order to allow for the fact that the various medians are based on very different numbers of observations. The frequencies, not published in the report, were provided by the RSC. The weighted regressions are reported on the right-hand side of Table 7.2, where it can be seen that the results are very different, especially the values of the constant terms for the higher age groups. It should be noted that the standard errors in weighted regressions are much lower than in the unweighted regressions, mainly because of the much larger number of observations used in the former.

Having estimated linear relationships between median earnings

Table 7.2   Linear regressions of annual earnings on responsibility score: 1983

Age group	Unweighted regressions			Weighted regressions		
	Constant	Slope	R^2	Constant	Slope	R^2
25–29	5 691.57	238.78	0.977	5 703.59	237.10	0.963
	(238.77)	(11.65)		(13.18)	(1.22)	
30–34	4 123.58	520.75	0.840	4 989.23	428.48	0.861
	(862.35)	(62.95)		(49.83)	(4.00)	
35–39	3 773.43	638.00	0.963	3 758.08	622.80	0.920
	(677.07)	(48.06)		(51.57)	(3.76)	
40–44	3 282.57	752.57	0.953	2 428.55	794.07	0.946
	(635.95)	(46.42)		(62.26)	(4.36)	
45–49	2 506.15	857.31	0.975	2 336.03	860.18	0.970
	(606.25)	(41.84)		(57.64)	(3.91)	
50–54	1 071.54	1 019.84	0.964	−112.97	1 086.65	0.966
	(867.08)	(59.83)		(79.85)	(5.24)	
55–59	512.31	1 087.69	0.967	−370.16	1 144.27	0.949
	(874.74)	(60.36)		(127.20)	(8.27)	
60–64	307.27	1 046.73	0.928	−1 157.88	114.80	0.943
	(1 489.79)	(97.783)		(247.56)	(15.19)	
All ages combined	369.10	948.43	0.951	−661.94	998.83	0.953
	(1 489.79)	(59.82)		(27.49)	(1.99)	

Note
Standard errors are given in parentheses immediately below the parameter estimates. Those in responsibility groups 4 and 5 (130 individuals over all age groups) were omitted.

and responsibility, using a more satisfactory procedure, it is then necessary to consider the appropriateness of the specification. From Table 7.2 it can be seen that both the constant term and slope coefficient vary systematically with age; the constant decreases steadily while the slope increases with age, but at a decreasing rate. These results may simply be interpreted as showing that although median earnings are linearly related to the responsibility score, higher levels of the latter make a larger contribution to earnings in the older age groups. But this is not a very satisfactory statement, as the responsibility score does not seem to be measuring the same type of phenomenon for the different age groups; the results suggest that further investigation into the nature of the relationship is required.

An Alternative Specification

The use of a linear relationship between earnings, y, and responsibility, x, immediately raises two points. First, the method of assessing the responsibility score imposes a maximum value of x beyond which no individual can move, yet there is no such constraint on the level of earnings. This suggests that the relationship between y and x may become relatively steeper as x approaches its maximum possible value (with x on the horizontal axis). The second, related, point is that the observations for younger age groups may be spread about higher levels. Thus if the 'true' relationship between y and x is non-linear, the linear regressions will simply provide approximations over different ranges of the observations.

Alternative specifications cannot be examined using individual data, since the RSC *Remuneration Survey* provides only summary measures of the earnings distribution for each age group and responsibility score. However, a good idea of the relationship can be seen by plotting median annual earnings against responsibility score, for various age groups. Such graphs suggest that it may be more appropriate to regress the logarithm of median earnings against the responsibility score. Thus if y_m denotes the median earnings and x denotes responsibility score, a weighted regression of

$$\log (y_m) = \alpha + \beta x \qquad (7.1)$$

may be carried out for each age group. Results are presented in Table 7.3. Comparison with the right-hand side of Table 7.2 shows that the coefficients in the non-linear form are estimated with much greater precision (the 't' values are considerably higher), and the values of R^2 are higher. A very important further result is that there is a much greater similarity between age groups than indicated from the estimates of the linear specification (although the youngest age groups have significantly lower values of β). This result is encouraging from the point of view of the method used to measure responsibility since, as observed earlier, large differences between age groups would otherwise seem to indicate that the responsibility score is not consistently measuring the same phenomenon. Thus, although the earlier discussion was critical of

Table 7.3   Weighted regressions of log $(y_m) = \alpha + \beta x$

Age group	α	β	R^2
25–29	8.709	0.029	0.961
	(0.0016)	(0.0002)	
30–34	8.734	0.040	0.913
	(0.0036)	(0.0003)	
35–39	8.724	0.050	0.957
	(0.0030)	(0.0002)	
40–44	8.689	0.058	0.977
	(0.0029)	(0.0002)	
45–49	8.746	0.058	0.984
	(0.0029)	(0.0002)	
50–54	8.645	0.068	0.984
	(0.0034)	(0.0002)	
55–59	8.676	0.069	0.975
	(0.0053)	(0.0003)	
60–64	8.636	0.068	0.962
	(0.0120)	(0.0007)	
All ages	8.399	0.076	0.993
combined	(0.0008)	(0.0001)	

the statistical methods used in the RSC report, the further analysis offers support for the use of the assessment schedule devised by the RSC. In view of these encouraging results the following section considers the integration of the relationship into the analysis of the variation in earnings over the working life.

It may perhaps be thought that the above results suggest the use of a multiplicative scale, as discussed earlier. It would be interesting to compare results, if the scores for the four different areas of responsibility were recorded separately. A multiplicative system at least has the 'advantage' of reflecting a greater value attached to obtaining high scores in *all* areas of responsibility. It may be that some younger individuals can rapidly attain autonomy in just a few areas of responsibility, and that the difficulty of achieving a wider spread of autonomy should be reflected in the measuring scale.

7.3   AGE AND EARNINGS

The Age-Earnings Profile

Since 1919 the Royal Society of Chemistry has published detailed information about the distribution of its members' earnings, decomposed into a number of age groups, and its reports have presented diagrams showing the profiles with age of various summary measures (in particular the octiles and the highest and lowest deciles). The main characteristics of these age-earnings profiles can be easily summarized: the distribution of earnings in each group is approximately lognormal; the arithmetic mean of the logarithms of earnings in each age group is a quadratic function of age; and the variance of logarithms is a linear function of age. The 1983 RSC *Remuneration Survey* provides information about the earnings of approximately 8 500 Fellows and members, grouped into eight age groups between 25 and 64, and 27 income groups (1983, Table 8, p. 5). Unfortunately it is not possible to obtain age and earnings distributions for precisely the same group of individuals included in the tables for responsibility and earnings. The age-earnings profiles are estimated for a sub-sample of the group used earlier. These data can be used to obtain the following results, where μ_t and σ_t^2 are respectively the arithmetic mean and the variance of the logarithms of earnings at age t, and that the 'hat' denotes estimated values along the fitted line:

$$\hat{\mu}_t = 7.642 + 0.0705t - 0.00058t^2$$
$$(0.0648)\ (0.000041)\ (0.00317) \tag{7.2}$$

$$\hat{\sigma}_t^2 = -0.0687 + 0.0040t$$
$$(0.00410)\ (0.00011) \tag{7.3}$$

The parameters in equations (7.2) and (7.3) were estimated simultaneously using the same iterative technique as discussed in Chapter 4.

Basic Relationships

This section combines the information about the relationship between earnings and measured responsibility, discussed in section 7.2, with the above well-established results concerning the growth of earnings with age. An important factor influencing the pattern of earnings change is the variation in responsibility with age, and any analysis must ensure that the three aspects are treated consistently. A valuable feature of the responsibility scale produced by the RSC, which is not possessed by the more usual ranking procedures, is that responsibility can be treated as a quasi-continuous variable. Thus there is a much greater potential for the integration of responsibility into formal analyses of earnings distributions.

The basic interrelationships may be seen as follows. From section 7.2, the logarithm of median earnings was found to be linearly related to responsibility, as in equation (7.3). The form of the relationship was very similar for all age groups, except for the youngest. From above, the mean of the logarithms of earnings is a quadratic function of age.

There has been no difficulty about estimating the mean of the logarithms of earnings directly for each group, as full frequency distributions are published by the RSC, but the fact that the logarithm of median earnings has been regressed against responsi-bility may initially appear to create a problem of inconsistency. However, there is one situation in which such a problem does not exist. The lognormal distribution has the convenient property that the mean of the logarithms of earnings and the logarithm of median earnings are equivalent; this is because log-earnings are normally distributed and hence have equal mean, mode and median. If the distribution of earnings within each responsibility level may be regarded as following the form of the lognormal distribution, then the estimates in section 7.2 may be regarded as equivalent to regressions of mean log-earnings on responsibility. It would obviously be desirable to test this assumption directly, but the required data are not available.

For presentation purposes it is most convenient to consider explicit functional forms relating y to x, and x to t, and then to examine their implications for the relationship between y and t. It is also useful to begin by considering *individual* earnings, although separate subscripts need not be used. Using the results obtained earlier, each individual's earnings are assumed to be related to that individual's responsibility score according to:

$$\log y_t = \alpha + \beta x_t + u_t \qquad (7.4)$$

where the coefficients α and β are the same for all individuals and age groups, and u_t is a stochastic term that governs individual variations, with $E(u_t) = 0$. Suppose further that changing responsibility with age can be described by the following:

$$x_t = a + bt - ct^2 + \varepsilon_t \qquad (7.5)$$

where a, b, and c are parameters and ε_t is stochastic with $E(\varepsilon_t) = 0$. Thus the average responsibility score is quadratic function of age. The empirical appropriateness of these assumptions about x_t will be examined in the following subsection; the purpose of the present analysis is to concentrate on the possible interrelations in the generation of earnings distributions. Substitution of (7.5) into (7.4) gives:

$$\log y_t = (\alpha + a\beta) + (\beta b)t - (\beta c)t^2 + (\beta \varepsilon_t + u_t) \qquad (7.6)$$

Taking expectations then produces, with $\mu_t = E(\log y_t)$,

$$\mu_t = (\alpha + a\beta) + (\beta b)t - (\beta c)t^2 \qquad (7.7)$$

This is precisely the quadratic equation which has been estimated above in (7.2). The result in (7.7) shows clearly how the coefficients in (7.2) depend on combinations of the coefficients in (7.4) and (7.5). Taking variances of (6), with $\sigma_t^2 = V(\log y_t)$, gives:

$$\begin{aligned}
\sigma_t^2 &= E(\beta \varepsilon_t + u_t)^2 \\
&= \beta^2 E(\varepsilon_t^2) + E(u_t^2) + 2\beta E(\varepsilon_t u_t)
\end{aligned} \qquad (7.8)$$

Since individuals are concentrated in the lower responsibility scores at younger ages, the process of increasing responsibility with age is likely to increase the dispersion of x_t as t increases. Hence it may be assumed that:

$$E(\varepsilon_t^2) = \sigma_0^2 + \sigma_\varepsilon^2 t \qquad (7.9)$$

(Again, this will be examined further below.) Suppose, furthermore, that $E(u_t^2) = \sigma_u^2$, for all t, and that $E(\varepsilon_t u_t) = 0$. Thus (7.8) reduces to

$$\sigma_t^2 = (\beta^2\sigma_0^2 + \sigma_u^2) + (\beta^2\sigma_\varepsilon^2)t \qquad (7.10)$$

which is of course precisely the equation that has been estimated in (7.3) above. The result in (7.10) shows how the extent to which the dispersion of earnings increases with age is affected by $\beta^2\sigma_\varepsilon^2$ that is, it depends on the increasing spread of the distribution of responsibility scores with age and on the coefficient relating responsibility to log-earnings. The above model therefore generates the well-established pattern of age-earnings profiles (the variation in both μ_t and σ_t^2 with t) and allows a much richer interpretation of the coefficients in terms of responsibility changes. The empirical relevance of (7.4), (7.7) and (7.10) has already been established, so it remains to consider the important assumptions reflected in (7.5) and (7.9).

Age and Responsibility

As mentioned earlier, the RSC provided details of the unpublished frequency distributions of responsibility scores for each age group, from the 1983 survey. These distributions of the cardinal measure of responsibility can be used to test the assumptions made earlier, but instead of carrying out separate least squares regressions using only the means and variances, an iterative procedure based on maximum likelihood, involving all the information available in the table, was used. The results are as follows:

$$\hat{\bar{x}}_t = -1.138 + 0.576t - 0.0051t^2$$
$$\qquad (0.4135) \ (0.00025) \ (0.0209) \qquad (7.11)$$

$$\hat{\sigma}_{xt}^2 = 0.256 + 0.2052t$$
$$\qquad (0.2935) \ (0.00780) \qquad (7.12)$$

where $\hat{\bar{x}}$ and $\hat{\sigma}_{xt}^2$ denote respectively the estimated mean and variance of responsibility at age t ($\hat{\sigma}_{xt}^2$ is of course equivalent to $E(\varepsilon_{xt}^2)$ in equation 7.9).

These results show that the assumption that responsibility score is a quadratic function of age is well supported, along with the linear increase in the variance of responsibility score with age. Although further analysis of the present data does not seem warranted, it can be argued that these results indicate a strong potential for the inclusion of the RSC's measure of responsibility into the analysis of earnings (of other groups of employees). It offers the prospect of a richer interpretation of the characteristics of age-earnings profiles.

8.   Earnings and Job Mobility

The literature on earnings change has increasingly suggested that the key processes generating earnings inequality are those operating within the firm. However, there has been little empirical work on these phenomena, largely reflecting data deficiencies. Very few data sets on earnings contain information about internal processes and those which do often measure them narrowly. For example, most surveys of labour mobility define it either as movement between firms or as such movement plus major, once-and-for-all changes of work type.

This chapter develops an empirical analysis of earnings using data derived from work histories which contain considerable information about internal processes. Emphasis is placed on evaluating the relative importance for earnings change of external and internal processes and on comparing the perspectives obtained from examining job changes in isolation and job mobility as a process operating over a longer time period. Such an emphasis demonstrates the need for future research to concentrate on the collection of both longitudinal and internal information.

This chapter is based on three surveys of male professional scientists in Australia and Britain, undertaken in 1985, and used in the previous two chapters. This group of workers is not representative of the labour force as a whole and consequently the results cannot be regarded as universally applicable. A number of implications are, however, drawn concerning research on earning distributions and, in particular, on the collection of information on the processes generating earnings.

Section 8.1 briefly discusses the economic literature relating to internal processes. Section 8.2 then explains the methods used to measure internal mobility. The relationships between changes in job duties and earnings are examined in section 8.4. Section 8.5 goes on to consider the cumulative effect of different mobility processes for earnings.

8.1   THE ANALYSIS OF INTERNAL PROCESSES

There are three main strands of research which have emphasized the need to link earnings change to internal phenomena. These are specific human capital theory, internal labour market (ILM) theory and insider/outsider analyses.

Human capital theory has not explicitly analysed the internal workings of firms but the more recent research using the approach has indicated the important role played by intra-firm processes in generating earnings differences. Borjas (1981), for example, found that the highest earners in a sample of mature men drawn from the US national longitudinal study were those showing the lowest levels of inter-firm mobility. This result occurred despite the fact that such moves were associated, on average, with substantial increases in earnings. Borjas explained this apparent paradox as a reflection of the greater degree of self-investment by the less mobile in specific human capital, that is, human capital which is useful only in the firm in which it is acquired. According to the basic postulates of human capital theory, workers will only invest in specific human capital if they expect a long period of employment with the same employer. Assuming that *ex post* tenure is a good proxy for *ex ante* tenure, it can be expected that the less mobile members of any sample will acquire more specific human capital than the more mobile and will, *ceteris paribus*, exhibit higher earnings. However, the specific human capital explanation of the higher earnings of the less mobile is not supported by detailed empirical analyses measuring the degree of specific human capital held by different workers. Furthermore, the approach has been subject to criticism by those who believe that the processes being conceptualized are different from the human capital hypothesis; see Blaug (1976) and Thurow (1983). Indeed, Borjas (1981, p. 376) accepted that 'It is very likely that the empirical findings are consistent with many alternative explanations.'

Internal labour market theory has been more concerned to develop an analysis of earnings change within firms which is an accurate representation of the processes concerned. It is suggested that the bulk of job mobility (defined as the change in job duties performed) results from the gradual accumulation of small changes in the tasks undertaken. These changes are not significant in themselves but, when viewed over a long period of time, represent a major change in the nature of the job. This gradual form of mobility is termed 'osmosis'.

Research using the internal labour market approach has not been able to develop a framework for analysing the link between internal mobility and earnings. Such research needs to develop an accurate measure of internal mobility which includes some proxy for osmotic mobility, and needs data pertaining to a long period. Interest in the internal processes of firms has also been promoted by more recent insider/outsider literature. This strand of thought was originally developed to explain a number of macroeconomic paradoxes and, in particular, the limited response of money wages to changes in the level of unemployment; see Solow (1985). Recent research has been taking a more microeconomic approach and has been examining questions such as the relative importance of internal (insider) and external (outsider) influences upon wage determination at the plant level; see Lindbeck and Snower (1986) and Blanchflower and Oswald (1987).

8.2   THE MEASUREMENT OF INTERNAL MOBILITY

The surveys have been described briefly in Chapter 6. They obtained information about the job mobility of individuals from the beginning of the first job to the time of the survey. This required respondents to list a variety of details about each job held during their working lives, including income, type of work undertaken, level of responsibility held, year of commencement and completion of job. The use of such a retrospective technique has been criticized for yielding inaccurate information due to faulty recall and *ex post* rationalization. In the present context there is, however, every reason to believe that the responses are reasonably accurate. The characteristics of respondents place them among the more accurate of survey respondents and, furthermore, the institutes concerned make extensive use of cross-sectional surveys so that their members are familiar with the types of classification and format used. In addition, comparisons made with data collected by the institutes confirmed that the respondents were representative of the population.

Measuring Mobility

The theoretical literature suggests that it is important to distinguish between three main types of mobility: inter-firm mobility, intra-firm mobility and within-job mobility. Mobility between firms has been the subject of most analysis, reflecting the ready availability of data on labour turnover (usually defined as movement between firms). Such mobility is also emphasized by theories of job search and the wage competition model. It is conventional to distinguish between voluntary and involuntary mobility between firms. The former is seen to reflect the worker's decision to seek more advantageous employment and the latter is seen to result from other pressures. The distinction between voluntary and involuntary mobility is not always definite, however, since some 'voluntary' job changes may be prompted by pressure from employers (constructive dismissal). In the present study a movement between firms was described as voluntary if it was made for 'immediate salary improvement', 'long-term prospects in fresh employment' or 'frustration'. It was classified as involuntary if it was made because of redundancy, dismissal or closure.

Internal mobility has been less comprehensively studied and is difficult to measure. There are two main problems. The first is how to distinguish between those changes in job duties which constitute job changes and those which do not. The second is how to measure those mobility processes which result from the gradual accumulation of small changes in job duties, that is, osmotic mobility.

Discrete job changes within the firm can be measured in two main ways. The first and most common method is to define them as changes in occupational status, according to a given classification, without a change of firm. This procedure has been criticized for underestimating internal mobility; see Cole (1979). An alternative method is the 'self-reporting' technique, in which the decision as to whether a change in job duties constitutes a job change is left to the respondent. The present study uses this technique; respondents were simply asked to consider posts with different titles within the same firm as separate jobs.

A number of researchers have contended that the bulk of job mobility during a working life results from gradual changes in the tasks undertaken, that is, by osmosis, and will therefore not be captured by examination of discrete job changes, either within or between firms; see Doeringer and Piore (1971), Hunter and Reid (1968) and Cole (1979). Such mobility has been subject to little empirical analysis, however, largely because of measurement difficulties. The surveys of scientists were specifically designed to capture this phenomenon. Participants were asked to indicate the level of responsibility and the type of work undertaken at the beginning and end of each job held. This information indicates the extent of changes in job duties which did not involve an internal job change; this will be referred to as within-job mobility and can be regarded as a measure of osmotic mobility.

The surveys therefore tapped two dimensions of intra-firm mobility. The first was the discrete change of jobs within the firm (as reported by respondents) and the second was the gradual change in job duties through time. These are referred to as within-firm job changes and within-job changes respectively.

Responsibility and Type of Work

Combining the information on the level of responsibility at the beginning and the end of each job with that concerning the reason for the discrete job changes, it was possible to examine the degree to which each of the types of job mobility outlined above was associated with changes in levels of responsibility. The precise path taken to a new level of responsibility within a job is not known. The Australian survey of chemists used a five-part classification based on the tasks undertaken by the individual, with emphasis on the extent of supervision given and received. The survey of physicists added an extra sentence to the statement of job duties which linked the responsibility scales to the usual academic scales. For present purposes it was only necessary to distinguish job changes which involved either no change or an upward or downward movement in responsibility. The Australian surveys, using just five groups, are, however, likely to record relatively fewer changes of responsibility than the British survey.

The British and Australian surveys used different classifications for responsibility, reflecting the differing methods used by the professional institutes in their remuneration surveys. Since 1978 the British RSC has used a detailed assessment schedule to obtain a responsibility 'score' for each of its members. This procedure has been examined in detail in Chapter 7.

An alternative perspective on the process of upward mobility is to examine the movement of workers into managerial and administrative work. The regular remuneration surveys of the various professional institutes have continually shown that one of the key elements in obtaining a high income in a scientific career is the move into managerial/administrative work. A feature of the institutes is that people who move into management or administration during their career retain their membership. Each questionnaire asked participants to specify whether the work undertaken at the beginning and the end of each job was primarily administrative/managerial or non-administrative/non-managerial.

8.3   CHANGES IN JOB DUTIES AND EARNINGS

The objective of this section is to examine the relative importance of the types of mobility outlined above, the nature of changes in job duties during the working life and the immediate effect of such changes on earnings. Most empirical analyses of mobility and earnings have concentrated on the impact of external changes and have generally found that most movements between firms yield significant increases in earnings and that voluntary moves are more likely than involuntary moves to yield earnings increases. Very little work has been undertaken on either internal mobility or on the effects of mobility on job status and the duties undertaken. Such information is, however, essential if a comprehensive picture of the mobility process is to be obtained and if the process of earnings change is to be understood.

External and Internal Changes

The job changes reported by respondents were divided into voluntary inter-firm, involuntary inter-firm, within-firm and a residual. The characteristics of each type of job change are shown in Tables 8.1 and 8.2, which indicate that a substantial proportion of the job changes reported were internal. Both groups of chemists reported that approximately 40 per cent of all job changes were internal and the Australian physicists showed a figure of 30 per cent. Analyses of job turnover thus neglect a great deal of the mobility process. The slightly lower figure for the physicists possibly reflects the higher proportion of academics among the Australian physicists, since previous research has found that the market for academics exhibits less internal mobility than those for other workers; see Whitfield (1983). The bulk of internal job changes involve promotion rather than just transfer. Tables 8.1 and 8.2 show that the ratio of promotions to transfers is approximately two for all three groups.

Inter-firm job changes are predominantly voluntary. Less than 20 per cent of all changes of firm result from redundancy, dismissal or closure. The most common reason given for changing firms was long-term prospects in fresh employment, reflecting the long time horizon of scientists in making their labour market decisions. It would therefore seem to be more appropriate to talk in terms of movements between job ladders rather than jobs, as suggested by Okun (1981).

The relative importance of internal and external job changes is

Table 8.1   Percentage earnings changes by reason for change: British chemists (all job changes)

Type of job change	No.	Q_1	M	Q_u
Voluntary inter-firm				
Immediate salary improvement	454	14.3	25.0	40.0
Long-term prospects in new employment	911	4.2	14.3	28.6
Frustration in present employment	470	0	10.0	22.2
Involuntary inter-firm				
Redundancy, dismissal or closure	328	−4.0	4.0	16.7
Within-firm				
Transfer within organization	514	0	0	10.0
Promotion within organization	1 065	3.5	11.1	20.0
Residual				
Health consideration	22	−6.7	3.4	14.3
Other	313	0	20.5	70.0

Note
Q_1 and Q_u are respectively the lower and upper quartiles, and M is the median.

Table 8.2   *Percentage earnings changes by reason for change:*
Australian scientists (all job changes)

Types of job change	Chemists				Physicists			
	No.	Q_1	M	Q_u	No.	Q_1	M	Q_u
Voluntary inter-firm								
Immediate salary improvement	144	13.9	24.7	44.4	37	9.1	26.3	100.0
Long-term prospects in new employment	757	0	10.0	30.5	381	0	16.3	45.5
Frustration in present employment	318	0	7.3	19.3	93	0	10.0	38.6
Involuntary inter-firm								
Redundancy, dismissal or closure	208	−4.0	6.3	22.1	82	−6.5	4.4	19.7
Within-firm								
Transfer within organization	358	0	0	8.0	103	0	0	7.9
Promotion within organization	674	0	5.8	14.3	190	3.5	9.0	16.1
Residual								
Health, personal, family, travel	51	−20.0	0	31.9	22	−14.6	0	20.0
Further studies	42	11.1	45.5	86.6	13	1.4	5.9	150.0
Fixed term contract	24	0	12.5	28.0	29	0	16.0	59.8

Note
Q_1 and Q_u are respectively the lower and upper quartiles, and M is the median.

related to the life cycle. External changes are more important in the early years of working life and internal changes are more important in later years. Table 8.3 shows the relative importance of external and internal changes for given experience groups. External mobility is more prevalent in the first ten years of working life for all three groups but internal mobility is more prevalent for those with more than 20 years of experience. It is also interesting to note that the relative magnitude of external mobility is greatest for Australian physicists and least for UK chemists for all experience groups.

Table 8.3 *The ratio of external and internal job changes and experience*

Experience (years)	UK chemists	Australian chemists	Australian physicists
≤5	1.9 (1 039/547)	2.0 (793/402)	3.6 (445/124)
6–10	1.2 (740/599)	1.3 (446/331)	1.7 (216/125)
11–15	0.9 (448/519)	1.1 (256/241)	1.4 (92/68)
16–20	0.6 (219/370)	1.0 (129/135)	1.0 (47/47)
>20	0.5 (253/462)	0.6 (114/190)	0.8 (41/50)

Note
Numbers in parentheses are absolute numbers of external and internal moves respectively.

Job Change and Earnings Change

Summary measures of the distribution of percentage earnings change for each type of job change are also shown in Tables 8.1 and 8.2. The larger percentage changes were experienced for voluntary changes and, not surprisingly, when a voluntary change is primarily motivated by the desire to obtain an immediate improvement in salary. Moves made due to frustration in present employment were, on average, less remunerative. Both internal promotions and involuntary moves yielded earnings increases, on average, but the median increase is less than for voluntary changes. For each sample, internal transfers resulted in zero median income change. Thus changes of firm and, to a lesser degree, internal promotions typically yield increases in income.

Changes in Responsibility

A decomposition based on the direction of change in responsibility is given in Table 8.4. Given the narrow definition of a job which is used, it is not surprising that most jobs do not involve a change in responsibility. Thus 60 per cent of jobs reported by British chemists, 76 per cent of those reported by Australian chemists and 78 per cent of those reported by Australian physicists involved no change in responsibility. The greater proportion of responsibility changes reported by British chemists probably reflects the more detailed responsibility scale used. It was found that a large number of the changes of responsibility level reported occurred within the confines of the same job. Of all changes of level reported, over 40 per cent occurred within the job for all three groups. This offers support for the hypothesis that much job mobility results from the accumulation of small-scale changes in job duties, that is, by osmosis.

Table 8.4   Direction of change in responsibility

Type of movement	British chemists			Australian chemists			Australian physicists		
	Down	No change	Up	Down	No change	Up	Down	No change	Up
Within-job	24	4 645	3 010	11	3 118	966	2	1 385	382
Within-firm	175	878	1 467	56	687	553	21	229	164
Voluntary inter-firm	364	736	1 257	216	888	429	73	472	198
Involuntary inter-firm	209	242	394	69	221	57	16	129	23

The importance of examining the processes of internal mobility is also indicated by showing the proportion of responsibility level changes occurring within the same firm, that is, within the same job and on change of job within the same firm. Of all changes in responsibility level reported, over 60 per cent occurred within the same firm, for all three groups surveyed.

A qualitative difference can also be observed for the different ways in which responsibility level can change. Changes of level within the job are predominantly upward; the ratios of upward to downward change range from 88 for Australian chemists to 191 for Australian physicists. Changes of level on change of job within the same firm are less likely to be positive; the corresponding ratios range between 8 and 10. Voluntary moves between firms show a much greater proportion of downward changes, with ratios of between 2 and 3. Equivalent ratios for involuntary changes of firm are all less than two and for Australian chemists are more likely to involve a fall in responsibility level than a rise.

A picture therefore emerges of responsibility level change which shows that it is predominantly located in processes operating within firms. The bulk of those changes taking place within firms occur within the same job and are almost always upward. Changes of level occurring on change of job within the firm are predominantly upward but approximately one-tenth involve a fall in level. A large number of movements between firms involve a change of responsibility and such moves were more likely to yield increases than decreases. However, between one-quarter and one-third of voluntary moves involved a fall in level and involuntary moves were more likely to result in a fall.

The relationships between the type of mobility, change in responsibility and change in earnings are also shown in Table 8.5. As the changes made within jobs can occur over quite different time periods, the percentages in that category refer to annual average changes in earnings adjusted for price changes over the

Table 8.5   Distribution of percentage earnings changes resulting from responsibility change

Type of job change	British chemists				Australian chemists				Australian physicists			
	No.	Q_l	M	Q_u	No.	Q_l	M	Q_u	No.	Q_l	M	Q_u
Upward responsibility changes												
Within-job	1 713	1.4	5.1	11.2	761	0.7	4.1	9.1	284	1.1	3.8	7.0
Within-firm	920	1.7	10.7	20.0	441	0	7.1	16.7	121	3.6	8.7	20.0
Voluntary inter-firm	958	8.3	20.0	34.5	338	4.7	18.5	40.0	143	2.0	19.1	57.9
Involuntary inter-firm	293	2.6	20.0	59.1	46	−2.0	11.1	33.3	17	0	16.1	50.0
Downward responsibility changes												
Within-job	9	−2.2	0.6	1.7	9	0	2.6	28.1	0	—	—	—
Within-firm	114	0	0	11.1	43	0	0	5.0	14	−6.3	0	0
Voluntary inter-firm	295	0	10.0	25.5	172	−10.0	2.9	17.0	51	−29.8	11.1	40.9
Involuntary inter-firm	170	−13.0	0	12.5	57	−17.4	0	11.6	12	−21.1	−11.3	10.3

Notes
The figures for within-job changes give the annual average percentage increase in earnings, adjusted for price increases, between the beginning and end of the job. Other values give the percentage change from the end of a job to the beginning of the next job. Q_l and Q_u are respectively the lower and upper quartiles, and M is the median.

period during which the job was held. The table shows that voluntary moves between firms which involved an increase in responsibility were associated with a median increase in earnings of approximately 20 per cent. Voluntary changes involving a fall in level also involved a substantial increase in earnings, although the magnitude was less than for those involving a rise. Involuntary change of firm involving a rise in level were more remunerative, on average, than voluntary changes involving a fall. However, involuntary moves involving a fall in level showed a median decrease in earnings.

Internal job changes which involved an increase in responsibility level showed positive median increases in earnings but the magnitude of the rise was less than for changes of firm involving an increase in level. The bulk of internal falls in responsibility were associated with no change in earnings. Within-job changes of responsibility are of a different type from the other changes and the earnings changes are not directly comparable. It is, however, notable that workers experiencing an increase in responsibility within the job showed a median increase in real earnings per annum of 4–5 per cent.

Managerial and Administrative Work and Earnings

The results of the analysis of moves into and out of management are shown in Table 8.6. They are broadly similar to those for change of responsibility level, to which they are loosely related. Moves into managerial/administrative positions predominantly occurred within the same firm and in the Australian surveys were more likely to have occurred within the same job than on a change of job within the same firm. Movements out of management largely occurred during external job changes and it is notable that involuntary changes were more likely to involve moves out of rather than into management.

The income changes associated with moves into and out of management, also shown in Table 8.6, were, on average, higher for external as opposed to internal moves. The median increase in earnings on a voluntary inter-firm move into management/administration was approximately twice that of an internal move. Movements out of management/administration were not usually accompanied by earnings increases although those changing firms voluntarily and moving out of management/administration did, on average, experience an earnings increase.

The results of this section have shown that from a short-term point of view it seems more rewarding to achieve promotion by moving between firms, while the gradual or 'osmotic' mobility taking place within jobs is associated with a relatively low annual average rate of increase in real earnings. These findings may perhaps be interpreted as supporting the argument that wages are attached to jobs rather than individuals, as stated by internal labour market theorists.

8.4 MOBILITY AND EARNINGS

The above analysis has examined each job or job change in isolation. This section takes a broader perspective and looks at the

Table 8.6 Managerial and administrative work and earnings changes

Type of job change	British chemists				Australian chemists				Australian physicists			
	No.	Q_1	M	Q_u	No.	Q_1	M	Q_u	No.	Q_1	M	Q_u
Movement into *management or administration*												
Within-job	247	2.1	5.7	10.5	256	0.8	4.3	9.8	66	0.5	2.8	6.1
Within-firm	288	2.7	11.6	23.1	172	0	7.1	14.3	46	3.7	7.9	17.1
Voluntary inter-firm	233	9.1	19.2	35.1	145	1.4	13.3	27.8	27	8.1	18.8	42.9
Involuntary inter-firm	59	0	11.1	33.3	14	0.7	8.6	40.0	8	0	2.8	33.9
Movement out of *management or administration*												
Within-job	28	−1.1	2.0	7.2	12	2.3	3.6	9.8	3	—	—	—
Within-firm	120	0	0	10.5	42	0	0	4.4	14	−6.3	0	3.3
Voluntary inter-firm	143	0	9.2	21.4	98	−9.1	1.9	18.2	21	7.1	33.5	78.3
Involuntary inter-firm	76	−10.0	0	10.0	38	−25.9	−4.0	12.5	5	−33.3	−12.5	5.6

Notes
The figures for within-job changes give the annual average percentage increase in earnings, adjusted for price increases, between the beginning and end of the job. Other values give the percentage change from the end of a job to the beginning of the next job. Q_1 = change at lower quartile; M = change at median; Q_u = change at upper quartile.

relationship between the different types of mobility and the earnings reported by the respondent at the time of the survey. The objective is to see the contribution of each of the types of mobility to earnings change. Section 8.2 indicated that movements between firms yield substantial increases in earnings but that the internal processes yield greater increases in job status. This raises the question of whether a change of firm is more remunerative in the long term than a change of jobs within the firm or a change of status within the same job. The analysis thus indicates the importance of the different types of mobility in the generation of high earnings and thereby provides evidence concerning the need to examine internal processes in research on earnings change.

The examination of the cumulative effect of mobility on earnings reported here involves the use of linear regression analysis in which the dependent variable is the logarithm of annual earnings at the time of the survey. The use of earnings at the time of the survey is of course less desirable than using a longer-term definition. The implication is therefore that the value of annual earnings at the time of the survey is a reasonable indicator of earnings in the long term. Respondents obviously have differing degrees of experience at the time of the survey and this could be expected to influence the level of their earnings. This factor can be partly allowed for by adding experience and experience squared as independent variables, as in conventional earnings equations.

The independent variables can be divided into those concerned with processes unrelated to mobility and those relating to the mobility process itself. The former are: a dummy variable taking the value of 1 if the respondent held a PhD and 0 if not; experience and experience squared (as suggested above); responsibility at the start of working life (for the British survey this variable was the responsibility score at the beginning of the first job and for the Australian surveys it was based on two dummy variables indicating whether or not respondents were in either responsibility levels 2 and 3 or 4 and 5); a dummy variable taking the value of 1 if the respondent was in managerial/administrative work in the first job and 0 if not.

The mobility variables were based on the types of mobility outlined earlier and whether or not the respondent had spent a period out of the labour market. The number of internal promotions, the number of internal transfers, the number of voluntary inter-firm moves and the number of involuntary inter-firm moves were included as separate independent variables. A dummy variable was also included which took the value of 1 if a move into management/administration occurred within any job. All of the regressions included a dummy variable taking the value of 1 if the respondent had spent a period of unemployment and 0 if not. The British regression had an additional dummy variable based on whether or not the respondent had spent a period out of the labour market.

Regression Results

The regression results for the three surveys are given in Table 8.7. All of the R^2s are relatively high for this type of cross-sectional analysis. Many of the coefficients are significantly different from zero, except for the mobility variables of Australian physicists. It therefore seems that the market for physicists differs from that for chemists. For physicists the mobility pattern seems less important for obtaining a high income than other variables such as experience and whether a respondent holds a doctorate. As suggested earlier, it is likely that this reflects the large number of academics in the physics sample relative to the predominance of people in industry and commerce among the chemists.

Among the non-mobility variables both the possession of a doctorate and the level of responsibility held at the beginning of the first job (in the British survey) are positively related to earnings at the time of the survey. The equivalent coefficients in the Australian regressions are smaller.

The coefficients on the mobility variables all take their expected signs, with the exception of the variable for voluntary inter-firm moves of Australian physicists, although this is not significantly different from zero. Interpretation of the coefficients is made easier if it is noted that, if b is the estimated coefficient on a variable, then $100(\exp(b) - 1)$ estimates the percentage increase in current earnings resulting from a unit increase in the variable.

These regression results on earnings and mobility pattern offer strong support for the importance of internal processes. Individuals who moved into management/administration within any job during their working lives are likely to earn considerably more than their counterparts who did not. For example, respondents to

Table 8.7 Regression analysis of current earnings on job mobility

Variable	British chemists	Australian chemists	Australian physicists
Constant	8.787	9.845	9.481
	(296.33)	(322.04)	(189.01)
Doctorate (=1 if PhD;	0.170	0.200	0.214
0 otherwise)	(10.76)	(7.20)	(5.13)
Experience	0.030	0.030	0.069
	(17.02)	(12.56)	(13.07)
Experience squared	−0.00032	−0.00031	−0.0012
	(−10.08)	(−7.60)	(−11.35)
Responsibility at start	0.024	—	—
	(8.60)		
Responsibility 2 and 3	—	0.048	0.109
at start		(1.66)	(2.35)
Responsibility 4 and 5	—	0.138	−0.109
at start		(0.80)	(−0.26)
No. of internal	0.068	0.046	0.034
promotions	(12.84)	(5.30)	(1.81)
No. of internal transfers	0.041	0.021	0.023
	(5.57)	(1.80)	(0.99)
No. of voluntary inter-	0.034	0.009	−0.012
firm moves	(5.83)	(1.01)	(−0.81)
No. of voluntary inter-	−0.038	−0.029	−0.010
firm moves	(−4.31)	(−2.49)	(−0.49)
Management in first job	—	0.106	−0.121
(=1 if in man./admin.)		(1.78)	(1.20)
Move to man./admin.	0.105	0.064	0.083
within any job	(6.31)	(2.61)	(1.64)
Period of unemployment	−0.108	−0.054	−0.145
	(−4.88)	(−1.93)	(−0.262)
Period out of labour	−0.058	—	—
market	(−2.85)		
R^2	0.414	0.416	0.426
n	1 895	794	520

Note
Dependent variable: logarithm of earnings in 1985. '*t*-values' are given in parentheses immediately underneath parameter estimates.

the British chemists' survey making such a move earned approximately 11 per cent more than those who did not; the equivalent figures for Australian chemists and physicists were 7 and 9 per cent respectively. Similarly, internal moves were positively linked to earnings at the time of the survey. Each promotion within the same firm yielded a 7 per cent increase in earnings for British chemists and each internal transfer yielded 4 per cent, on average. The benefits from such internal mobility were less for Australian physicists and chemists but were still substantial.

In all of the surveys, each voluntary inter-firm move was less remunerative than either of the internal types of mobility. Thus the higher immediate increase in earnings associated with such voluntary mobility, reported above, is offset by other factors associated with external mobility. These include, for example, a lower rate of increase of earnings in the new job, a lower possibility of future promotion or a greater possibility of involuntary mobility.

Involuntary inter-firm moves were negatively related to earning at the time of the survey. In the British survey each job change of this type resulted in earnings which were approximately 4 per cent lower on average than would otherwise have been the case. The equivalent figures for the Australian chemists and physicists were 3 and 1 per cent respectively. It was also found that a period of unemployment at any stage in the career had a major negative impact on earnings at the time of the survey. For British chemists earnings were approximately 10 per cent lower for those indicating a period of unemployment, 5 per cent lower for Australian chemists and 14 per cent lower for Australian physicists.

The major conclusion of this chapter is that a great deal of upward mobility, defined as improvements in either job status or real earnings, takes place within the organization. Such mobility commonly takes the form of changes that occur within the confines of jobs with similar job titles as well as discrete job changes within firms. This can be regarded as an indicator of the magnitude of the osmotic form of mobility which many researchers have asserted to be important. This chapter also indicates that internal mobility processes are extremely significant in generating observed earnings differences among chemists and physicists.

These findings are compatible with a wide variety of theories. It is possible that differential internal mobility reflects variations in investment in human capital as Borjas has suggested, or segmented promotion hierarchies as internal labour market theorists might stress. It is not possible to discriminate between these theories on the basis of the information presented here. However, the chapter has shown, albeit for a specific occupational group, that the use of work-history information which includes data on intra-firm processes can yield important insights into the mechanisms generating the distribution of earnings.

A number of implications can be drawn from the results. The first and most fundamental is that the analysis of earnings distributions must involve explicit attempts to move away from cross-sections to longitudinal series and must examine intra- as well as inter-firm processes. There is, however, a dearth of appropriate data and there is consequently a need for researchers to spend more time collecting data on the processes of earnings change. Economists have been extremely reluctant to engage in data collection, unlike researchers in other social sciences. They have also been less keen to open the 'black box' of the employing organization than, say, industrial relations and sociology researchers. However, it would seem that further progress in understanding the generation of earnings distributions requires that such reluctance be overcome.

PART III

Demographic Effects

9. Financing Pensions in an Ageing Population

In recent years the pensions debate has been dominated by forecasts of ageing populations in virtually all industrialized economies, although the extent of population ageing is likely to vary significantly. Public pension schemes are typically of the defined-benefit type (rather than being based closely on the history of contributions by each individual) and are financed on a pay-as-you-go basis. This encourages a view of pension financing in simple terms of a current transfer from the working to the retired population. The argument that future generations of workers will not be prepared to suffer the burden of pension financing is then often used to suggest that basic state pensions will have to be reduced.

The main issues are, however, much more complex. An emphasis on demographic variables often ignores the changing labour force participation, especially of women, associated with slower population growth, and the relative cost reductions in other areas of public expenditure (such as infant and maternal health care). Furthermore, a proper assessment of the burden of financing such transfer payments requires comparison of net transfers among three generations rather than simply two.

It is also important to recognize that pension and tax structures generally have much more flexibility than is often appreciated. For example, a characteristic of more recent pensioners is that they are on average better off than previous cohorts. A larger proportion have had access to private pension schemes and have experienced much higher incomes during their working lives. Hence the burden of financing transfers to poorer pensioners can to some extent be shared between those workers *and* pensioners who are relatively richer. Furthermore, many tax structures effectively 'claw back' some of the pension transfers, so that the *net* transfer is not as high as it may initially appear. For example, in most countries pensions are included as part of taxable income, and additional revenue will be obtained from indirect taxes arising from expenditure of the transfers. The latter is particularly relevant in those countries which have a consumption tax such as the Value Added Tax (VAT) in the European Community. A more direct method of reducing net transfers and concentrating payments on the relatively poorer pensioners is the use of means testing, which may be regarded as a special type of pension tax. Such means-testing plays an important part in the Australian state pension scheme, though it is not widely used elsewhere.

This chapter examines the policy implications of ageing populations in alternative pension and tax structures. Because of the complexity of such schemes, the detailed implications are far from obvious and numerical results are therefore given for a wide variety of situations. Two major types of scheme are compared. The first type has a means-tested, taxable state pension which is financed only from income taxation. This may be regarded as a stylized version of the Australian scheme. The second structure examined has a basic taxable pension which is not means-tested. This pension is financed using a combination of income taxation and a consumption tax similar to a Value Added Tax, along with special contributions which are related to gross earnings. The latter contributions are therefore similar to the British National Insurance Contribution (NIC) scheme.

The precise structure of the two schemes is presented in section 9.1. Section 9.2 then provides a detailed analysis of the government's budget constraint in each scheme. This is a crucial prerequisite for any examination of the trade-offs between taxes and pensions. The effects of an ageing population are then examined in section 9.3. Alternative policy choices, involving changes in taxes and benefits within each scheme, are also considered. Informed policy debate requires a clear understanding of the orders of magnitude involved in such choices.

9.1 ALTERNATIVE SYSTEMS

The state pension is usually the most complex, and therefore least well understood, transfer scheme in any country. In order to concentrate on the major issues involved, it is necessary to consider simplified systems which nevertheless capture the main elements of those schemes used in practice. This section presents the two basic types of pension scheme, which are examined in detail in later sections. Both systems use an income tax schedule which has a tax-free threshold and a single marginal tax rate applied to income measured above the threshold. The approach may be extended to deal with multi-rate schedules, but this is not the major focus of attention in the present chapter. The analysis concentrates on the problem of financing a basic pension and excludes consideration of any earnings-related component. Problems associated with dependants' benefits are also ignored and the models deal with individuals as the unit of analysis. In addition, eligibility conditions, which are often quite complex, are ignored. Hence just two groups are considered, those over retirement age, all of whom are pensioners, and workers.

A Means-Tested Pension

The first system considered is one in which pensioners receive a basic pension which is subject to income taxation and is means tested according to gross income. The income test is very similar to that used in Australia. Denote the basic pension by b and consider a pensioner whose gross non-pension income is y. If income is below a lower limit, y_e, then the full pension is received. When y exceeds y_e, the pension is reduced by a proportion, s, of income in excess of the lower limit. Thus the pension is reduced by an amount $s(y - y_e)$. This implies that no pension is received once y reaches an upper limit, y_u, which is equal to $y_e + b/s$.

An equivalent way of viewing this type of income test is to regard each individual as receiving an unconditional pension of b, but then paying a special 'pension tax' on non-pension income. The pension tax, $P(y)$, is therefore given by:

$$
\begin{aligned}
P(y) &= 0 & \text{for } y \leqslant y_e \\
&= s(y - y_e) & \text{for } y_e < y < y_u \\
&= b & \text{for } y \geqslant y_u
\end{aligned}
\tag{9.1}
$$

In assessing each pensioner for income taxation, it is necessary to avoid the double taxation of the pension tax by making this tax deductible. Suppose the income tax threshold for pensioners is a_r. Then if the marginal tax rate is denoted t, the income tax paid on a non-pension income of y, denoted $T_r(y)$, is given by:

$$T_r(y) = t[(y + b) - \{a_r + P(y)\}] \qquad (9.2)$$

Here $y + b$ is total income and $a_r + P(y)$ measures the total allowance against that income for tax purposes. The following analysis uses the assumption, following the Australian system, that $b = a_r$, so that $T_r(y)$ can be rewritten as:

$$T_r(y) = t\{y - P(y)\} \qquad (9.3)$$

and taxable income is equal to non-pension income less the amount of pension tax paid.

This first model contains only an income tax applied to workers. If a worker's income is denoted by w, and the tax-free threshold applied to workers is a, then the tax revenue $T(w)$ is given by:

$$
\begin{aligned}
T(w) &= 0 &&\text{for } w \leq a \\
&= t(w - a) &&\text{for } w > a \qquad (9.4)
\end{aligned}
$$

Because of the various thresholds used in the income tax and pension tax systems, the total amount paid depends on the precise forms of the distributions of workers' and pensioners' incomes. It is not sufficient merely to know the arithmetic mean values of y and w, which may be denoted $\bar{y}$ and $\bar{w}$. In general, $F(w)$ and $H(y)$ are used to denote the cumulative distribution functions of w and y respectively. Hence, $F(w)$ represents the proportion of workers whose income is less than or equal to w. In producing numerical examples below, it will be necessary to specify the precise forms of these distributions, but for the time being they may be stated in general terms.

A Basic Pension with Indirect Taxes

The means-tested scheme will be compared with one which provides an unconditional basic pension, but in which there is also an indirect tax similar to VAT, along with special contributions similar to NICs. The effect of the consumption tax is to tax some of the transfer payment paid to each pensioner.

If the tax threshold for pensioners is the same as that for workers, of a, then the tax paid by pensioners $T_r(y)$ is given by:

$$T_r(y) = t\{(y + b) - a\} \tag{9.5}$$

When $b > a$, all pensioners will pay income tax. The income tax schedule facing workers is assumed to be the same as in the first scheme described above; that is, equation (9.4).

NICs, $C(w)$, are assumed to be a constant proportion, c, of the gross income of workers, applied between two limits w_e and w_u. The British system took this form for some years, and more formally it is given by:

$$
\begin{aligned}
C(w) &= 0 & &\text{for } w < w_e \\
&= cw & &\text{for } w_e \leqslant w < w_u \qquad (9.6) \\
&= cw_u & &\text{for } w \geqslant w_u
\end{aligned}
$$

Like the income tax system, it would be possible to examine a more complex NIC scheme using the approach shown below.

Both workers and pensioners must pay a VAT type of consumption tax. If VAT involves a proportional rate, v, applied to total consumption expenditure exclusive of VAT, then the equivalent rate expressed as a tax-inclusive rate is given by $v/(1 + v)$. If workers and pensioners save a proportion s_w and s_r respectively of their net income, then the amount of VAT paid, $V(w)$ and $V_r(y)$ respectively, is given by:

$$V(w) = (1 - s_w)\{w - T(w) - C(w)\}\{v/(1 + v)\} \tag{9.7}$$

$$V_r(y) = (1 - s_r)\{y - T_r(y)\}\{v/(1 + v)\} \tag{9.8}$$

In order to concentrate on the differences between the different types of scheme, it will be assumed in what follows that $s_w = s_r = 0$. This is a convenient assumption which could easily be relaxed.

Comparing Marginal Tax Rates

In making comparisons between the two basic schemes described above, for a given basic pension, b, there is no point comparing values of the marginal income tax rate, t, required to finance pensions, for given values of v and c. The use of additional taxes in the second scheme will clearly produce lower values of t. It is therefore necessary to examine the effective overall marginal rate of tax in the multi-tax system. Consider a worker in the second scheme whose income, w, is such that income tax and NIC are paid. With $s_w = 0$, the total tax paid is given by:

$$T(w) + C(w) + \{w - T(w) - C(w)\}\{v/(1 + v)\}$$
$$= \{T(w) + C(w) + vw\}/(1 + v) \qquad (9.9)$$

Appropriate substitution from (9.4) and (9.6) into (9.9) then gives total tax of:

$$w\{(t + c + v)/(1 + v)\} - at/(1 + v) \qquad (9.10)$$

For those workers with income between w_e and w_u, the effective marginal tax rate is equal to $(t + v + c)/(1 + v)$. The effective average tax rate can be found to be given by $\{v + c + t(1 - a/w)\}/(1 + v)$. For the first type of scheme, with only the income tax facing workers, the marginal rate is t and the average rate is $t(1 - a/w)$. These comparisons need to be kept in mind in section 9.3.

The two schemes differ in the number and type of policy instruments available to governments. The basic pension, b, and the income tax schedule facing workers, determined by a and t, are common to both schemes. In the means-tested scheme the instruments also include the pension tax rate and pension tax threshold income level. In the multi-tax scheme additional instruments include the NIC earnings limits and contribution rate, along with the VAT rate. However, freedom to choose these variables independently is restricted by the government's budget constraint. This is the subject of the next section.

9.2 THE GOVERNMENT BUDGET CONSTRAINT

Income tax and VAT are used in order to finance other forms of government expenditure, in addition to state pensions. Policy variables can only be adjusted subject to the constraint that expenditure on pensions plus the expenditure for other purposes is equal to the sum of tax revenue from all sources from the retired and working populations. In reality, there are many other forms of government revenue, but these can be ignored here given the focus of this chapter; they may be considered as financing other expenditure which also remains fixed when changing pension variables. The approach used below is to express each component of the government's budget constraint precisely in terms of the tax and pension structure, along with demographic variables and the distribution of income of both pensioners and workers. The resulting equation is then imposed in order to solve for the marginal income tax rate, given the other policy variables.

The Means-Tested Pension

In the first structure considered above, total government expenditure (on both pensions and other relevant forms) must equal the total income tax revenue from both the retired and working populations, plus the revenue from the pension tax (arising from the means testing of the pension). The taxable income of all pensioners combined is, using (9.3), the total non-pension income less the total amount of pension tax paid. With a constant marginal tax rate of t, the budget constraint may be expressed as:

$$\left\{\begin{array}{c}\text{government}\\\text{expenditure}\end{array}\right\} = t\left\{\begin{array}{c}\text{workers'}\\\text{taxable}\\\text{income}\end{array}\right\} + t\left\{\begin{array}{c}\text{pensioners'}\\\text{non-pension}-\\\text{income}\end{array}\begin{array}{c}\text{pension}\\\text{tax}\end{array}\right\} + \left\{\begin{array}{c}\text{pension}\\\text{tax}\end{array}\right\}$$

Solving for the tax rate therefore gives:

$$t = \frac{\left\{\begin{array}{c}\text{government}\\\text{expenditure}\end{array}\right\} - \left\{\begin{array}{c}\text{pension}\\\text{tax}\end{array}\right\}}{\left\{\begin{array}{c}\text{workers'}\\\text{taxable}\\\text{income}\end{array}\right\} + \left\{\begin{array}{c}\text{pensioners'}\\\text{non-pension}\\\text{income}\end{array}\right\} - \left\{\begin{array}{c}\text{pension}\\\text{tax}\end{array}\right\}} \qquad (9.11)$$

This equation shows that when government pension expenditure increases, either because of a change in the pension itself or an increase in the number of pensioners, the tax rate must increase. But the change in pension expenditure may also be accompanied by an increase in the total non-pension income of pensioners, which reduces the required tax rate. An increase in the total pension tax revenue reduces the required tax rate, although pension tax appears in both the numerator and denominator of (9.11), because government expenditure is necessarily less than the tax base.

Detailed comparisons require the components of (9.11) to be derived precisely in terms of the pension and tax structure. The following derivations are largely intuitive. More formal derivations are given in the notes to this chapter. First, if there are N pensioners, the total non-pension income is simply N multiplied by the arithmetic mean value of y, $\bar{y}$. An individual worker's taxable income, if $w > a$, is equal to $w - a$. Hence the total taxable income of all workers is given by the total income above the threshold, reduced by an amount, a, for each worker above the threshold. Given the distribution function of workers' income defined earlier, the proportion of workers above a is $1 - F(a)$. Consequently if there are L workers and $1 - F_1(a)$ denotes the proportion of *income* obtained by those above a, the total income above the threshold is $L\bar{w}\{1 - F_1(a)\}$, where $\bar{w}$ is the arithmetic mean value of w. Workers' aggregate taxable income is therefore expressed as:

$$L\bar{w}[\{1 - F_1(a)\} - (a/\bar{w})\{1 - F(a)\}] \qquad (9.12)$$

It is convenient to write the term in square brackets in (9.12) as $g_1(a, \bar{w})$, so that:

$$\text{workers' taxable income} = L\bar{w}g_1(a, \bar{w}) \qquad (9.13)$$

The term g_1 allows for the effect of the tax-free threshold, and it is clear that if $a = 0$, $g_1 = 1$.

The evaluation of the total pension tax paid is somewhat more awkward. Since the pension tax operates above a threshold and has a maximum value of the pension itself, as in the case of workers' income tax, the total tax can be expressed as a proportion of total pensioners' non-pension income; the proportion depends on the parameters of the scheme, which in this case are b, s, and y_e, as well as average income. Writing this proportion as $g_2(b, s, y_e, \bar{y})$ gives:

$$\text{pension tax revenue} = N\bar{y}g_2(b, s, y_e, \bar{y}) \qquad (9.14)$$

It is shown in the notes and further reading that g_2 is equal to:

$$(b/\bar{y})\{1 - H(y_u)\} + s\{H_1(y_u) - H_1(y_e)\} -$$
$$s(y_e/\bar{y})\{H(y_u) - H(y_e)\} \qquad (9.15)$$

In this expression $H_1(y)$ represents the proportion of total income obtained by those pensioners with incomes less than or equal to y. The first term in curly brackets in (9.15) represents the proportion of pensioners who pay the maximum pension tax of b; the second term in curly brackets represents the total income of those who are liable to the pension tax (imposed at the rate, s); the third term in curly brackets denotes the proportion of pensioners who pay the pension tax. There is a direct comparison between the structure of the expressions for g_1 and g_2, because both are taxes imposed on income measured in excess of a threshold; the pension tax has the added complication of the upper limit, y_u, above which no additional pension tax is paid.

Finally, if E denotes the government non-pension expenditure per person (workers and pensioners combined), the total government expenditure is given by:

$$Nb + (N + L)E \qquad (9.16)$$

Substituting (9.12) to (9.16) into (9.11) gives the tax rate required to finance any given pension as:

$$t = \frac{Nb + (N + L)E - N\bar{y}g_2}{L\bar{w}g_1 + N\bar{y} - N\bar{y}g_2} \qquad (9.17)$$

It is convenient to define the *dependency ratio*, D, as N/L and the *replacement ratio*, R, as $b/\bar{w}$ (that is, the ratio of the basic pension to the average income of workers). Equation (9.17) can be written as:

$$t = \frac{DR + (1 + D)(E/\bar{w}) - D(\bar{y}/\bar{w})g_2}{g_1 + D(\bar{y}/\bar{w})(1 - g_2)} \tag{9.18}$$

Popular debate on pension financing can be seen to emphasize the role of the term DR in equation (9.18) which shows that increasing dependency and replacement ratios will raise the tax rate imposed on workers. But the role of $\bar{y}$ and g_2 (influenced by the system of means testing and the precise distribution of pensioners' incomes) is also very important.

The Basic Pension with Indirect Taxes

The second pension and tax structure presented in section 9.1 has additional taxes, but does not have means testing. The derivation of relationships proceeds as before. Consider first the total tax paid by workers, which is the sum of direct and indirect taxes, and given by:

$$t \left\{ \begin{array}{c} \text{workers'} \\ \text{taxable} \\ \text{income} \end{array} \right\} + \left\{ \begin{array}{c} \text{workers'} \\ \text{NICs} \end{array} \right\}$$

$$+ \frac{v}{1 + v} \left[\left\{ \begin{array}{c} \text{workers'} \\ \text{total} \\ \text{income} \end{array} \right\} - t \left\{ \begin{array}{c} \text{workers'} \\ \text{taxable} \\ \text{income} \end{array} \right\} - \left\{ \begin{array}{c} \text{workers'} \\ \text{NICs} \end{array} \right\} \right]$$

This can be arranged to get:

$$\frac{1}{1 + v} \left[t \left\{ \begin{array}{c} \text{workers'} \\ \text{taxable} \\ \text{income} \end{array} \right\} + \left\{ \begin{array}{c} \text{workers'} \\ \text{NICs} \end{array} \right\} + v \left\{ \begin{array}{c} \text{workers'} \\ \text{total} \\ \text{income} \end{array} \right\} \right] \tag{9.19}$$

To this must be added the total tax revenue of pensioners, who do not pay national insurance contributions. Hence the expression in (9.19) can be converted to give total revenue by substituting 'total taxable income' for the first term in curly brackets and 'total income' for the third term in curly brackets. The result must then be equated to government expenditure to get the budget constraint, which can then be solved for t to give:

$$t = \frac{(1 + v)\left\{\begin{array}{c}\text{government}\\\text{expenditure}\end{array}\right\} - \left\{\begin{array}{c}\text{workers'}\\\text{NICs}\end{array}\right\} - v\left\{\begin{array}{c}\text{total}\\\text{income}\end{array}\right\}}{\left\{\begin{array}{c}\text{total taxable}\\\text{income}\end{array}\right\}}$$

(9.20)

Using the notation introduced earlier, total income is given by $L\bar{w}$ plus $N(\bar{y} + b)$; notice that the pension must be added to pensioners' other income. The national insurance contributions of workers is c multiplied by a proportion of workers' total income, with the constant of proportionality depending on the income thresholds and the income distribution. This may be written $g_3(w_e, w_u, \bar{w})$, so that:

$$\text{total NICs} = cL\bar{w}g_3(w_e, w_u, \bar{w})$$

(9.21)

It is shown in the notes to this chapter that g_3 is given by:

$$g_3 = \{F_1(w_u) - F_1(w_e)\} + (w_u/\bar{w})\{1 - F(w_u)\}$$

(9.22)

The first term reflects the total income of those with income between the limits w_e and w_u, while the second term reflects the fact that all those above the upper limit w_u pay a fixed contribution.

Taxable income of workers has already been derived in equation (9.13), so it is only necessary to obtain the taxable income of pensioners. Following the above approach this can be written as a proportion, $g_4(a, b, \bar{y})$, of $N\bar{y}$, so that

$$\text{pensioners' taxable income} = N\bar{y}g_4(a, b, \bar{y})$$

(9.23)

In considering the term g_4, two possibilities arise. If $b > a$ it is clear that all pensioners must pay income tax regardless of their value of y. Hence total taxable income is $N(\bar{y} + b - a)$ and $g_4 = 1 + (b - a)/\bar{y}$. Alternatively if $b < a$, those with incomes below

$a - b$ will not pay tax and the corresponding value of g_4 is given by:

$$g_4 = \{1 - H_1(a - b)\} - \{(a - b)/\bar{y}\}\{1 - H(a - b)\} \quad (9.24)$$

Substituting these results in (9.20) gives the marginal tax rate as:

$$t = \frac{(1 + v)\{Nb + (N + L)E\} - cL\bar{w}g_3 - v\{L\bar{w} + N(\bar{y} + b)\}}{L\bar{w}g_1 + N\bar{y}g_4} \quad (9.25)$$

Rewriting this in terms of the dependency and replacement ratios, gives:

$$t = \frac{(1 + v)\{DR + (1 +D)(E/\bar{w})\} - cg_3 - v\{1 + D(R + \bar{y}/\bar{w})\}}{g_1 + D(\bar{y}/\bar{w})g_4} \quad (9.26)$$

which may usefully be compared with (9.18). The effect of means testing compared with an unconditional pension may be seen directly by setting $c = v = 0$ in (9.26) to give:

$$t = \frac{DR + (1 + D)(E/\bar{w})}{g_1 + D(\bar{y}/\bar{w})g_4} \quad (9.27)$$

Means testing thus reduces the numerator of t by $D(\bar{y}/\bar{w})g_2$ and replaces g_4 with $(1 - g_2)$. For most cases the income tax rate in the means-tested system is the lower rate but, as illustrated in section 9.3, this is not always true.

9.3 AGEING POPULATIONS AND THE TAX RATE

The above results, which express the marginal income tax rates in terms of other variables, can be used to obtain precise orders of magnitude for a wide variety of alternative tax and population structures. First, consider the effects of an ageing population, reflected by increasing values of the dependency ratio, D, when other features of the system remain unchanged. It should be remembered, however, that this type of comparison reflects the worst situation because increased dependency is likely to be accompanied by other changes, including reductions in other government expenditure, E, and increases in average pensioner incomes, $\bar{y}$.

This type of partial effect of population ageing in each system may be examined by obtaining the partial differential, $\partial t/\partial D$, for equations (9.18) and (9.26). For the means-tested system similar to that used in Australia, and using the convenient simplification that $e = E/\bar{w}$ and $x = \bar{y}/\bar{w}$, it can be found that:

$$\frac{\partial t}{\partial D} = \frac{g_1(R + e - g_2x) - ex(1 - g_2)}{\{g_1 + Dx(1 - g_2)\}^2} \tag{9.28}$$

For feasible values, the numerator of (9.28) is positive, so that the income tax rate increases as D increases, but at a declining rate since D appears in the denominator. The importance of the ratio of average pensioner to average worker incomes, x, is also clear from this result. It will, however, be seen that for practical orders of magnitude, the denominator of (9.28) is dominated by the term g_1, so that $\partial t/\partial D$ is approximately constant over a wide range of D; the relationship between t and D is thus close to a straight line. The increase in t as D increases will be lower, the lower is the pension and hence the replacement ratio. This results directly from the appearance of R in the numerator of (9.28), and indirectly from the fact that the term g_2 is a function of the basic pension, b.

Consideration of the second structure, with an unconditional pension financed with a mixture of direct and indirect taxation, is slightly more awkward, but it can be shown that partial differentiation of (9.26) gives:

$$\frac{\partial t}{\partial D} = \frac{g_1\{R + e(1 + v) - vx\} - xg_4\{e(1 + v) - (v + cg_3)\}}{\{g_1 + Dxg_4\}^2} \tag{9.29}$$

Again the marginal income tax rate increases with D at a slightly declining rate, but for relevant ranges of values the relationship between t and D will be found to be close to linear.

Income Distributions

The various terms g_1 to g_4 depend not only on average pensioner and worker incomes but also on their distribution. Some assumptions about the form of these distributions are therefore required. The forms chosen must provide a reasonable approximation to reality and must be quite tractable, in view of the need to calculate proportions of people and total income within specified ranges. The lognormal distribution meets both of these requirements, and is used in all of the calculations reported below. Hence w and y are assumed to be distributed as $\Lambda(\mu_w, \sigma_w^2)$ and $\Lambda(\mu_y, \sigma_y^2)$ respectively, where μ and σ^2 denote the mean and the variance of logarithms. A property of the lognormal distribution is that $\bar{w} = \exp(\mu_w + \sigma_w^2/2)$, and similarly for $\bar{y}$. In view of the importance of increasing pensioner incomes, calculations will be reported below for alternative values of $\bar{y}$. However, the results all apply to the following parameter values: $\sigma_y^2 = 0.5$; $\sigma_w^2 = 0.3$; and $\mu_w = 10.446637$. These values imply that $\bar{w} = \$40\ 000$. Comparisons are made for $\bar{y}$ equal to $\$8\ 000$ and $\$16\ 000$, for which μ_y takes the values 8.7372 and 9.43035 respectively. The income tax threshold, a, is set at $\$5\ 000$ and the non-pension expenditure per person is $\$7\ 000$ throughout.

Some Comparisons

The effect of increasing dependency is illustrated in Figure 9.1 for the means-tested pension scheme combined with income taxation, where $y_e = \$2\ 000$, $s = 0.5$ and $\bar{y} = \$8\ 000$. The threshold income level above which means testing applies and the pension tax (taper) rate are similar to those in Australia. Results are shown for four levels of the basic pension, ranging from $\$4\ 000$ to $\$10\ 000$. As indicated above, the schedules are approximately linear, with the slope increasing as the basic pension increases. A higher value of $\bar{y}$ reduces the slopes. The values shown in Figure 9.1 may be contrasted with the simplistic framework that is often used in pension debates; there is a basic non-taxable pension and a proportional income tax scheme, $\bar{y} = 0$ and in this case $E(N + L) + bN = tL\bar{w}$ and $t = RD + e(1 + D)$. For $R = 0.25$ (corresponding to $b = 10\ 000$ and $\bar{w} = 40\ 000$) and $E = 7\ 000$, it can be seen that a doubling of D from 0.2 to 0.4 would imply an increase in t by a factor of 1.33. The corresponding case in Figure 9.1 implies an increase in the marginal income tax rate by a factor of approximately 1.25; furthermore the average tax rate increase is correspondingly lower.

Figure 9.2 illustrates the second structure. Results are shown for the same range of basic pension, b, and dependency ratio, D, and where there is a consumption tax at the rate $v = 0.15$ with national insurance contributions applied to income between \$8 500 and \$75 000 at the rate of 0.075. These values are similar to those in the UK. As in Figure 9.1, $\bar{y} = 8\,000$. Comparison with means testing alone may be made by setting $c = v = 0$ in the non-means-tested scheme, shown in Figure 9.3. Figures 9.1 and 9.3 show, as expected, that the marginal income tax rates are generally lower where means testing is used, but other features are the same. An exception to this general rule is where the basic pension is relatively high and the value of $\bar{y}$ is relatively low; for values of D above about 0.45 and a pension of \$10 000 with $\bar{y} = \$8\,000$ the means-tested scheme actually requires a higher value of t. The explanation for this is the different tax structure applying to pensioners in the two schemes; in the means-tested scheme the

Figure 9.1   The means-tested system

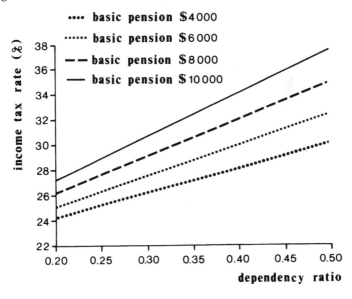

Figure 9.2   A basic pension with value added tax and national insurance contributions

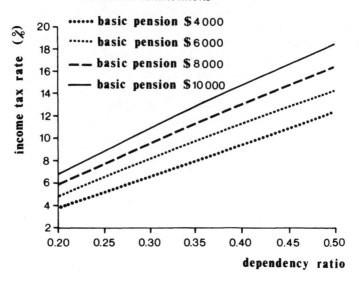

Figure 9.3   Effective tax rates with no means testing

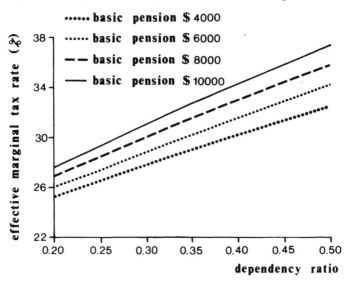

threshold is equal to the basic pension, so as the latter rises the taxable income of pensioners falls. For a higher value of $\bar{y}$ than that used in Figures 9.1 and 9.3, there is a much larger difference between required tax rates, with that required in the means-tested structure being much lower.

It has been argued that in comparing the different structures it is more appropriate to measure the overall effective marginal tax rate in the scheme using a combination of different taxes. Furthermore, overall average tax rates should be compared at given income levels. Figure 9.4 shows marginal and average rates (calculated at $\bar{w}$) for the means-tested scheme, with two values of

Figure 9.4   Marginal and average tax rates with means testing

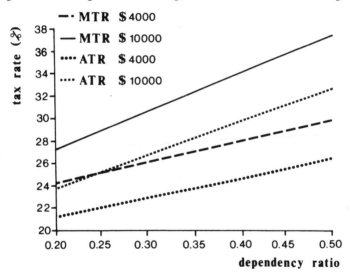

the basic pension, and other values corresponding to those used in Figure 9.1. These may be compared with the lower overall effective marginal and average rates shown in Figure 9.5, which in other respects corresponds to Figure 9.2. The interesting result which arises when comparing Figures 9.4 and 9.5 is that the marginal and effective overall rates are much closer together in the structure which uses the combination of income and consumption taxes with the NIC. This means that, for each value of b and

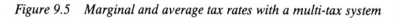

Figure 9.5 Marginal and average tax rates with a multi-tax system

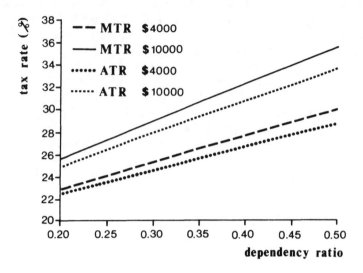

most values of *D*, the effective marginal rate is *lower* with the multi-tax system than when means testing is used with only an income tax, but the average tax rate is *higher*.

It has been suggested that recent policy debates have typically ignored the extent to which pensioners, on average, receive higher incomes from sources other than state pensions. This means that the burden of financing transfer payments to low income pensioners is shared between relatively richer workers *and* pensioners. The effect of increasing dependency, with a higher value of $\bar{y}$, is shown in Figures 9.6 and 9.7 for the case where $\bar{y} = \$16\ 000$ but the other parameters are the same as for Figures 9.4 and 9.5. Figure 9.6 applies to the system which uses means testing combined with only an income tax, while Figure 9.7 applies to the second scheme. Both figures give overall effective marginal tax rates and average tax rates (evaluated at $\bar{w}$), so they are directly comparable. In this case it is found that for dependency ratios in excess of 0.25 (when $b = \$4\ 000$) or 0.30 (when $b = \$10\ 000$), the marginal tax rate is higher in the multi-rate scheme than in the scheme using means testing. However, the average tax rates are consistently lower in the latter scheme.

Figure 9.6   A higher average pensioner income: means testing

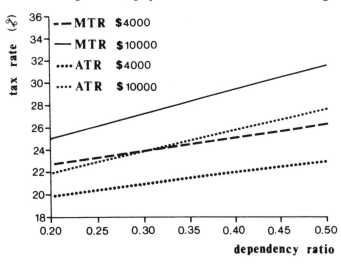

Figure 9.7   A higher average pensioner income: a multi-tax scheme

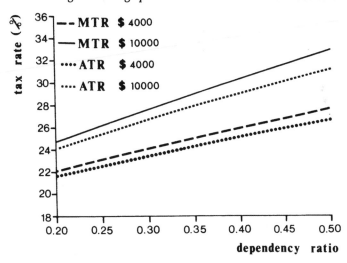

The analytical results can also be used to examine the orders of magnitude involved when changing other parameters of the systems. Of particular interest in the means-tested scheme are the effects of changing the pension tax rate, s, and the threshold, y_e, above which the tax is paid (or means testing begins to operate). For example, it is found that if the value of s is increased from 0.5 to 0.75, while y_e is simultaneously increased from \$2 000 to \$4 000, the required income tax rate is virtually unchanged at all levels of the dependency ratio. This type of change nevertheless has implications for redistribution, since it involves greater transfers to those at the lower end of the distribution of pensioner incomes, at the expense of the relatively better-off pensioners, while those for whom the pension tax is b in each case are not affected.

For the multi-tax system combining income tax, VAT and NIC, it is of interest to examine the changes in the various rates which are deficit neutral. Such changes may be obtained from equation (9.26) by taking the total differential, allowing for variations in only t, v and c:

$$dt = -\left\{\frac{1 + Dx - e(1 + D)}{g_1 + g_4 Dx}\right\} dv - \left\{\frac{g_3}{g_1 + g_4 Dx}\right\} dc \quad (9.30)$$

For example, deficit neutral changes in just v and c can be examined by setting $dt = 0$ in (9.30). Alternatively, a shift from income taxation towards VAT may be examined by setting $dc = 0$. Other alternatives are of course available.

The approach used here has the advantage of generating the detailed implications of alternative policy proposals. For example, Gruen (1985, p. 621) suggested that the taper rate, or pension tax rate, in the Australian pension scheme should be reduced 'to 25 per cent or at most 33 per cent. One way in which the cost of this reform could be reduced is if the income-free area associated with the pension were abolished.' Many proposals, unlike Gruen's, do not even consider the fact that a policy to increase expenditure must be accompanied by suggestions relating to its finance and an analysis of the combined package. This proposal may be examined by setting y_e equal to zero, while reducing the value of s in the means-tested scheme, and then finding the new rate of income tax required to ensure that these changes are deficit neutral. In a wide range of situations (depending on the level of the basic pension and the average non-pension income of pensioners, along with the dependency rate) it was found that a slight increase in the income tax rate would be required to finance the change. However, this increase was less than one percentage point in all cases. Where b and $\bar{y}$ are relatively low (at 4 000 and 8 000 respectively), the use of $s = 0.33$ and $y_e = 0$ involved approximately the same tax rate as when $s = 0.5$ and $y_e = 2\ 000$.

It has been seen that in each type of system there are many complex interdependencies among the various taxes, so that much care needs to be taken in making comparisons of tax rates. Although the schemes examined abstract from many complexities, an advantage of the approach is that it allows computations of a vast range of alternative policies to be carried out. It is argued that a clear appreciation of the orders of magnitude involved in policy choices is an important prerequisite for rational policy debate.

NOTES AND FURTHER READING

Consider the income tax revenue from workers in both schemes examined above. Aggregate revenue is given by:

$$Lt \int_a^\infty (w - a)dF(w)$$

$$= Lt \left[\int_a^\infty wdF(w) - a \int_a^\infty dF(w) \right]$$

$$= Lt \left[\left\{ \bar{w} - \int_0^a wdF(w) \right\} - a \left\{ 1 - \int_0^a dF(w) \right\} \right] \qquad (9.31)$$

This can be simplified using the concept of the first moment distribution, $F_1(w)$, defined by $F_1(w) = \int_0^w udF(u) \Big/ \int_0^\infty udF(u) = \int_0^w udF(u) \Big/ \bar{w}$, with $F(w) = \int_0^w f(u)du = \int_0^w dF(u)$. Evaluating the integrals for $w = a$ allows (9.31) to be written as:

$$Lt\bar{w}[\{1 - F_1(a)\} - (a/\bar{w})\{1 - F(a)\}] \qquad (9.32)$$

$g_1(a, \bar{w})$ is the term in square brackets in (9.32).

Secondly, consider the pension tax raised in the first scheme, which uses the means-tested pension; this is given by:

$$N \left[s \int_{y_e}^{y_u} (y - y_e)dH(y) + b \int_{y_u}^{\infty} dH(y) \right] \quad (9.33)$$

The first term in (9.33) gives the pension tax paid by those between the limits y_e and y_u, while the second term is the tax paid by all those above y_u. Simplification of (9.33) follows the same approach as that used to obtain (9.32), using instead the first moment distribution of pensioners' incomes $H_1(y) = \int_0^y u dH(u)/\bar{y}$. Thus, revenue from the pension tax is:

$$N \left[s \left\{ \int_0^{y_u} (y - y_e)dH(y) - \int_0^{y_e} (y - y_e)dH(y) \right\} + b \left\{ 1 - \int_0^{y_u} dH(y) \right\} \right]$$

$$= N\bar{y}[(b/\bar{y})\{1 - H(y_u)\} + s\{H_1(y_u) - H_1(y_e)\} - s(y_e/\bar{y})\{H(y_u) - H(y_e)\}]$$

$$(9.34)$$

The term in square brackets in (9.34) is $g_2(b, s, y_e, \bar{y})$. Here it should be remembered that $y_u = y_e + b/s$.

Thirdly, consider the total revenue raised from national insurance contributions in the second scheme. This is given by:

$$Lc \left[\int_{w_e}^{w_u} w dF(w) + w_u \int_{w_u}^{\infty} dF(w) \right] \quad (9.35)$$

A similar approach shows that (9.35) can be simplified to:

$$Lc\bar{w}[\{F_1(w_u) - F_1(w_e)\} + (w_u/\bar{w})\{1 - F(w_u)\}] \quad (9.36)$$

The term in square brackets in (9.36) is $g_3(w_e, w_u, \bar{w})$.

Finally, consider the total income tax paid by pensioners in the second scheme, for the case where $b < a$. This is given by:

$$Nt \int_{a-b}^{\infty} (y + b - a)dH(y) \quad (9.37)$$

Following the same procedure as that used to get (9.31), shows that this is equal to:

$$Nt\bar{y} \left[\{1 - H_1(a - b)\} - \left(\frac{a - b}{\bar{y}} \right) \{1 - H(a - b)\} \right] \quad (9.38)$$

and $g_4(a, b, \bar{y})$ is the term in square brackets in (9.38).

For extensive reviews of population ageing and social security in a variety of countries, see OECD (1988) and Heller et al. (1986). The issues are examined in Creedy and Disney (1989a). On the need to allow for three generations see Prest (1970). For detailed analyses of the Australian scheme, see Foster (1988) and Creedy and Disney (1989b).

10. Aggregate Consumption in a Life-Cycle Model

Despite the extensive and impressive amount of work which has been stimulated by the insights offered by the life-cycle model, some aspects of the theory and its testing have been rather neglected. It can be argued, for example, that the influence of household size and the variation in both household size and earnings over the life cycle have not been fully integrated into the basic analysis. The associated problems of aggregation have also been neglected, despite the foundation of the approach in individual maximizing behaviour and its predominant use in the specification of aggregate consumption functions.

A review of the life-cycle hypothesis of saving was provided by Modigliani (1986), who made very little reference to demographic aspects. However, after briefly noting the life cycle of earnings, he added that

> consumption also varies with age, largely reflecting variations in family size, as one might expect if the consumer smooths consumption *per equivalent adult*. . . . Now the life cycle of family size, at least in the United States, has a very humped shape rather similar to that of income, though with a somewhat earlier peak. (1986, p. 304)

The purpose of this chapter is to examine how the changing distribution of household size with age, and the changing distribution of income with age, can be integrated into a simple life-cycle model. Earlier treatments of household size are briefly considered in section 10.1, which also presents the model used later. The chapter then examines several aggregation problems which have been neglected in previous discussions. Section 10.2 considers aggregation over households and section 10.3 goes on to examine two approaches to aggregation over ages. The final results enable changes in the ratio of aggregate consumption to aggregate income over time (or between countries) to be related explicitly to changes in the life-cycle pattern of earnings and household size.

10.1 THE TREATMENT OF HOUSEHOLD SIZE

Earlier Approaches

The first study to consider the influence of household size and composition on life-cycle saving seems to have been that of Fisher (1956). After modifying the basic model, Fisher nevertheless concluded from his empirical analysis that 'theoretical expectations as to the influence of family size upon savings, then, receive limited support' (1956, p. 200). In the reply by Modigliani and Ando (1957), they suggested an extension to Fisher's approach which seems to have been widely accepted, and may briefly be summarized here.

The basic life-cycle model was expressed as

$$C_t = \gamma_t^i V_i \qquad\qquad i = 1, ..., L \qquad\qquad (10.1)$$

where L is the (fixed) length of life, C_t is the consumption planned at period i for period t, V_i represents total resources at period i, and γ_t^i depends on the form of utility function U and the rate of interest r, but is independent of total resources V_i. The approach of Modigliani and Ando (1957, p. 111) simply involved adapting equation (10.1) by writing

$$\gamma_t^i = \gamma_t'^i \{1 + \alpha_t^i (J_t^i - 1)\} \qquad\qquad (10.2)$$

Here J_t^i is the expectation at i of the number of individuals in the family at time t, and α_t^i is the marginal cost assigned at i to each additional member of the household (after the head) in period t. Equation (10.2) therefore involves a rather unusual type of equivalent adult scale; each member after the first is given the same weight depending only on the age of the head of the household. This seems unnecessarily restrictive and the formulation does not fully take into account the relative shapes of the age profiles of household size and income, as well as the correlation between the two.

A Simple Model

It would perhaps seem more natural to formulate a life-cycle consumption model directly in terms of income and consumption per equivalent adult. The arguments of the utility function can therefore be written C_t/h_t instead of simply C_t, where h_t represents the following equivalent household size obtained in the conventional way. In the following presentation lower-case letters will be used to denote variables measured in terms of 'per equivalent household member'.

In the popular case of the additive separable utility function, with constant intertemporal elasticity of substitution, η, the utility function where the head of the household is aged i years is given by

$$U_i = \sum_{t=1}^{L} \zeta^{-(t-i)} c_t^{-\beta} \qquad (10.3)$$

where the time preference rate is $\zeta - 1$ and $\beta = -(1 - 1/\eta)$. This must be maximized subject to the constraint that:

$$\sum_{t=1}^{L} \left(\frac{t}{1+r}\right)^{t-i} c_t = w_i + \sum_{t=i}^{L} \left(\frac{1}{1+r}\right)^{t-i} y_t = v_i \qquad (10.4)$$

where w_i is accumulated savings (net worth), v_i is wealth, and y_j is income per equivalent adult. Writing $\delta = 1 + r$, the maximization of (10.3) subject to (10.4) can be seen to give the standard result that

$$c_t = \gamma_t^i v_i \qquad (10.5)$$

with

$$\gamma_t^i = \left(\frac{\delta}{\zeta}\right)^{\eta t - i} k_i \qquad (10.6)$$

and

$$k_i = \left\{ \sum_{t=i}^{L} (\zeta \delta \beta)^{-\eta(t-1)} \right\}^{-1} \qquad (10.7)$$

It can be seen from (10.6) that when $\delta = \zeta$ the consumption profile is flat, and the elasticity of substitution, η, cannot be identified. When $i = 0$ the planned consumption stream over the remainder of the life cycle in the equivalent adult terms is thus given by:

$$c_t = \left(\frac{\delta}{\zeta}\right)^{\eta t} k_0 v_0 \qquad (10.8)$$

where $v_0 = \sum_{t=0}^{L} \delta^{-t} y_t$. This result forms the basis of the following sections.

10.2 AGGREGATION OVER HOUSEHOLDS

Equation (10.8) gives the familiar result that the logarithm of consumption (per equivalent adult) increases linearly with age, since:

$$\log c_t = \log (k_0 v_0) + \{\eta \log (\delta/\zeta)\} t \qquad (10.9)$$

On the assumption that the parameters of the utility function are the same for all households, but that expected incomes and household size vary, the problem considered in this section is that of finding the average planned consumption in each age group. It is assumed that expectations are based on observed differences between age groups, suitably adjusted for expected inflation and growth of real incomes. It is required to show explicitly how average household consumption in each age group depends on the precise way in which the joint distribution of income and household size is expected to vary over the life cycle. As mentioned earlier, average consumption per equivalent adult cannot simply be taken as being equal to a ratio of two averages.

The Joint Distribution of Consumption and Household Size

Now a reasonable working assumption is that household consumption and size are jointly lognormally distributed in each age group. Thus, neglecting the t subscripts for convenience, the joint distribution of C and h is given by

$$\Lambda(C, h | \mu_c, \mu_h, \sigma_c^2, \sigma_h^2, \varrho) \qquad (10.10)$$

where Λ denotes the lognormal distribution function, μ_c, and μ_h are the means of the logarithms of consumption and household size, σ_c^2 and σ_h^2 are the corresponding variances of logarithms, and
ϱ is the correlation coefficient between the logarithms. Then using
the result in Aitchison and Brown (1957, p. 12), consumption per equivalent adult in each age group is distributed as follows:

$$\frac{C}{h} \text{ is } \Lambda\left(\frac{C}{h}\bigg|\mu_c - \mu_h, \sigma_c^2 + \sigma_h^2 - 2\varrho\sigma_c\sigma_h\right) \qquad (10.11)$$

The general result is required that for the lognormal distribution $\Lambda(x|\mu, \sigma^2)$ the arithmetic mean of x is equal to $\exp(\mu + \sigma^2/2)$. Applying this result to the distribution of C/h from (10.11), it can be seen that:

$$E\left(\frac{C}{h}\right) = \exp\{\mu_c - \mu_h + \tfrac{1}{2}(\sigma_c^2 + \sigma_h^2 - 2\varrho\sigma_c\sigma_h)\}$$

$$= \frac{E(C)}{E(h)} \exp(\sigma_h^2 - \varrho\sigma_c\sigma_h) \qquad (10.12)$$

Returning to the consumption profile, taking expected values of (11.8) gives:

$$E\left(\frac{C}{h}\right) = \left(\frac{\delta}{\zeta}\right)^{\eta t} k_0 E(v_0) \qquad (10.13)$$

And substituting for $E(h) = \exp(\mu_h + \sigma_h^2/2)$, this can be written as

$$E(C) = k_0 E(v_0) \exp\left\{\eta t \log\frac{\delta}{\zeta} + \varrho\sigma_c\sigma_h + \mu_h - \sigma_h^2/2\right\} \qquad (10.14)$$

Equation (10.14) shows explicitly how the arithmetic mean household consumption at each age depends on the parameters of the common utility function, the relative dispersions of consumption and household size, their correlation, and medium household size.

Variations with Age

In order to know how $E(C)$ varies with age, using equation

(10.14), it is necessary to specify the way in which household size varies with age.

Empirical studies of life-cycle variations in income, household size and consumption support the hypothesis that μ_h is a quadratic function of t. Hence it is possible to write:

$$\mu_{ht} = m_0 + m_1 t - m_2 t^2 \tag{10.15}$$

The process of household formation and contraction suggests that the dispersion of household size, as reflected in the term σ_{ht}^2, would also increase to a maximum, after which it would fall. The evidence supports this argument to some degree but the extent of the variation in σ_{ht}^2 with t is not large. As a first approximation it is perhaps not too unreasonable to assume that σ_{ht}^2 is constant at σ_h^2: while not strictly accurate this assumption does not do too much injustice to the evidence and makes further analysis much more tractable. Similarly, it will be assumed that σ_{ct}^2 and ϱ are constant at σ_c^2 and ϱ, so that the relative dispersion of household consumption and the correlation between consumption and household size are the same in each age group. These assumptions make the term $\varrho\sigma_c\sigma_h$ in equation (10.14) much more tractable than it would otherwise be, and in fact it can be seen that the use of more general profiles would anyway have a negligible effect on the time profile of $E(C_t)$.

The appropriate substitution into (10.14), after rearranging, gives the result that:

$$\log E(C_t) = q_0 + q_1 t - q_2 t^2 \tag{10.16}$$

with

$$
\begin{aligned}
q_0 &- \log\{k_0 E(v_0)\} + m_0 + \varrho\sigma_c\sigma_h - \sigma_h^2/2 \\
q_1 &= m_1 + \eta \log\left(\frac{\delta}{\zeta}\right) \\
q_2 &= m_2
\end{aligned}
\tag{10.17}
$$

Hence the logarithm of average planned consumption in each age group is a quadratic function of age. While few studies provide sufficient information for the average value of consumption per equivalent adult to be obtained, many give the arithmetic mean household consumption in a number of age groups to which (10.16) may be directly applied.

10.3 AGGREGATION OVER AGES

Having aggregated over households, the process of aggregation over ages must then be considered. This section shows how the overall average consumption/average income ratio can be obtained. It will then be possible to examine explicitly the effects on this ratio (and therefore also the savings ratio) of changes in demographic variables and the age-earnings profile. This could be used in both time series and cross-country studies of aggregate consumption. It is first necessary to specify a distribution of age of heads of households. It has been suggested in Creedy (1985) that a reasonable empirical assumption is that the distribution is normal. Hence if age, t, is Normally distributed with mean and variance m_p and s_p^2 respectively, the distribution function is given by:

$$F(t) = N(t|m_p, s_p^2) \qquad (10.18)$$

Average Consumption

Average consumption, $\bar{C}$, over all household and age groups is thus given by:

$$\bar{C} = \int E(C_t)dN(t) \qquad (10.19)$$

where integration is over the complete age distribution of heads of households. The substitution of (10.16) and (10.18) into (10.19) gives:

$$\bar{C} = \frac{1}{s_p\sqrt{2\pi}} \int \exp\left(q_0 + q_1 t - q_2 t^2\right) \exp\left\{-\tfrac{1}{2}\left(\frac{t-m_p}{s_p}\right)^2\right\} dt \quad (10.20)$$

Expanding and collecting terms gives:

$$\bar{C} = \frac{k_0 E(v_0)}{s_p\sqrt{2\pi}} \int \exp\left(w_0 + w_1 t - w_2 t^2\right) dt \qquad (10.21)$$

with:

$$w_0 = m_0 + \varrho \sigma_c \sigma_h - \sigma_h^2/2 - m_p^2(2s_p^2)$$
$$w_1 = m_1 + \eta \log\left(\frac{\delta}{\zeta}\right) + m_p/s_p^2 \qquad (10.22)$$
$$w_2 = m_2 + 1/(2s_p^2)$$

It is possible to simplify the expression in (10.21) further. Consider the general expression:

$$\int \exp\left(a + bt - ct^2\right)dt \qquad (10.23)$$

By completing the square and rearranging, it can be found that (10.23) is equivalent to

$$\exp\left(a + \frac{b^2}{4c}\right) \int \exp\left\{-\frac{1}{2}\left(\frac{t - \frac{b}{2c}}{1/\sqrt{2c}}\right)^2\right\} dt$$

and using the formula for the Normal distribution, this in turn becomes

$$\frac{\pi}{\sqrt{c}} \exp\left(a + \frac{b^2}{4c}\right) N\left(t \left| \frac{b}{2c}, \frac{1}{2c}\right.\right) \qquad (10.24)$$

However, in the present context integration is over the complete age distribution, so that the Normal integral in the expression (10.24) can be taken as being equal to unity. Hence (10.21) can be simplified to give:

$$\bar{C} = \frac{k_0 E(v_0)}{s_p \sqrt{2w_2}} \exp\left\{w_0 + \frac{w_1^2}{4w_2}\right\} \qquad (10.25)$$

Average Income

It has not so far been necessary to consider explicitly the changing distribution of income with age, since $E(v_0)$ is a constant and does not depend on t. The model used here is that described in Chapter 4. Household income in each age group is lognormally distributed with mean and variance of logarithms μ_t and σ_t^2, so that Y_t is

$\Lambda(Y_t|\mu_t, \sigma_t^2)$. It is of course required to obtain an expression for arithmetic mean household income, to be compared with mean consumption in equation (10.25). Hence the distribution of Y, rather than $y = Y/h$, is required. The parameters change with age according to the following profiles:

$$\mu_t = \mu_0 + \mu_1 t - \mu_2 t^2 \qquad (10.26)$$

$$\sigma_t^2 = \sigma_0^2 + \sigma_1^2 t \qquad (10.27)$$

Although mean log-income increases quadratically with age, arithmetic mean income is not a quadratic function of age, since using the general result for the lognormal distribution stated earlier:

$$E(Y_t) = \exp(\mu_t + \sigma_t^2/2) \qquad (10.28)$$

Arithmetic mean income over all households and age groups, $\bar{Y}$, is given by:

$$\bar{Y} = \int E(y_t) dN(t|m_p, s_p^2) \qquad (10.29)$$

Substitution of (10.26), (10.27) and (10.28) into (10.29), along with the functional form for the distribution of age of household head, can be seen to give (after some manipulation along the same lines used as in deriving equation (10.21)):

$$Y = \frac{1}{s_p\sqrt{2\pi}} \int \exp(p_0 + p_1 t - p_2 t^2) dt \qquad (10.30)$$

with:

$$\begin{aligned}
p_0 &= \mu_0 + \sigma_0^2/2 - m_p^2/(2s_p^2) \\
p_1 &- \mu_1 + \sigma_1^2/2 + m_p/s_p^2 \\
p_2 &= \mu_2 + 1/(2s_p^2)
\end{aligned} \qquad (10.31)$$

The integral in (10.30) can also be simplified using the general result given in (10.24), so that:

$$\bar{y} = \frac{1}{s_p \sqrt{2p_2}} \exp\left(p_0 + \frac{p_1^2}{2p_2}\right) N\left(t \left| \frac{p_1}{2p_2}, \frac{1}{2p_2}\right.\right) \tag{10.32}$$

As before, the normal integral in (10.32) can be taken as approximately equal to unity. Hence the ratio of average consumption to average income in the population as a whole is found to be:

$$\bar{C}/\bar{y} = k_0 E(v_0)(p_2/w_2)^{1/2} \exp\{w_0 - p_0 + w_1^2/(4w_2) - p_1^2 - p_1^2/(4p_2)\} \tag{10.33}$$

Equation (10.33) thus shows how the aggregate consumption/income ratio depends on the parameters of the utility function, the variation in the distributions of household size and income with age, and the age distribution of heads of households. It can be used to show how the ratio varies over time as the profiles or age distribution changes, or to examine differences between countries. It has the advantage that the basic statistical components of the model are realistic, and the aggregation procedure has been carried out explicitly.

Lifetime Income per Equivalent Adult

The decomposition of the aggregate consumption/income ratio into its various demographic components is not however complete, since the term $E(v_0)$, the average value of expected lifetime income per equivalent adult, also needs to be examined. As the previous analysis has used continuous distributions for the age of the household head, it is appropriate here to write:

$$v_0 = e^{-\delta t}y_t dt \tag{10.34}$$

and

$$E(v_0) = \int e^{-\delta t}E(y_t)dt \tag{10.35}$$

It has been assumed that household income, Y, and household size, h, are lognormally distributed in each age group with mean of logarithms μ_t and μ_{ht} respectively. It is reasonable to assume that Y and h are jointly lognormally distributed, with a correlation in each age group of θ_t. Hence the result in Aitchison and Brown (1957, p. 12) again gives the result that:

$$y_t = Y_t/h_t \text{ is } \Lambda \left(\frac{Y_t}{h_t} \middle| \mu_t - \mu_{ht}, \sigma_t^2 + \sigma_{ht}^2 - 2\theta_t \sigma_{ht} \sigma_t \right) \quad (10.36)$$

This may be compared with equation (10.11) above, concerning the distribution of consumption per equivalent adult. This result, while in many ways very convenient, is slightly awkward for present purposes because of the term $2\theta_t \sigma_{ht} \sigma_t$, and it was earlier assumed that $\sigma_{ht} = s_h$ for all t. It is perhaps also reasonable for present purposes to assume that σ_t^2 remains constant at, say, σ_0^2. In fact it can be seen that σ_1^2 only appears in (10.33) as part of p_1, which is itself dominated by the other components μ_1 and m_p/s_p^2. Hence the final results will not be sensitive to this assumption. Assuming also that $\theta_t = \theta$, for all t, it can be seen that:

$$E(y_t) = \exp \left(\mu_t - \mu_{ht} + \sigma_0^2/2 + \sigma_h^2/2 - \theta \sigma_h \sigma_0 \right) \quad (10.37)$$

Following the same stages as used earlier, it can be found that:

$$E(v_o) = \frac{\sqrt{\pi}}{u_2} \exp \left(u_0 + \frac{u_1^2}{4u_2} \right) N \left(t \middle| \frac{u_1}{2u_2}, \frac{1}{2u_2} \right) \quad (10.38)$$

with:

$$u_0 = \mu_0 - m_0 + \tfrac{1}{2}(\sigma_0^2 + \sigma_h^2 - 2\theta \sigma_0 \sigma_h)$$
$$u_1 = \mu_1 - m_1 - \delta \qquad\qquad\qquad (10.39)$$
$$u_2 = \mu_2 - m_2$$

Now $w_0 - p_0 + u_0 = \sigma_h(\varrho \sigma_c - \theta \sigma_0) = \sigma_{hc} - \sigma_{hy}$, where the two terms are the covariances between consumption and household size and income and household size respectively. Hence, taking the normal integral in (10.38) to be approximately unity, equation (10.33) becomes

$$\bar{C}/\bar{y} = k_0 \left(\frac{\pi p_2}{w_2 u_2} \right)^{0.5} \exp \left\{ \sigma_{hc} - \sigma_{hy} + \tfrac{1}{4} \left(\frac{w_1^2}{w_2} + \frac{u_1^2}{u_2} - \frac{p_1^2}{p_2} \right) \right\}$$
$$(10.40)$$

Equation (10.40) represents the complete 'demographic decomposition' of the aggregate consumption/income ratio in a life-cycle model.

Median Consumption and Income

The derivation of median household consumption and median income may also be carried out for the basic model used above; indeed the process is more straightforward since the dispersion parameters of the various distributions are no longer relevant. The median is, however, less commonly used in aggregate studies. It is necessary to begin from the basic result stated in equation (10.8). Taking expectations of (10.8)

$$E(\log c_t) = z + \left\{ \eta \log \frac{\delta}{\zeta} \right\} t \qquad (10.41)$$

where $z = E(\log k_0 v_0)$. The left-hand side of (10.41) is the average value of the logarithm of consumption per equivalent adult in age group t. Since the relevant distributions are lognormal, this term is equivalent to the logarithm of geometric mean consumption per equivalent person, and the latter is also equal to the logarithm of the medium value. From the result in (10.15) it can be seen that

$$E(\log c_t) = \mu_{ct} - \mu_{ht} \qquad (10.42)$$

and of course μ_{ct} is $E(\log C_t)$, or log-median consumption in age group t. Hence substitution of (10.15) and (10.42) into (10.41) gives:

$$E(\log C_t) = (z + m_0) + \left(m_1 + \eta \log \frac{\delta}{\zeta} \right) t - m_2 t^2 \qquad (10.43)$$

Median household consumption in the tth age group is then simply the exponential of (10.43). The log-median household consumption over all ages, $\log C_M$, is then obtained by using the normal age distribution of household heads in (10.18). Thus:

$$\log C_M = \quad E(\log C_t) dN(t | m_p, s_p^2) \qquad (10.44)$$

When substituting (10.43) into (10.44) the only awkward term involves the expected value of t^2 for a normal distribution: this is obtained using the standard result for moments about the origin in relation to those about the mean, in particular that the variance is equal to the mean squared value minus the square of the mean. Hence

$$\log C_M = (z + m_0) + \left(m_1 + \eta \log\frac{\delta}{\zeta}\right)m_p - m_2\left(s_p^2 + m_p^2\right) \quad (10.45)$$

The same approach can then be used to obtain the log-median household income $\log Y_M$, using (10.26) whence:

$$\log Y_M = \int \mu_t dN(t)$$
$$= \mu_0 + \mu_1 m_p - \mu_2(s_p^2 + m_p^2) \quad (10.46)$$

So the ratio of C_M to Y_M can be obtained using equations (10.45) and (10.46). Much less information is therefore required about the distributions of consumption, household size and income when only median values are required.

The results are useful for the examination of changes in consumption/income ratios over time, and for comparisons among countries. Furthermore, the aggregate consumption functions generally used in applied work do not allow discrimination among alternative theories, and the present approach offers some potential for more extensive tests of the basic life-cycle hypothesis.

NOTES AND FURTHER READING

Several studies, including Thurow (1969) and Nagatani (1972), argued that consumption follows current earnings more closely than in the basic life-cycle model, largely because of uncertainty about future earnings. But these studies ignored household variations and did not consider aggregation. Aggregation was considered explicitly by Blinder (1975), but he ignored household size. Friedman commented that, 'although the interdependence between [age, size of household] and the distribution of income may be important for some problems it may not be for this aggregation. The interdependence enters in a rather complex way and the assumption [of independence] remains an approximation even when interdependence exists' (1957, p. 19). This chapter argues that aggregation needs to be considered in more detail.

The 'representative consumer' was used by Heien (1972) in examining demographic effects and Weber (1970) in studying the effects of interest rates on aggregate consumption. Weber assumed that earnings grow at a constant rate, and made no allowance for household size. In his analysis of the interest elasticity of savings, Summers (1981) refers to his model as a 'realistic life cycle model', yet the profiles of income and household size, and the problems of aggregation, are not examined. A basic statement in terms of consumption per equivalent adult was made in Lansberger (1970) although he did not pursue the analysis further.

In the above life-cycle model, the marginal rate of substitution between c_t and c_i depends only on $(t - i)$ and not on the point in time. Tastes remain unchanged and if expectations are proved correct the original plan must be followed. The household thus follows Strotz's (1956) 'strategy of precommitment'. The case of uncertain lifetime has been examined in Yaari (1964). It can be seen that k_0 is approximately equal to $1 - (\zeta\delta^\beta)^{-\eta}$. Furthermore, it is possible to show that net worth per equivalent adult at t, w_t, depends in a simple way on income before and after period t. The present value, at period 0, of period t's net worth is given by:

$$\delta^{-t}w_t = (1 - G_t)\sum_{j=0}^{t-1}\delta^{-j}y_j = G_t\sum_{j=t}^{L}\delta^{-j}y_j \qquad (10.47)$$

where

$$G_t = (1 - g^t)/(1 - g^{L+1}) \text{ and } g = (\zeta\delta^\beta)^{-\eta} \qquad (10.48)$$

A model involving consumption per equivalent adult was used by White (1978), with simple profiles of income and household size, and the aggregation problems were not examined; a representative household's consumption was 'grossed-up'. The simulated aggregate savings rate was found to be lower than actual savings, and on this basis White rejected the life-cycle model.

PART IV

Taxation

11. Individual Choice and the Tax Structure

In examining income tax progression it is usual to concentrate on income redistribution and/or incentive effects using a single period framework. The basis for progression is seen in terms of value judgements concerning inequality. The purpose of the present chapter is to consider the choice of income tax progression in terms of its ability to alter the time stream of post-tax income. It is seen that high income individuals may be prepared to pay a higher proportion of lifetime income in taxation, when the benefits from intertemporal adjustment outweigh the loss arising from the additional tax.

The starting point of the analysis is Buchanan's (1967) treatment of progression. Instead of considering progression and redistribution, Buchanan examines the choice of tax structure for an individual facing a fixed tax obligation. Alternatives are compared in a two-period framework, subject to the constraint that they embody *equal present values of future tax obligations* (1967, p. 227). The essential feature of Buchanan's approach is that instead of considering progression in terms of 'externally selected ethical norms' (1967, p. 225), he uses the institutional choice approach with which he is closely associated. The advantage of this approach is that it allows 'progression to be examined in an individualistic reference system'; that is, it allows 'the choice calculus of the individual as he evaluates alternative tax structures. . . . Progression need not be discussed only in terms of its impact on a set of separate persons at different income levels' (1967, p. 226).

Section 11.1 develops the analysis of individual intertemporal allocation, and section 11.2 goes on to consider progression with more than one individual but with each person facing the same tax structure. Section 11.3 then examines the argument, first made by Buchanan and Forte (1964), that in some circumstances an individual may prefer a specific tax on an item or set of items of consumption, thereby reversing the usual static results.

11.1   PROGRESSION AND INTERTEMPORAL ALLOCATION

A crucial component of Buchanan's two-period model is the assumption that if individuals wish to borrow they must pay a higher rate of interest than that at which the government can borrow. The framework may therefore be described as one of capital market 'imperfection', where the individual's borrowing rate of interest exceeds the lending rate of interest. An individual who expects a rising income stream, and who wishes to borrow in order to enjoy a relatively smoother consumption stream, will therefore prefer to delay the payment of as much of his tax obligation as possible. By delaying the payment of tax, the obligation (in terms of a present value evaluated at the government's borrowing rate) can still be met and consumption smoothed by borrowing less. The individual can therefore adjust the budget constraint by suitable choice of tax structure. In the perfect capital market framework, where the budget constraint is a straight line, the budget line cannot be altered by adjusting the timing of tax payments.

Buchanan's Numerical Examples

Buchanan presents his argument using only numerical examples for two individuals, A and B. The first individual is assumed to have a pre-tax income stream of $1 000 and $2 000 in periods 1 and 2 respectively, while the corresponding stream for person B is assumed to be $600 and $1 710. The assigned tax obligation for each individual is obtained by imposing a proportional tax of 33.6 per cent on each individual's income in each period and assuming a government rate of interest of 5 per cent. Hence A's obligation is $0.336(1 000 + 2 000/1.05) = $976.19, while B's obligation is $0.336(600 + 1 710/1.05) = $748.80.

Buchanan's examples assume the same tax-free threshold, in a single-step progressive structure, for each individual. With a threshold of $500, A's tax obligation can be met with a tax rate (applied to income above the threshold) of 50.6 per cent, while B's obligation can be met with a tax rate of 59.8 per cent. In comparing Table 11.1 with Buchanan's tables it should be stressed that the above values have been recalculated for greater accuracy (in particular Buchanan used a tax rate for B of 59.7 per cent). It is not difficult to show that the time streams of post-tax income for the individuals in Table 11.1 are flatter than would be obtained for a proportional tax; the relevant figures are not reproduced here. Buchanan therefore argues that progressive tax structures are preferred by both individuals, given a desire for a steady stream of consumption. However, it is argued below that these examples do not sufficiently explore the mechanics of individual optimization.

Table 11.1   Time profiles of income and taxation

Tax obligation	Person A 976.19		Person B 748.80	
	period 1	period 2	period 1	period 2
Pre-tax income	1 000	2 000	600	1 710
Tax Bill under single-step progression threshold = $500	253.09	759.26	59.79	723.46
Post-tax income	746.91	1 240.74	540.21	986.54

Further Analysis

The basic framework of analysis is shown in Figure 11.1, where the axes measure after-tax income. The budget constraint facing an individual with after-tax income of y_1 and y_2 in periods 1 and 2 respectively is shown as the kinked line ABC. The slope of the flatter section AB is given by $-(1 + r)$, where r is the government's borrowing rate and the individual's lending rate. The slope of BC is however $-(1 + r + \delta)$ where δ is the extent to which the individual must pay more than the government to borrow. With a given pre-tax income profile of z_1, z_2 and a given tax obligation, the line AD cannot be shifted. However, BC can be shifted outwards by delaying the payment of tax. In some circumstances,

Figure 11.1   Income tax in a two-period model

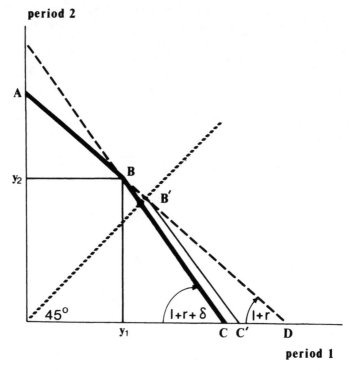

to be made explicit below, it is possible to shift the constraint until
the line B'C' is reached and after-tax income is the same in each
period. The borrower can therefore reach a higher indifference
curve by the suitable choice of a tax structure. These points can
be seen as follows.

Suppose that the tax-free threshold is denoted a, and the
marginal tax rate is denoted t. Then for an individual, post-tax
income in each period is given by:

$$y_i = at + z_i(1 - t) \text{ for } z_i \geq a; \quad i = 1,2 \qquad (11.1)$$

If T denotes the tax obligation, in terms of the present value to
the government of the stream of tax payments, then for $z_i \geq a$:

$$T = t(z_1 - a) + t(z_2 - a)/(1 + r) \qquad (11.2)$$

and a can be expressed in terms of t, using

$$a = \frac{\{z_1 + z_2/(1 + r)\} - (T/t)}{1 + 1/(1 + r)} \qquad (11.3)$$

If $z_2 = z_1(1 + \theta)$, (11.3) can be rearranged to give:

$$a = \frac{z_1(2 + r + \theta) - T(1 + r)/t}{2 + r} \qquad (11.4)$$

Consider the present value of after-tax income, W, evaluated using the individual's borrowing rate of interest. This specifies the point C in Figure 11.1. Then:

$$W = at\left(\frac{2 + r + \delta}{1 + r + \delta}\right) + z_1(1 - t)\left(\frac{2 + r + \delta + \theta}{1 + r + \delta}\right) \qquad (11.5)$$

Consider variations in W as t varies, subject to the condition that the tax obligation, T, is always met. Then:

$$\frac{\partial W}{\partial t} = \left(\frac{2 + r + \delta}{1 + r + \delta}\right)\left(a + t\frac{\partial a}{\partial t}\right) - z_1\left(\frac{2 + r + \delta + \theta}{1 + r + \delta}\right) \qquad (11.6)$$

From (11.3) it can be seen that:

$$\frac{\partial a}{\partial t} = \frac{T(1 + r)}{t^2(2 + r)} \qquad (11.7)$$

As t is increased, the threshold a must also be increased in order to keep the present value, evaluated using r, constant. Substitution of (11.7) and (11.2) into (11.6) gives, after some tedious manipulation:

$$\frac{\partial W}{\partial t} = \frac{\theta\delta z_1}{(1 + r + \delta)(2 + r)} \qquad (11.8)$$

The right-hand side of (11.8) shows that if θ and δ are greater than zero, an increase in the marginal tax rate, accompanied by an appropriate increase in the threshold, will unambiguously increase W. Therefore the point C moves outwards, allowing a higher indifference curve to be reached. The fact that the constraint facing a lender, who is somewhere along the section AB, cannot be shifted by changing the tax structure is also demonstrated since this corresponds to the case where $\delta = 0$. It must be stressed that $\theta > 0$ does not necessarily result in the individual wishing to borrow; this will (as discussed further below) depend on the rate of time preference of the individual.

Equation (11.8) also shows that $\partial W/\partial t$ does not depend on t, so that the borrower has every incentive to raise t to its highest possible value of unity. This result has a straightforward explanation. Tax payments are delayed by raising the threshold to its highest value, thereby minimizing taxable income in the first period (when income is lowest). But the ability to raise the threshold, a, is limited by the fact there must be enough taxable income to meet the tax obligation, even with a tax rate of unity.

There are two possibilities here. If there is sufficient income in the second period to pay the tax, then the best situation for the individual is to set the threshold above the first period's pre-tax income, with the marginal tax rate equal to 1. This means that no tax is paid in the first period and the tax obligation is met with a threshold given by:

$$a = z_2 - T(1 + r) \qquad (11.9)$$

If, however, income in the second period is insufficient, then the best the individual can do is to set $t = 1$, with the value of the threshold determined from equation (11.4). This gives:

$$\frac{a}{z_1} = 1 - \left\{ \frac{(T/z_1)(1 + r) - \theta}{2 + r} \right\} \qquad (11.10)$$

Since all income above the threshold is taxed at 100 per cent, this obviously means that post-tax income is the same in both periods. In both cases the marginal tax rate is pushed to its maximum of unity.

Maximum Progression

An implication of the above argument is that Buchanan's numerical examples do not take the analysis sufficiently far. As long as an individual has $\theta > 1$ (a rising income profile) and wishes to borrow (depending on the rate of time preference in relation to the interest rate), there is a clear preference for the most progressive scheme ($t = 1$) consistent with the tax obligation being met. Buchanan acknowledged that his examples are arbitrary, but individuals A and B would actually prefer the situation shown in Table 11.2.

Person B, who has $\theta = 1.85$, can meet the tax obligation from the second period's income, with $t = 1$, but the stream of post-tax income is not flat. However, person A, for whom $\theta = 1.0$, must pay tax in both periods, but can adjust the threshold in order to obtain an even flow of post-tax income. The effect on the steeper section of the budget constraint may be seen by a comparison of the present values of post-tax income, evaluated using the borrowing rate of the individual. With $r = 0.05$, suppose that $\delta = 0.01$; Buchanan's examples do not go far enough to require an assumption about δ. The present values of post-tax income, from the income streams in Table 11.1, are found to be $1 917.42 and $1 470.91 for individuals A and B respectively. But the income streams in Table 11.2 give present values of $1 919.70 and $1 471.47 for A and B respectively. Both individuals are clearly better off given the tax structures of Table 11.2, since as borrowers they can reach higher indifference curves. (It is in making these comparisons that the inaccuracies in Buchanan's second table, even without the obvious misprint, become significant because the

Table 11.2   Preferred profiles of income and taxation

	Person A		Person B	
Marginal tax rate	1.0		1.0	
Tax-free threshold	987.81		923.76	
	period 1	period 2	period 1	period 2
Tax Bill	12.19	1 012.19	0	786.24
Post-tax income	987.81	987.81	600	623.76

ranking of the present values would seem incorrectly to be reversed.)

The question of whether or not an individual will actually borrow may be considered explicitly only when an assumption about the utility function is made. Suppose the isoelastic form is used, as in Chapter 2, whereby:

$$U(c_1, c_2) = c_1^{-\beta} + \frac{1}{1 + \xi} c_2^{-\beta} \qquad (11.11)$$

The parameter ξ denotes the rate of time preference while $\beta = -(1 - 1/\eta)$, where η is interpreted as the intertemporal elasticity of substitution. Then, as shown in Chapter 2, the individual borrows if:

$$\xi > (1 + r + \delta) \left\{ \frac{y_1}{y_2} \right\}^{1/\eta} - 1 \qquad (11.12)$$

Thus for individual A, where $y_1 = y_2$, it is necessary for ξ to exceed the borrowing rate of interest, of 0.06, whatever the elasticity of substitution, before he will borrow. For individual B, it can be found that if $\eta = 1.2$ the individual borrows if $\xi > -0.26$, which is of course highly likely. A likely situation for individual A is that the optimal position is the new corner solution, at B' in Figure 11.1.

11.2   INTERTEMPORAL AND INTERPERSONAL ALLOCATION

The question arises of the conflict that exists if it is required to impose common values of a and t on both individuals. The interdependence of equity and efficiency must be considered explicitly. As Buchanan observed, 'the interdependence between the share-assignment problem and the institutional efficiency problem is evident in the example. It is not possible that both uniformity in rates among separate persons, *and* predetermined liability shares can be maintained over more than one alternative' (1967, p. 233). Buchanan seemed to take the view that the distributional effects of introducing a common rate structure would typically outweigh any efficiency effects. By this it is meant that some taxpayers would choose a proportional rather than a progressive tax structure even though as individuals, each with a fixed amount of revenue to render, they would have chosen progression. Thus he argued that:

> Individual A, the high-income receiver, finds that distributional and efficiency objectives come into conflict, and, in the normal case, the distributional elements assume considerably more importance. Hence, we should expect the traditional intergroup conflicts over tax institutions. The individual who expects to receive the relatively higher income is led to support the selection of fiscal institutions that are inefficient because of the nature of the political bargaining process in which he must engage. (1967, p. 234)

However, the possibility that in some circumstances the high income individual will trade off an increase in the tax burden in return for the intertemporal efficiency gains needs to be considered explicitly.

A Tax/Progressivity Trade-Off

Suppose that tax burdens are initially set, as in Buchanan's framework, by a proportional tax system applied to each individual's income in each period. The problem is to determine whether there is a revenue-neutral progressive tax structure that makes the high income individual better off despite having to pay a higher proportion of the total tax revenue.

If p is the proportional tax rate, then total revenue (evaluated at the government's borrowing rate of interest) is given by:

$$T = p \left\{ \sum_i z_{1i} + \frac{1}{1+r} \sum_i z_{2i} \right\} \quad (11.13)$$

where z_{ji} is person i's income in period j. Under the progressive tax, the tax revenue is given by:

$$T = t \left\{ \sum_i (z_{1i} - a) + \frac{1}{1+r} \sum_i (z_{2i} - a) \right\} \quad (11.14)$$

The expression in (11.14) can be adjusted for any situation where

$z_{ji} < a$. However, the threshold, a, would never be increased beyond the income level of the richest person during the first period, because as soon as all tax payments have been shifted to the second period there are no further intertemporal gains to be secured. For revenue neutrality, equate (11.13) and (11.14) and rearrange to get:

$$t = \frac{p\left\{\Sigma z_{1i} + \dfrac{1}{1+r}\Sigma z_{2i}\right\}}{\left\{\Sigma(z_{1i} - a) + \dfrac{1}{1+r}\Sigma(z_{2i} - a)\right\}} \tag{11.15}$$

From (11.15) the tax paid by each individual in each period, and therefore the tax burden expressed as a present value, can be examined for alternative values of the tax threshold. The present value of post-tax income (evaluated at the borrowing rate of individuals) can also be evaluated for each tax structure.

An example is given in Table 11.3 for the situation where person A has an initial income of $1 000 and a growth rate (θ) of 1.0, but person B has initial income of $500.00 with a growth rate of 4.2. Suppose further that $p = 0.10$, $r = 0.10$ and $\delta = 0.03$. It can be seen that the present value of net income of the richer individual increases until $a = 500$, despite the fact that the tax burden increases. This result does not actually depend on the particular values chosen for p, r, δ and so on. All that is required for agreement to be reached about some degree of progression is that the first period income of the richer person does not exceed that of the poorer person, and that the lifetime incomes are 'sufficiently close'. The pre-tax income profiles must therefore either 'cross' or begin at a common point. The agreed tax structure will have the tax-free threshold set at the first period income level of the richer person, and the marginal rate at whatever is needed to raise the required tax revenue. Buchanan's pair of individuals could not agree on a progressive structure because the richer individual has a higher income in *both* periods. With the income streams of Table 11.3, the use of a tax-free threshold of $500 (combined with a marginal rate of 0.151) involves only a small change in the distribution of the tax burden between the individuals. Larger changes, produced when the difference between lifetime incomes is greater, soon outweigh the efficiency gains of progression.

Table 11.3   A tax–progressivity trade-off

Tax-free threshold	Marginal tax rate	Person A		Person B	
		Tax burden	Net income	Tax burden	Net income
0	0.10	281.82	2 492.92	286.36	2 520.80
100	0.107	281.65	2 493.17	286.53	2 520.83
200	0.116	281.47	2 493.47	286.72	2 520.86
300	0.125	281.24	2 493.81	286.94	2 520.90
400	0.137	280.98	2 494.21	287.20	2 520.95
500	0.151	280.67	2 494.70	287.51	2 521.00
600	0.163	272.25	2 503.16	295.93	2 512.81

11.3   DIRECT AND INDIRECT TAXATION IN A TWO-PERIOD MODEL

As a sequel to the analysis of income taxation, Buchanan argued that if consumption is divided into 'basic needs' and 'residual needs', and if basic needs differ between periods by more than income, an individual may prefer a specific tax on residual consumption. This section provides a formal analysis of this question, using a framework which captures the division between basic and residual needs. The following approach divides consumption in each period into committed consumption and supernumerary consumption (along the lines of the linear expenditure system), and examines a commodity tax imposed as a proportion of supernumerary or residual consumption. Buchanan's argument was largely intuitive, based on discussion of marginal rates of substitution. The analysis presented below shows that the standard argument in favour of income taxation carries over to the two-period model, subject of course to the condition that the income stream is exogenous.

The Framework of Analysis

Instead of writing the individual's optimization problem explicitly, consider again a two-period diagram, Figure 11.2, in which the axes measure supernumerary consumption in each period. If the borrowing rate of interest facing the individual is ϱ and the lending

Figure 11.2   Committed consumption in each period

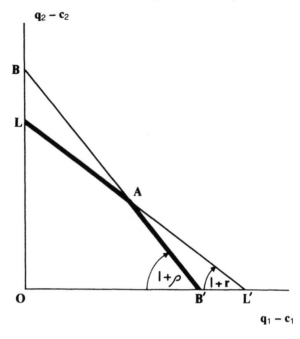

rate is r, then the existence of capital market imperfections means that $\varrho > r$ and the budget constraint is the kinked line LAB′. The range AB′ applies to the individual who borrows, while LA applies to a lender. Given that the individual faces a tax liability of T (expressed in present value terms), what kind of tax structure makes the feasible region OLAB′ as large as possible? Is there any place in such a tax structure for a specific commodity tax?

Denote total tax-exclusive consumption expenditure in each period as q_i and income as y_i. Suppose that the individual faces committed expenditure in each period of c_i, and that the consumption tax involves a proportional rate, s, applied to supernumerary consumption $q_i - c_i$. Suppose further that the income tax has the marginal rate, t, with a tax-free threshold of a. Assume that the interest on loans is not tax deductible, and that interest income is not taxable. In fact the last assumption is not important, as it will be seen below that the only situation that is relevant is where the individual borrows in the first period. The tax liability facing the individual can then be expressed, if $y_i > a$, as:

$$T = s\{(q_1 - c_1) + (q_2 - c_2)/(1 + r)\} + t\{(y_1 - a)$$
$$+ (y_2 - a)/(1 + r)\} \qquad (11.16)$$

The tax payments in each period are discounted using the government's borrowing rate, r.

Maximum First-Period Consumption

The individual cannot alter the slope of the lines LL′ and BB′, since these depend on the respective interest rates, but consider the maximum possible amount the borrower could consume in the first period, corresponding to point B′ in Figure 11.2. First, the line BB′ is defined by the following equation:

$$\{(q_1 + s(q_1 - c_1)\} + \{q_2 + s(q_2 - c_2)\}/(1 + \varrho)$$
$$= \{y_1 - t(y_1 - a)\} + \{y_2 - t(y_2 - a)\}/(1 + \varrho) \quad (11.17)$$

This states that the present value of tax-inclusive consumption must equal the present value of net-of-income-tax income, where both terms are evaluated using the borrowing rate of interest, ϱ. At the point corresponding to B′, consumption in the second period is limited only to committed expenditure so that $q_2 - c_2 = 0$. It is useful to define 'supernumerary gross income' in each period as $y_i^* = y_i - c_i$, and letting $q_i^* = q_i - c_i$, the substitution of $q_2^* = 0$ into (11.17) gives, after rearrangement, the result that at B′:

$$q_1^* = \frac{1}{1 + s}\left[\{y_1^* - t(y_1 - a)\} + \frac{1}{1 + \varrho} \{y_2^* - t(y_2 - a)\} \right] \quad (11.18)$$

Furthermore, substitution of $q_2^* = 0$ into (11.16) gives, for the tax constraint, the result that:

$$T = sq_1^* + t\left[\left(y_1 + \frac{y_2}{1 + r}\right) - a\left(1 + \frac{1}{1 + r}\right)\right] \qquad (11.19)$$

It is convenient to write $y_2 = y_1(1 + \theta)$ and $\varrho = r + \delta$, so that (11.19) becomes:

$$T = sq_1^* + \frac{t}{1 + r}\{y_1(2 + r + \theta) - a(2 + r)\} \quad (11.20)$$

Let supernumerary gross income grow by the rate ψ, so that $y_2^* = y_1^*(1 + \psi)$. If committed consumption grows by the rate ξ, it can be shown that:

$$\psi = (\theta y_1 - \xi c_1)/(y_1 - c_1) \quad (11.21)$$

Appropriate substitution for y_2^* into (11.18) then gives:

$$q_1^* = \frac{1}{1 + s}[y_1^*(2 + r + \delta + \psi) - t\{y_1(2 + r + \delta + \theta)$$

$$- a(2 + r + \delta)\}]\, \frac{1}{1 + r + \delta} \quad (11.22)$$

Choice of Tax Structure

The individual's choice problem regarding the tax structure therefore involves the maximization of q_1^*, given by (11.22), subject to the constraint given by (11.20). Again, it is not necessary to write down the constrained optimization problem formally. This may be considered more directly by using (11.20) to solve for s, substituting the result in (11.22) and rearranging to get, after some manipulation:

$$q_1^*(1 + r + \delta) = y_1^*(2 + r + \delta + \psi) - T(1 + r + \delta)$$

$$+ \frac{\delta t}{1 + r}\{y_1(1 + \theta) - a\} \quad (11.23)$$

The first point to stress about (11.23) is that when $\delta = 0$, the maximum value of q_1^* cannot be affected by the tax structure. This means that the segment of the budget constraint that applies if the individual lends in the first period cannot be shifted outwards by a change in the tax structure. Secondly, the term ψ, which reflects the changing time profile of committed consumption (along with θ, as seen from equation (11.21)), appears only in the first term of (11.23). Hence the choice of the tax structure is independent of the value of ψ. This immediately contradicts a major argument of Buchanan and Forte.

The third implication of (11.23) is that the borrower, the only case that is relevant, simply prefers the tax structure that maximizes the amount of income tax paid in the second period, given by $t\{y_1(1 + \theta) - a\}$. This arises because the individual discounts the future tax liability at a higher discount rate than the government. This is subject of course to the constraints $s \geqslant 0$, $0 \leqslant t \leqslant 1$ and $a \geqslant 0$ along with (11.20). The expression would need to be modified slightly if income in the second period is sufficiently large and the tax liability sufficiently low so that the tax-free threshold exceeds the income in the first period. The substantive results are, however, unchanged. The individual prefers to increase t to its highest possible value of unity, and reduce the threshold, a, to its lowest possible value consistent with the tax liability being met. This means that the value of s will be pushed to zero, so there is no role for the tax on supernumerary consumption. For example, suppose that $r = 0.10$, $\delta = 0.05$, $\theta = \psi = 1.0$, and $y_1 = 1\,000$, with $y^*_1 = 700$. If the tax liability is 1 000, the individual prefers an income tax schedule with a tax-free threshold of 953 and a marginal tax rate of 100 per cent. A positive value of s would require either a higher value of the threshold or a lower marginal rate, either of which would produce a lower value of q^*_1.

12. Revenue and Inequality Neutral Changes in the Tax Mix

This chapter examines some general aspects of a shift from direct to indirect taxation, in particular from a multi-rate income tax towards a general consumption tax. The aim of the chapter is *not* to produce specific policy proposals but to provide a framework which allows the implications of any proposal to be examined. In view of the fact that recipients of transfer payments pay the consumption tax arising from their expenditure, it is necessary to examine the precise interrelationships among an income tax, a system of transfer payments, and a consumption tax. Furthermore, the progressivity of a system can only be judged from its overall effects, rather than individual components. Even with a highly simplified structure of taxes and transfers, analytical results cannot be obtained, so examples are given using a micro-simulation model.

The consumption tax structure is considered in section 12.1. The analysis abstracts from the important administrative issues relating to the way in which the tax is collected; the emphasis is on the relationship between the tax paid and total expenditure, allowing for specified commodity groups to be exempt from the consumption tax. Section 12.2 then considers a simple form of transfer payment, namely a minimum income guarantee, along with the income tax structure. The appropriate adjustment of the level of income support in response to a change in (or introduction of) a general consumption tax is considered. In addition to using a multi-rate income tax structure, section 12.2 introduces a more general income tax function which has just four parameters. This highly flexible function is useful in obtaining a clear view of the way in which the variation in marginal and average tax rates needs to be changed in order to achieve any desired policy result. Section 12.3 examines results based on the use of a micro-simulation approach. The progressivity of any tax and transfer system is judged by its effect on the inequality of the distribution of net (after-tax-and-transfer) income. Alternative measures of inequality are reported, involving different implicit value judgements concerning inequality aversion. No attempt has been made to allow for the possible effects of taxes and transfer on work incentives or on tax evasion. Furthermore, unlike most of the work in this book, the framework uses a single year only so that intertemporal issues are ignored.

12.1 CONSUMPTION TAX STRUCTURES

It is often suggested that a general consumption tax which is imposed at a fixed rate on total expenditure must be regressive. The argument is based on the observation, from cross-sectional data, that higher income groups save a larger proportion of disposable income. However, it is too simplistic in view of the need to consider the interest income taxation arising from savings and the tax on the ultimate consumption of savings, combined with the well-known point that with a life-cycle framework the cross-sectional consumption function is misleading. These longer period aspects are not examined in the present chapter, however, which concentrates on the use of special exemptions that are typically used in order to introduce a degree of progression into the rate structure. For example, one of the most firmly established empirical regularities concerns the low income elasticity of the demand for food: the proportion of expenditure on food decreases as total expenditure increases. It is not surprising that food is typically exempt from consumption taxation (such as the Value Added Tax in Europe). The introduction of exemptions implies that the consumption tax *rate* must be relatively higher. The following analysis attempts to establish the relevant orders of magnitude involved. For example, it is not clear *a priori* whether the objective of maintaining progressivity constant can be met by using such exemptions, or whether it is more conveniently met by appropriate adjustments to transfer payments or the schedule of income tax rates.

Expenditure Patterns

Some idea of the variation in expenditure on specified commodity groups with aggregate expenditure can be obtained from the Australian *Household Expenditure Survey* 1984. Weekly expenditure was divided into 14 commodity groups, and the proportions of expenditure, for all households combined, obtained. Further details of the data and the calculations are given in the notes at the end of this chapter. The most systematic reduction in the proportion of expenditure on any group is indeed for food. Other commodity groups for which expenditure declines as a proportion of total expenditure include fuel and power, medical care and health, and current housing costs. Hence a variety of progressive consumption tax structures can be constructed, using different combinations of these groups. The following analysis uses six such alternative structures. A greater degree of disaggregation would perhaps be desirable, but the groups used here are sufficient for the purpose of examining the interdependencies involved.

Tax-Exempt Categories

If q denotes total expenditure, then the existence of a set of tax-exempt goods implies a relationship between q and the proportion of expenditure on exempt goods, denoted $r(q)$. Suppose that the tax-exclusive consumption tax rate is v, which implies a tax-inclusive rate of $v/(1 + v)$. The amount of consumption tax paid, $V(q)$, is therefore given by:

$$V(q) = \left(\frac{v}{1 + v}\right) \{1 - r(q)\} \qquad (12.1)$$

Information about the form of $r(q)$ was obtained by dividing households into 30 total weekly expenditure groups. The average value of $r(q)$ was calculated for households within each group for alternative tax structures defined according to the categories of tax-exempt goods. The tax-exempt categories used to define six alternative consumption tax structures are given in Table 12.1. In considering an appropriate functional form for $r(q)$, a useful restriction is that as q falls, the value of $r(q)$ rises to some finite proportion rather than approaching the relevant axis asymptotically. This requirement clearly rules out a double-log relationship between $r(q)$ and q, but the following modification was found to provide a very good approximation:

$$r(q) = \alpha/(q + \theta)^\beta \qquad (12.2)$$

Hence, $r(q)$ is equal to α/θ^β when $q = 0$, rather than being infinitely large (where $\theta = 0$). A problem with (12.2) is that it is non-linear in the parameters, so that ordinary least squares regression methods cannot be used. An iterative procedure based on the method of maximum likelihood was therefore used to provide the results for the structures described in Table 12.1. Estimates for the six alternative structures are given in Table 12.2. An assumption required in using these results is that the expenditure pattern is independent of the tax structure. While this is not realistic, the profiles of $r(q)$ obtained may reasonably be used for the examples below. The results in Table 12.2 were obtained using weekly expenditure, and therefore need to be converted to annual terms. The appropriate values of α, β and θ for use with annual expenditure are given in Table 12.3.

12.2   TRANSFERS AND INCOME TAXATION

A Minimum Income Guarantee

Consider the following simple transfer system which guarantees a basic minimum real level of consumption. If an individual's income, after the payment of income taxation, is below the specified level, b, then income is brought up to the level, b. This may be administered in a variety of ways, but these differences are not important here. The minimum income guarantee is a

Table 12.1   Tax-exempt categories

Structure	Exempt categories
1	Food
2	Food + fuel and power
3	Food + medical care and health
4	Food + fuel and power + medical care and health
5	Food + current housing costs
6	Food + fuel and power + medical care and health + current housing

Table 12.2   *Estimates of* $r(q) = \alpha/(q + \theta)^{\beta}$ *for alternative structures*

Structure	log α	β	θ	Residual variance
1	2.598	0.653	233.33	0.00657
	(0.819)	(0.108)	(107.17)	
2	2.535	0.634	164.48	0.00592
	(0.597)	(0.080)	(67.67)	
3	2.360	0.591	218.96	0.01225
	(1.026)	(0.136)	(143.45)	
4	2.338	0.580	156.88	0.01103
	(0.768)	(0.104)	(92.91)	
5	1.132	0.374	61.656	0.01318
	(0.418)	(0.059)	(49.72)	
6	1.416	0.389	59.17	0.01521
	(0.446)	(0.063)	(50.23)	

Note
Standard errors are in parentheses. Number of expenditure groups = 30.

reasonable approximation to the final result of more complex transfer systems used in many countries.

In the present context it is necessary to adjust the basic minimum, *b*, in order to allow for the effect of the consumption tax. This is because a change in the tax mix will involve a change in the consumption tax rate (and may also be associated with a change in the structure of tax-exempt categories of expenditure). It is not sufficient merely to use the tax structure of equation

Table 12.3   *Consumption tax structures (annual expenditure)*

Structure	α	β	θ
1	177.51	0.653	12 131.60
2	154.59	0.634	8 554.00
3	109.66	0.591	11 388.00
4	102.41	0.580	8 158.80
5	13.58	0.374	3 208.40
6	19.16	0.389	3 078.40

(12.2), with b substituted for q, to find the amount of consumption tax paid on b, and then to add that amount to b. The additional expenditure, which effectively arises from the reimbursement of consumption tax on b, itself attracts further consumption tax. Hence if b^* is the adjusted value of b, the following condition must hold: the consumption tax paid on b^*, plus the basic minimum b, must be equal to the adjusted value itself, b^*. Hence:

$$b^* = b + b^*\{1 - r(b^*)\}\{v/(1 + v)\} \qquad (12.3)$$

with $r(b^*)$ obtained using (12.2). Although (12.3) implies that:

$$b^*\{1 + vr(b^*)/(1 + v)\} = b(1 + v) \qquad (12.4)$$

the resulting equation is non-linear in b^*, and can only be solved using numerical methods. In the experiments described below, an iterative search procedure is used to solve (12.4) every time the consumption tax rate or structure is changed.

The Income Tax Structure

The income tax structure in Australia has varied considerably in the number of marginal tax rates and thresholds used. Since expenditure data for 1984 are used the starting point is the 1984–85 tax structure shown in Table 12.4. This has six steps in the schedule, with a maximum rate of 60 per cent applied to income measured above $35 788. Given the reliance upon income tax in Australia, along with the erosion of the tax base resulting from many arbitrary exemptions, combined with the failure to

Table 12.4   Income tax rates and thresholds: Australia 1984–85

Threshold ($)	Marginal tax rate
4 595	0.2667
12 500	0.30
19 500	0.46
28 000	0.4733
35 000	0.5533
35 788	0.60

adjust thresholds for inflation, the tax rates are high by international standards.

It is useful to keep in mind that the income tax paid on income above any specified tax threshold in a multi-rate system can always be written in terms of an effective single threshold and tax rate. Consider the tax paid $T(y)$, between the thresholds a_k and a_{k+1}, when the marginal tax rate operating between these limits is constant at t_k. Then $T(y)$ can be written as:

$$T(y) = (y - a_k^*)t_k \qquad a_k < y < a_{k+1} \qquad (12.5)$$

where a_k^* is equal to the threshold a_k, less the ratio of the tax paid on the previous ranges, to the current marginal rate, t_k.

When considering possible changes in income taxation designed to reduce revenue, it is convenient, instead of dealing with an arbitrary number of thresholds, to keep in mind just four basic characteristics of a tax schedule. These are the tax-free threshold below which no tax is paid, the lowest and the highest marginal tax rates used, and the rate at which the marginal rate increases between the two limits. A general tax function, involving just four parameters to capture these characteristics, is the following:

$$\begin{aligned} T(y) &= 0 & y &\leq a \\ &= (y - a)(t_2 - hy^{-k}) & y &> a \end{aligned} \qquad (12.6)$$

where

$$h = (t_2 - t_1)a^k \text{ and } k < 1$$

The parameter k governs the variation in marginal rates between t_1 and t_2 above the threshold, a. The function in (12.6) provides a good approximation to many multi-rate schedules actually used, and of course any particular form (depending on the parameters) can be converted into a multi-step schedule. The marginal income tax rate for any $y > a$ is given by:

$$\frac{\partial T}{\partial y} = (t_2 - hy^{-k}) + (y - a)khy^{-(1+k)} \qquad (12.7)$$

Effective Tax Rates

It is necessary to examine the way in which the various taxes combine to produce overall effective marginal and average tax rates for given values of income, y. With $q = y - T(y)$, for those not in receipt of the minimum income guarantee, the sum of income tax and consumption tax payments, $R(y)$, is given by:

$$R(y) = T(y) + q\{1 - r(q)\}\{v/(1 + v)\} \qquad (12.8)$$

The overall effective marginal tax rate is thus given by:

$$\frac{\partial R}{\partial y} = \frac{\partial T}{\partial y} + \left(\frac{v}{1 + v}\right)\left(1 - \frac{\partial T}{\partial y}\right)\left\{1 - \frac{\alpha}{(q + \theta)^\beta}\left(1 - \frac{\beta q}{q + \theta}\right)\right\} \qquad (12.9)$$

For the four-parameter income tax schedule of (12.6) it is necessary to substitute for $\partial T/\partial y$ using (12.6). For the multi-step function, $T(y)$ is given by (12.6), for which the marginal income tax rate is constant at t_k. In the simple case where $r(q) = 0$ and all goods are subject to the consumption tax at the fixed rate, then (q) is:

$$\frac{\partial R}{\partial y} = \frac{\partial T/\partial y + v}{1 + v} \qquad (12.10)$$

Those who receive the basic minimum income guarantee face a marginal effective tax rate of unity and a negative average tax rate.

Progressivity of Taxes and Transfers

The progressivity of the system cannot be measured in terms of the structure of marginal and average tax rates, but is measured by the overall effect on the dispersion of incomes. In view of the non-linear nature of the transformation between gross income and income after all taxes and transfers, it is not possible to obtain explicit measures of inequality. The results are therefore based on a simulated 'population' of 10 000 individuals. For comparison purposes several measures of inequality are reported, including the coefficient of variation, the variance of logarithms and Atkinson's inequality measure for three degrees of 'inequality aversion'. The simulated distribution of gross income was based on a lognormal distribution having a mean and variance of logarithms of 10 and 0.5 respectively, which are appropriate for the tax structure used. These values imply an arithmetic mean income of $28 368.

12.3 CHANGING THE TAX MIX

This section presents the main results of the simulation analyses of revenue-neutral shifts from direct taxation towards some form of general consumption tax. The procedure is as follows. First the redistributive and revenue effects of a given tax structure are examined. Then a change in the income tax schedule, producing less revenue from income tax, is imposed. For a given consumption tax structure (depending on the exempt categories as discussed earlier), the value of the consumption tax rate, v, which generates the same total net revenue (that is, revenue after the payment of the minimum income guarantee) is found. The required value of v is obtained using a numerical search procedure, since explicit solutions are not available in view of the nature of the consumption tax schedule. Given the consumption tax rate required for revenue neutrality, the various measures of inequality can then be calculated.

Cutting Top Income Tax Rates

A simple way to cut income tax revenue is to eliminate the top income tax rate of the multi-rate tax structure. This is indeed what was done in the UK in 1979 when a significant shift towards value-added taxation was made. The desire to cut top rates was based on standard incentive arguments. Suppose that the top threshold and associated rate are eliminated from the Australian tax structure shown in Table 12.4, and that the additional revenue is obtained from a consumption tax, using the alternative structures given in Table 12.3. The results are shown in Table 12.5. The first column of the table gives results for the basic case where only income taxation is used, and where a minimum income guarantee of $8 000, in real terms, is available. The remaining six columns give results for the six consumption tax structures of Table 12.3, for different tax-exempt categories. The increase in the consumption tax rate required for revenue neutrality, as the number of exempt categories increases, is seen from the fifth row of the table. The nominal minimum income guarantee, after adjusting for the consumption tax, does not necessarily increase when moving from left to right along the columns, because more of the expenditure arising from transfer payments is exempt.

The measures of inequality in Table 12.5 are for the distribution of income after all taxes and transfers. If the effect of income taxation alone is considered, the measures of inequality (in the order given in the table) are 0.5610, 0.3037, 0.1619, 0.2130 and 0.2625 for the basic tax structure of Table 12.4. When the top marginal rate is eliminated, the income tax system considered in isolation is less progressive, with values of 0.5862, 0.3149, 0.1689, 0.2209 and 0.2708 respectively. It can be seen that none of the consumption tax structures is able to compensate for this increase in dispersion. Hence, what seems like a minor change to the income tax system, involving a very low consumption tax rate to achieve revenue neutrality, cannot be made to be progressivity

Table 12.5   Eliminating the top rate of income tax

	Basic case: Income tax only	Basic case with top income tax rate eliminated, and consumption tax structure					
		1	2	3	4	5	6
Income tax/capita	9 631	9 370	9 370	9 370	9 370	9 370	9 370
Nominal Minimum Income Guarantee	8 000	8 103	8 100	8 101	8 099	8 096	8 088
Transfer payments/capita	198	209	209	209	209	208	208
Prop. receiving transfers	0.109	0.112	0.112	0.112	0.112	0.112	0.112
Consumption tax rate	0	0.018	0.019	0.019	0.020	0.021	0.023
Consumption tax/capita	0	273	278	275	279	273	269
Coefficient of variation	0.5429	0.5666	0.5663	0.5664	0.5662	0.5662	0.5658
Variance of logarithms	0.2437	0.2517	0.2515	0.2517	0.2515	0.2521	0.2515
$I(1.2)$	0.1388	0.1446	0.1445	0.1445	0.1444	0.1445	0.1443
$I(1.6)$	0.1781	0.1845	0.1844	0.1844	0.1843	0.1843	0.1841
$I(2.0)$	0.2138	0.2204	0.2202	0.2203	0.2201	0.2202	0.2200

Notes
N = 10 000; Real value of minimum income guarantee is $8 000; Consumption tax structures are in Table 12.3; 1984–85 income tax structure is in Table 12.4.

neutral however many categories of expenditure are exempted
from the consumption tax. This result still holds if there is a
consumption tax in operation before the shift, so that the consumption tax *rates* are higher. The result is also unaffected by
changes in the real minimum income guarantee.

Comparison of the inequality measures across the columns
indicates that there is very little difference between the different
consumption tax structures. This is not really surprising in the
present example because the consumption tax *rates* are so low.
Indeed, there is very little reduction compared with a consumption
tax system which has no exemptions at all. However, for higher
tax rates (either starting from the use of a consumption tax
combined with income tax, or having a much larger shift towards
consumption tax), the role of exemptions becomes more
important. Nevertheless, increasing the number of exemptions
beyond food and fuel and power is found to have very little effect.
The well-established reduction in the proportion of expenditure
on food as total expenditure increases really dominates the consideration of introducing progressivity into the consumption tax
structure.

Progressivity Neutral Changes

It is possible to examine, for the tax change considered in the
previous subsection, the consumption tax rate required in order to
obtain a progressivity neutral tax shift. The precise rate will
depend on the consumption tax structure used and the inequality
measure chosen. Suppose, for example, that the first consumption
tax structure is used (where food is the only tax-exempt category)
and it is required to achieve the same dispersion of income after
all taxes and transfers according to Atkinson's measure, $I(2.0)$.
The elimination of the top income tax rate is found to require a
consumption tax rate of 0.074. This implies a nominal minimum
income guarantee of $8 420 (received by 12.6 per cent of the
population), along with consumption tax revenue per capita of
$1 067. The net tax revenue increases to $10 191 per capita, which
contrasts with the value of $9 433 before the tax shift. A progres-
sivity neutral tax shift is hence revenue increasing, while a revenue
neutral shift reduces progressivity, if only the top rate is cut. The
question therefore arises of whether a more extensive change in

Table 12.6   A revised tax structure

Threshold ($)	Marginal tax rate
5 000	0.18
10 000	0.28
20 000	0.40
30 000	0.52
40 000	0.59

the income tax structure could achieve both revenue and progressivity neutrality.

The tax structure of Table 12.4 involves a rather uneven increase in the marginal tax rate. Consider, however, the revised rate structure given in Table 12.6. The effect of moving from the structure of Table 12.4 to that of Table 12.6 is to reduce the total income tax revenue per person, and at the same time reduce the degree of progressivity. Thus the inequality measures of income after the deduction of income tax are given by (in the same order as in Table 5): 0.5585, 0.3074, 0.1629, 0.2148, 0.2655 respectively. With the exception of the coefficient of variation, all these measures are higher than for the basic tax structure of Table 12.4, given above.

The inequality measures of income, after all taxes and transfers, for the revised tax structure are given in Table 12.7. In each case the *rate* of consumption tax has been adjusted to ensure that net revenue is the same as the basic case of Table 12.5.

In Table 12.7 only the first two tax structures have been shown as there is little difference between the others. Comparison with the first column of Table 12.5 shows that the shift from direct to indirect taxation, involving the revised tax structure (rather than simply cutting top marginal rates) can achieve a slight overall reduction in inequality while reducing the progressivity of the income tax structure considered in isolation. With this revised structure, there is a greater shift towards the consumption tax. The adjusted (nominal) value of the minimum income guarantee is therefore higher than in Table 12.5, and is approximately $8 350, but the proportion of the population receiving transfer payments is almost one percentage point lower than in Table 12.5. This is

Table 12.7   Inequality of net income for revised tax structure

Dispersion of net income	Consumption tax structure	
	1	2
Coefficient of variation	0.5371	0.5364
Variance of logarithms	0.2411	0.2405
I(1.2)	0.1376	0.1373
I(1.6)	0.1768	0.1764
I(2.0)	0.2124	0.2119
Consumption tax rate	0.064	0.067

because marginal income tax rates are lower for lower incomes, so that fewer people have post-income-tax incomes which fall below the nominal minimum. The total transfer payments per capita are consequently slightly lower.

A large range of possible tax shifts can combine revenue and progressivity neutrality; the permutations are increased for income tax structures having a large number of marginal rates in the multi-step function. The analysis of alternatives can therefore usefully be carried out using the general tax function described earlier, which has just four easily interpreted coefficients; this is considered in the following subsection.

The General Tax Function

The general tax function provides a convenient method of searching for a tax shift, involving specified changes in, say, a, t_1 and t_2, while allowing k and v to be adjusted in order to achieve revenue and progressivity neutrality. Other combinations are of course possible depending on the choice of income tax parameter to be flexible, but it seems most appropriate to think in terms of a policy designed to cut, say, the initial or top marginal tax rates. An iterative procedure then involves changing one or more of the parameters, a, t_1 and t_2, and then finding the consumption tax rate, v, which (for a specified consumption tax structure) achieves revenue neutrality for the original value of k. A check is then made to examine whether or not a measure of inequality of income (net of taxes and transfers) has decreased. Although in principle the result depends on which measure is used, the five inequality measures are found to move together very closely. If the shift is found to be regressive, the value of k is increased slightly and the process is repeated. A change in k obviously influences both net transfers and consumption tax revenue, even if the rate, v, is unchanged. This process converges to a combination of k and v which gives revenue and progressivity neutrality for a given consumption tax structure and specified change in the income tax schedule.

For example, suppose that the income tax function has values of a, t_1, t_2 and k of 5 000, 0.65, and 0.3 respectively. The value of $I(2.0)$ for the distribution of income after income taxation is found to be 0.2719. If the real minimum income guarantee is, as before, equal to 8 000, no goods are exempt from the consumption tax and the rate, v, is 0.05, then the nominal minimum is \$8 396 (received by 13.2 per cent of the population) and the measure $I(2.0)$ is equal to 0.2213. If t_1 and t_2 are reduced to 0.2 and 0.55 respectively, and food is made exempt from the consumption tax, the search procedure outlined above shows that values of 0.50 and 0.083 for k and v respectively produce revenue and progressivity neutrality. This involves a higher nominal minimum income of \$8 470, but in view of the reduced tax rates, transfers are received by a smaller proportion, 13.0 per cent, of the population (although total transfers increase). The change to the income tax system involves a reduction from \$10 101 to \$9 822 in income tax revenue per capita, along with an increase in the dispersion of post-income-tax income to 0.2747.

The analysis has therefore shown that changes in the income tax structure, which lower rates and reduce the progressivity of income tax considered on its own, can be combined with a shift towards a consumption tax in order to achieve both revenue and progressivity neutrality.

NOTES AND FURTHER READING

The data are taken from the data collected by the Australian Bureau of Statistics 1984 household expenditure survey. For each household, expenditure was divided into 14 main categories: current housing costs,

fuel and power, food, alcoholic beverages, tobacco, clothing and foot-
wear, household furnishing and equipment, household services, medical
care and health, transport, recreation, personal care, miscellaneous goods
and services, and other housing costs. The sample contains 2 085 households. The households were divided into 30 total expenditure classes, and
then the proportion of expenditure on each of the 14 commodity groups
was calculated. These proportions were calculated as arithmetic means in
each class. Thus, with each total expenditure class, if e_{ih} is the expenditure
of the ith household on the h commodity group, e_i is total expenditure,
and f is the number of households in the class, the proportion is
$\sum\limits_{i}^{f} (e_{ih}/e_i)/f$. This method differs from proportions calculated by dividing
the total expenditure in each commodity by the total expenditure in the
class; that is,

$$\left(\sum_{i}^{f} e_{ih}\right) \Big/ \left(\sum_{i}^{f} e_i\right).$$

The methods differ because the average of ratios is not the same as the
ratio of averages. However, it was found that the estimation of the
functions $r(q)$, for alternative categories of exempt goods, was insensitive
to the method used to calculate the proportions.

An analysis of the 1979 Budget in the UK was made by Kay and Morris
(1979). Using a linear tax structure, and ignoring the role of transfer
payments, they argued on the basis of effective rates that the Budget was
approximately neutral in its effects on progressivity. Creedy and Gemmell
(1984) used a non-linear model allowing for transfer payments and, using
inequality measures of the distribution of net income, suggested that the
change was regressive. This chapter extends that analysis by allowing
transfer payments to be adjusted in response to tax changes, providing a
more comprehensive treatment of consumption taxation (and allowing for
even more non-linearity), adding a multi-step tax function and providing
a procedure for producing changes which are simultaneously revenue and
distribution neutral. The complexity of such a tax shift has recently been
stressed by Warren (1990), in the context of the Australian tax debate.

The analysis ignores administrative and compliance aspects of alternative arrangements such as the Value Added Tax or the Retail Sales Tax.
The term 'exempt' is often used in the context of small firms which are
exempt from registration for the Value Added Tax. Here it refers to
commodity groups which effectively have a zero rate. Exports, which are
typically zero rated, are ignored here.

The Draft White Paper (1985) argued that while consumption taxes are
regressive, because of differing propensities to save, any desired degree
of overall progressivity can be achieved through the income tax and
transfer payments structure. It ignored the intertemporal aspects of
saving, but suggested that a consumption tax penalizes those who dissave,
and dismissed the role of such exemptions in achieving desired redistributive effects (1985, p. 120). However, the argument confused the issue

by stressing that the exemption of items such as food gives a higher *absolute* benefit to high income groups.

The double-log form for $r(q)$ was in fact used by Creedy and Gemmell (1984) and does provide a very good fit (as measured by the multiple regression coefficient). But the improvement provided by the form used here is sufficient to warrant the extra non-linearity.

The form of (12.2) is equivalent to a Pareto Type II distribution; the method of estimation used is described in Creedy (1985). On the Atkinson inequality measure, see Atkinson (1971). The use of a measure of inequality, or even a variety of measures, may not be sufficient if concern is with the experience of specific groups of individuals.

13. Changing the Tax Mix and Unions' Wage Demands

Despite the considerable interest during the 1980s in the analysis of trade union behaviour, there were few discussions of the effects of tax changes on unions' wage demands. The subject was discussed briefly by Oswald (1982, p. 588), who gave sufficient conditions under which a rise in the marginal rate of income tax, applied to income measured above a threshold, would lead to an increase in wage demands. Hersoug (1984) examined the effects of 'revenue neutral' changes in progressivity and 'progressivity neutral' changes in revenue. He used a simple non-linear tax function which has a constant value of the elasticity of the post-tax wage with respect to the pre-tax wage; this elasticity was also used as a measure of progressivity. Sampson (1986) considered the effect of a 'revenue neutral' shift to indirect taxation in a unionized economy, using an income tax function in which tax is a constant proportion of income measured above a single tax-free threshold, and a proportional value added tax (VAT) applied to all expenditure. All the above studies used the model of a 'simple monopoly union' in which the union is assumed to specify its wage demand while the firm has complete discretion over the level of employment (so that employment is on the standard labour demand curve); see McDonald and Solow (1981).

A limitation of the studies by Hersoug (1984) and Sampson (1986) is their specification of what is meant by a revenue neutral tax change. Hersoug assumes that the average tax rate is constant for the single union under consideration, while Sampson assumes that the average rate is constant for some arbitrary wage level (sometimes associated with the average wage). Both authors therefore examine only a single union. It is argued, however, that in practice any government will be concerned with total tax revenue derived from all wage levels; it must ensure that changes in the tax structure leave aggregate revenue unchanged. It is important to consider changes in the tax structure quite separately from changes in overall tax revenue, though of course governments may combine both types of policy in a single package.

Changes in progressivity and in aggregate revenue, allowing for a large number of unions and a complete distribution of wages, have been considered in Creedy and McDonald (1988a) for both the constant elasticity tax function used by Hersoug and the simple linear tax function. Progressivity is defined more appropriately in terms of the difference between a measure of dispersion of pre- and post-tax wage distributions. 'Pure' increases in aggregate revenue (keeping progressivity constant) and decreases in progressivity (keeping aggregate revenue constant) are both shown to increase the wage demands of *all* trade unions. Shifts from direct to indirect taxation which keep aggregate revenue constant are examined in Creedy and McDonald (1992) for simple monopoly unions and for a model in which all unions are assumed to reach a Nash equilibrium in bargaining with firms over the level of both employment and wages. It is shown that an increase in the tax-free threshold, combined with an appropriate rise in the VAT rate, will reduce the wage demands of all unions. However, a reduction in the marginal income tax rate, combined with a revenue neutral rise in the VAT rate, is most likely to lead to an increase in the wage demands of all unions. In view of the effects of the overall progressivity of the tax system of these two types of tax structure change, the results obviously complement those of Creedy and McDonald (1988).

All the above analyses are limited to simple tax structures using, for example, a single rate of income tax. In practice the tax systems of most countries use a series of rates; the marginal tax rate follows a number of discrete 'steps' but remains constant within specified bands or thresholds. In the United Kingdom the major shift from direct to indirect taxation, that took place as a result of the 1979 Budget, was brought about by simply eliminating the highest rates of income tax and leaving all other rates unchanged.

This chapter extends the previous results by considering a multi-rate tax system that can easily be applied to most countries. The effect on unions' wage demands of eliminating the top marginal rate in such a system, while raising the VAT rate in order to keep aggregate tax revenue constant, is examined. Since the effect is ambiguous only for those previously paying the top marginal rate, it is sufficient for present purposes to deal with just a two-step tax function. Section 13.1 briefly describes the model of union behaviour used and the wage demands resulting from the tax system. Section 13.2 examines the effects on wage demands of the specified change in the tax mix. The complete evaluation of these effects is seen to require the full specification of revenue neutral changes; this is the subject of section 13.3

13.1 SIMPLE MONOPOLY UNIONS

The model of union behaviour is taken from the analysis of McDonald and Solow (1981) in which unions are regarded as trading employment for real wages. The union is assumed to maximize the utility function:

$$W = n\{U(y) - D\} + (m - n)U(b) \tag{13.1}$$

where D is the disutility of work and b is the level of unemployment benefits. The union is therefore regarded as maximizing the expected utility of each of its identical members. It is convenient to rewrite (13.1) as

$$W = n\{U(y) - U(x)\} + mU(b) \tag{13.2}$$

where $U(x) = U(b) + D$ and x is the opportunity cost of working. The framework is one in which a monopolistic union, all of whose m members have the same wage, w, sets the wage and allows employment, n, to be determined according to the labour demand function, $n = n(w)$.

It might be argued that a more appropriate framework of analysis is one in which unions and firms bargain over both wages and the level of employment. There has been much recent research into the analysis of alternative bargaining processes, surveyed by Oswald (1986) and Ulph and Ulph (1988). The justification for concentrating on the simple monopoly union model here is that the comparative static predictions of the various models are very similar, although they produce different wage and employment *levels*.

The Optimal Wage

Utility, W, must be maximized with respect to w, subject to the constraint that $n \leq m$. For interior solutions, the first-order condition for a maximum is obtained by writing W as a function of w and setting $W'(w) = 0$. Hence

$$W'(w) = n'(w)\{U(y) - U(x)\} + n(w)U'(y)y'(w) = 0 \qquad (13.3)$$

where the real post-tax wage is written as $y = y(w)$, the nature of the function depending on the structure of taxation. The first-order condition (13.3) can be rearranged as

$$\phi = \varepsilon\xi \qquad (13.4)$$

where $\phi = -wn'(w)/n$ is minus the wage elasticity of demand for labour, $\varepsilon = yu'(y)/\{U(y) - U(x)\}$ is the elasticity of the excess of the utility from working over that of the opportunity cost of working, with respect to the post-tax wage, and $\xi = wy'(w)/y$ is the elasticity of the real post-tax wage with respect to the pre-tax wage.

The Tax Structure

Consider the following income tax structure, where $T(w)$ represents the tax paid on a gross wage of w:

$$
\begin{aligned}
T(w) &= 0 & w &< a \\
&= t_1(w - a_1) & a_1 &< w < a_2 \\
&= t_1(a_2 - a_1) + t_2(w - a_2) & w &> a_2 \qquad (13.5)
\end{aligned}
$$

The system therefore has two thresholds, a_1 and a_2, and two marginal rates t_1 and t_2; there are two steps in the function. Suppose that there is a consumption tax levied at the single rate, v, on the tax-exclusive price of all goods. The VAT is assumed to be fully shifted to consumers in the form of an increase in the retail price of the good. It must also be acknowledged that the analysis of unions is quite 'partial' in the sense that they are not assumed to take account of any implied changes in the amount of

unemployment benefits that may need to be financed as a result
of changes in wage demands. If the pre-tax price of each good is
normalized to unity, the post-tax price is $1 + v$ and the real net-
of-tax wage, y, is given by:

$$y = \frac{a_1t_1 + w(1 - t_1)}{1 + v} \qquad a_1 < w < a_2$$

$$y = \frac{a_2t_2 - t_1(a_2 - a_1) + w(1 - t_2)}{1 + v}$$

$$= \frac{a_1t_1 + a_2(t_2 - t_1) + w(1 - t_2)}{1 + v} \qquad w > a_2 \qquad (13.6)$$

The policy to be considered here involves eliminating the second
'step' in the income tax schedule and simultaneously increasing
the consumption tax rate in order to maintain total revenue at a
constant level. This policy involves making $t_2 = t_1$. It may be added
here that the overall (effective) marginal tax rate for anyone facing
a marginal income tax rate of t is not equal to the sum of t and v
but is given by $t + (1 - t)v/(1 + v)$. This is because for an extra
unit of income only $1 - t$ is available for spending, and the tax-
exclusive rate of v must be translated into a tax-inclusive rate of
$v/(1 + v)$.

Risk-Neutral Unions

It can be shown that substitution of the tax structure into the first-
order condition (13.4) gives an explicit solution for the optimal
wage only where the union has a simple linear utility function
$U(y) = y$. For this reason the following discussion is limited to the
risk-neutral case. However, this assumption is not as restrictive as
it may initially appear to be. If the members are assumed to have
constant relative risk aversion, then the wage demand can be
solved numerically for alternative values of the Arrow-Pratt
measure of aversion. Although wage *levels* are different, it is
found that the comparative static effects of risk aversion are
negligible in the present context.

In view of the two-step nature of the tax structure, two types of
interior solution need to be considered according to the value of

w in relation to the tax thresholds. Substitution into the first-order condition and rearrangement gives:

$$w = \frac{\phi}{\phi - 1} \frac{\{x(1 + v) - a_1 t_1\}}{(1 - t_1)} \qquad \text{for } a_1 < w < a_2$$

(13.7)

$$w = \frac{\phi}{\phi - 1} \frac{[x(1 + v) - \{a_1 t_1 + a_2(t_2 - t_1)\}]}{(1 - t_2)} \qquad \text{for } a_2 < w$$

(13.8)

It can be seen that in each case the optimal wage is given by the pre-tax wage corresponding to a real after-tax wage equal to the opportunity cost of working, multiplied by a factor that depends on the elasticity of demand for labour. The situation where $w < a_1$ is not considered explicitly here. Notice that the minimum wage any union would accept is that wage whose post-tax real value is equal to the opportunity cost of working. Since the latter is largely dominated by unemployment benefits, which are usually lower than the threshold a_1, this case can reasonably be neglected.

13.2   CHANGES IN THE TAX MIX

Effects of Wage Demands

Suppose that there is a shift towards indirect taxation, achieved by eliminating the second 'step' in the income tax schedule. Define v^* as the VAT rate that gives the same total revenue, in a one-step income tax function, as before the policy change.

In examining the effects of such a change in the tax structure on wage demands it is necessary to consider separately those unions whose wages are between a_1 and a_2, and those whose wages exceed a_2. For the first group the only relevant effect on the tax structure is an increase in the consumption tax rate from v to v^*. From equation (13.7), which gives the optimum wage in terms of the elasticity of demand for labour and the parameters of the tax system for those with $a_1 < w < a_2$, it can be seen that $\partial w / \partial v > 0$. Hence those who initially paid income tax at the lower rate t_1 will unequivocally raise their wage demands.

For those with a wage initially above a_2, the new equilibrium wage, w^*, is given, after appropriate substitution into (13.7), by:

$$w^* = \frac{\phi}{\phi - 1} \frac{\{x(1 + v^*) - a_1 t_1\}}{(1 - t_1)} \qquad (13.9)$$

Then the change in the optimal wage is given by

$$w^* - w = \frac{\phi}{\phi - 1} \left[\frac{x(1 + v^*) - a_1 t_1}{1 - t_1} - \frac{x(1 + v) - \{a_1 t_1 + a_2(t_2 - t_1)\}}{1 - t_2} \right] \qquad (13.10)$$

After much manipulation, this can be rewritten as:

$$w^* - w = \frac{\phi}{(\phi - 1)(1 - t_1)(1 - t_2)}[x\{(v^* - v)$$
$$- (t_2 v^* - t_1 v)\} + (t_2 - t_1)\{a_1 t_1 + a_2(1 - t_1) - x\}] \qquad (13.11)$$

Wage demands will increase so long as the term in square brackets in (13.11) is positive. To consider the necessary conditions for this to occur, define θ and ψ as:

$$\theta = \{(v^* - v) - (t_2 v^* - t_1 v)\}/(t_2 - t_1) \qquad (13.12)$$

$$\psi = a_1 t_1 + a_2(1 - t_1) \qquad (13.13)$$

Notice that ψ is the post-income tax value of a wage equal to a_2. A necessary condition for wage demands to decrease is that:

$$x > \psi/(1 - \theta) \qquad (13.14)$$

It is therefore necessary to consider the orders of magnitude involved. This requires precise information about the change in the VAT rate needed to achieve revenue neutrality in aggregate, and is examined in the following section.

13.3   REVENUE NEUTRAL CHANGES

This section derives the implications for the consumption tax rate, v, of a policy change involving the elimination of the second step in the income tax function, such that total tax revenue remains unchanged at the initial wage distribution. The imposition of this kind of *ex ante* revenue neutrality is standard in the public finance literature. Allowing for endogenous changes in the distribution raises enormous complexities. In order to examine aggregate revenue it is necessary to specify some distribution of wages for all workers. The approach taken here is to impose an exogenous distribution function $F(w)$; some wage levels may be determined by monopolistic unions of the type considered here while other wages will be determined by quite different processes.

Total Tax Revenue

For the income tax schedule specified above the tax raised per person, R_t, is given by:

$$R_t = t_1 \int_{a_1}^{a_2} (w - a_1)\, dF(w) + t_1(a_2 - a_1) \int_{a_2} dF(w)$$
$$+ t_2 \int_{a_2} (w - a_2) dF(w) \qquad (13.15)$$

This expression can be simplified by using the concept of the first moment distribution. The 'first incomplete moment distribution' of an essentially positive variable is denoted $F_1(w)$ and is defined as:

$$F_1(w) = \frac{\int^w u\, dF(u)}{\int u\, dF(u)} \qquad (13.16)$$

The denominator of (13.16) is simply the arithmetic mean (that is, the first moment of w about the origin), denoted $\bar{w}$. Hence $F_1(w)$ represents the proportion of total wages obtained by those below w, who in turn comprise a proportion $F(w)$ of wage earners. The relationship between $F_1(w)$ and $F(w)$ is the familiar Lorenz curve of income distribution. Using (13.16) it can be seen that in general:

$$\int_a w \, dF(w) = \bar{w}\{1 - F_1(a)\} \tag{13.17}$$

Using this result it can be found that, after much manipulation, (13.15) can be reduced to the following convenient expression:

$$R_t = \bar{w}[t_1 G(a_1) + (t_2 - t_1)G(a_2)] \tag{13.18}$$

where the function $G(\,)$ is defined as:

$$G(a) = \{1 - F_1(a)\} - (a/\bar{w})\{1 - F(a)\} \tag{13.19}$$

This type of function plays a fundamental part in the analysis of non-linear tax schedules and tax/transfer models. If the term in square brackets in (13.18) is denoted Z, then

$$R_t = \bar{w}Z \tag{13.20}$$

The per capita value of disposable income is thus $\bar{w}(1 - Z)$. Assuming that all disposable income is consumed, and noting that a tax rate of v on the tax-exclusive price translates into a rate of $v/(1 + v)$ on the tax-inclusive price of goods, the per capita revenue raised by the consumption tax, R_v, is therefore

$$R_v = \frac{v}{1 + v} \, \bar{w}(1 - Z) \tag{13.21}$$

Total per capita tax revenue, R_2, can thus be written as:

$$R_2 = \bar{w}\left\{Z + \frac{v}{1 + v}(1 - Z)\right\} \tag{13.22}$$

The subscript on R is used here to indicate that it is the revenue obtained from a system that uses a two-step income tax schedule. It can be seen from (13.22) that the effective average tax rate is a weighted average of unity and the tax-inclusive consumption tax rate, with weights depending on the two income tax thresholds, the corresponding marginal rates, and the form of the distribution function $F(w)$.

From (13.18), the per capita income tax raised by an income tax system which has just one threshold and one marginal rate is obtained simply by setting $t_2 = t_1$, and is $\bar{w}t_1G(a_1)$. Total per capita revenue from such an income tax and a consumption tax combined, R_1, therefore follows directly from (13.22) with Z replaced by $t_1G(a_1)$. Hence:

$$R_1 = \bar{w}\left[t_1G(a_1) + \frac{v}{1+v}\{1 - t_1G(a_1)\}\right] \quad (13.23)$$

Eliminating the Top Marginal Rate

The above results can then be used to find the consumption tax rate, v^*, that gives the same total revenue in a one-step income tax function as with a two-step function combined with a consumption tax rate of v. Revenue neutrality requires, from (13.22) and (13.23):

$$Z + \frac{v}{1+v}(1 - Z) = t_1G(a_1) + \frac{v^*}{1+v^*}\{1 - t_1G(a)\} \quad (13.24)$$

It is useful to define $\delta = v/(1 + v)$ and $\delta^* = v^*/(1 + v^*)$. After some manipulation, and substituting for Z from (13.18), it can be found that (13.24) reduces to:

$$\frac{\delta^* - \delta}{1 - \delta} = \frac{(t_2 - t_1)G(a_2)}{1 - t_1G(a_1)} \quad (13.25)$$

Writing the right-hand side of (13.25) as k, the value of v^* can be obtained from

$$\delta^* = k + \delta(1 - k) \quad (13.26)$$

and

$$v^* = \delta^*/(1 - \delta^*) \quad (13.27)$$

The effect on a union's wage demands of a revenue neutral change in the tax mix, arising from a flattening of the rate structure, can now be investigated in detail. The following subsection returns to the condition specified in equation (13.14), using the result in (13.27).

A Numerical Example

The above analysis of revenue neutral changes applies to any distribution of wages. Investigation of orders of magnitudes requires, however, an explicit assumption about the form of $F(w)$, from which the appropriate values of the function $G(.)$ may be calculated. Suppose that wages are lognormally distributed with mean and coefficient of variation of income of 6 000 and 0.5 respectively. The absolute value of the mean is not important here, since comparisons can be made in terms of wage levels and tax thresholds relative to the mean. The coefficient of variation of 0.5 is an appropriate order of magnitude for Britain. If $a_1 = 2\,000$ it can be found that $G(a_1) = 0.7$; and if $a_2 = 8\,000$, then $G(8\,000) = 0.1$. Suppose that $t_1 = 0.3$, $t_2 = 0.4$ and $v = 0.10$. It can be found, on substituting in (13.27), that $v^* = 0.1128$. Furthermore, $\psi = 5\,400$ and $\theta = -0.022$. Hence from (13.14) it is seen that wage demands will decrease if x exceeds 5 283, which is 88 per cent of the arithmetic mean wage. This is a rather high value of the opportunity cost of working.

A value for x of 88 per cent of the mean wage can be placed in perspective by considering the associated pre-tax wage. Substituting for x, and the other parameters, into equation (13.8), a labour demand elasticity of 2 implies an optimal wage that is 2.5 times the arithmetic mean wage. It therefore seems most unlikely that any union's members will have such a high opportunity cost of working. Hence it appears that the policy of flattening the income tax rate structure, accompanied by a revenue neutral increase in the consumption tax rate, is likely to increase the wage demands of all trade unions. Such a policy would therefore have the effect of increasing inflation and unemployment.

It must be acknowledged that there is some uncertainty about the wide applicability of the model of trade union behaviour used here. Nevertheless the results would be expected to apply to any situation in which workers were prepared to trade employment for wage increases, and vice versa. The approach could also be used to examine the implications for unions' wage demands of alterna-

tive types of policy change involving changes in the parameters of
the tax system.

NOTES AND FURTHER READING

On comparative static properties of different models, see Ulph and Ulph
(1988, p. 11). In fact the conditions derived above also relate precisely to
the Nash solution for efficient bargains between the union and firm. It is
shown in Creedy and McDonald (1988) that in the determination of the
optimal wage, only the term involving the elasticity of labour demand is
affected. This enters in a simple proportional manner, as shown in
equations (13.7) and (13.8); so that the condition for wages to increase
when a tax parameter changes is not affected.

In a general equilibrium setting the change in the tax structure may also
be allowed to alter the structure of demand and hence prices, but this
complication is ignored here. If the demand shift is isoelastic, then the
wage demands are anyway unchanged by a change in (pre-tax) prices; see
McDonald and Solow (1981). On the special case of Cobb-Douglas
technology, see Ulph and Ulph (1988, p. 13). Any attempt to allow for
the effects of policy on the wage distribution would require a complete
model of the determination of the wage distribution and is outside the
scope of the present chapter.

On the use of the function $G(\ )$ in tax/transfers models see Creedy
(1985, pp. 131–45). The numerical values apply to a lognormal distribution with mean and variance of the logarithms of wages of 8.5879 and
0.2231 respectively. Values of the function $G(.)$ for such a distribution
are reported in Creedy (1985, p. 143), from which the following values
are taken. Calculation of the G function is made easier in the case of the
lognormal distribution by the convenient relationship between F and the
first moment distribution function F_1.

14. Financing Higher Education and Majority Voting

When considering higher education finance and individual choice there are many interdependencies and complexities. This chapter abstracts from many of the complexities in order to concentrate on the relationship between the private decision to invest in higher education and government funding of education through the tax system. In particular, the chapter is concerned with the question of when it would be in the interests of the uneducated majority of individuals to support the financing of a proportion of the costs of education out of general tax revenue. The precise form of support is a grant to pay a proportion of the cost per student. An important assumption is that education is considered as an investment good which generates positive externalities leading to growth. It is argued that a public choice approach avoids the limitations that can arise when viewing investment in education solely from the individual perspective or solely from the institutional perspective; this is debated at length by Majumdar (1983).

The interdependencies examined may be briefly described as follows. If a higher proportion of costs are financed through the tax system, then more individuals will invest in higher education and taxes must increase. This means that a proportion of costs are obtained from the educated as deferred payments in the form of extra taxation. The higher tax facing the uneducated is mitigated somewhat by the effect of the increase in earnings, from private returns alone, on the tax base. Furthermore, the positive effect of a larger proportion of educated individuals on the growth rate of the economy will increase the incomes of the non-educated, who may become better off even though they have to pay extra taxes.

It is not possible, without an explicit model of these interdependencies and the tax system, to form any conclusions about the

210

likely orders of magnitude involved. An appropriate model is developed in section 14.1, and used in section 14.2 to obtain results for alternative systems. First, however, it is useful to compare the present approach with earlier studies.

Earlier Studies

The willingness of a majority to support the funding of education through the tax system has been considered by previous writers, using rather different approaches to that considered here. Bös (1980) produces a median voter model of the demand for education. However, he does not consider education as an investment but models education as a private consumption good; individuals can consume different levels of education simply by buying more education at the given fee. The state's costs are met from a progressive system of taxation and the remaining individual costs are levied on the educated in the form of fees. Under a progressive tax system, and with a positively skewed distribution of incomes, public provision involves redistribution towards the median voter.

A different approach is taken by Johnson (1984), who develops a model where education increases skills and earning capacity but, as in Bös's model, there is no opportunity cost in terms of forgone earnings. Johnson argues that those with low ability, and who do not find it directly profitable to invest in education, can benefit from a subsidy towards the cost of educating the more able if there is complementarity between skills in the production process.

Johnson divides the population into three groups – low, medium and high skilled. The medium-skilled can become high-skilled workers by investing in education but the low-skilled cannot improve on their skill level. If there are productivity gains to the low-skilled which arise from an increase in the number of high-skilled workers, the low-skilled will benefit indirectly from subsidies towards the cost of educating medium-skilled workers. The cost to the low-skilled workers, in the form of higher taxes, of inducing the medium-skilled to invest in their own education is compared with the productivity (and hence wage) increase accruing to the low-skilled. With sufficient complementarity between the low- and high-skilled workers, the low-skilled subsidize the education expenses of the medium-skilled.

The following section develops a framework of analysis which allows for both private and public good aspects of education, treated as an investment rather than a consumption good. The revenue implications of any subsidy scheme are dealt with explicitly and education involves forgone earnings in view of the time required to acquire skills. A continuous distribution of ability is used.

14.1 THE MODEL

The framework of analysis is a two-period cohort model in which individuals either work or receive higher education in the first period, and all individuals work in the second period. Income in the first period is denoted by $y_i (i = 1,...,N)$. This is determined by the individual's endowment which affects both income in the first period and the ability to benefit from higher education, in that those with a higher value of y obtain a higher private rate of return from education. The endowment may be regarded as depending on ability and family background; the precise transformation of these factors to produce y does not need to be considered explicitly for present purposes.

Education involves an opportunity cost, such that a proportion, $1 - h$, of y is forgone by each individual undergoing higher education. The cost per person is denoted c, of which a proportion, $(1 - \varrho)$, is borne by the individual. The remainder, ϱc, is financed from income taxation. Income in the second period is higher than that in the first period by a proportion s_i, for individual i, if educated. However, education is assumed to raise earnings of all members of the cohort through a general increase in productivity; the rate of increase, g, depends on the proportion, p, of the cohort that is educated; thus $g = g(p)$. Those who do not invest in higher education benefit (proportionately) equally from the productivity growth, but otherwise have a constant earnings stream.

Educational Choice

It is first necessary to determine which individuals will become educated, for given values of the parameters of the model. Assume that the supply of education is demand determined, and the income tax system involves a proportional rate of tax, t, on all income. If the rate of interest is denoted r, then the present value of net lifetime earnings of the ith person, if educated, V_i^E, is given by:

$$V_i^E = hy_i(1 - t) - c(1 - \varrho) + y_i(1 + s_i + g)(1 - t)/(1 + r) \quad (14.1)$$

It is not necessary to assume that the private cost of education is all paid in the first period. It could be financed by a loan, to be repaid with interest in the second period; the present value is the same whichever assumption is made, so long as capital markets are perfect. The effects of imperfect capital markets on wealth inequality in a single period framework have been examined by Hare and Ulph (1982).

Assume that the cost of education per person, c, remains constant as the number of individuals who are educated increases. It might, however, be argued that in view of the existence of many fixed costs, the average cost per student would be expected to fall. The implications of decreasing costs are examined in the notes to this chapter.

The present value of net lifetime earnings of those without education, V_i^N, is given by:

$$V_i^N = y_i(1 - t) + y_i(1 + g)(1 - t)/(1 + r) \quad (14.2)$$

The ith individual chooses higher education if $V_i^E > V_i^N$. There is some value of y_i, called the 'educational choice margin', for which $V_i^E = V_i^N$. All those with y below this margin will not choose higher education. Equating (14.1) and (14.2) and rearranging gives:

$$\frac{s_i(1 - t)}{1 + r} + \{(h - 1)(1 - t)\} - \frac{c(1 - \varrho)}{y_i} = 0 \quad (14.3)$$

Suppose that s_i is proportional to the individual's endowment, y_i, so that:

$$s_i = uy_i \quad (14.4)$$

which is consistent with observed age-earnings profiles. It is assumed that u remains constant as ϱ is allowed to vary. However, it might be argued that the private returns to higher education would be expected to fall as the proportion of people educated increases. The sensitivity of the results to variations in the value of u will therefore be examined. Substituting (14.4) into (14.3) gives the educational choice margin, y^*, as the root of the quadratic:

$$y^{*2}u\left\{\frac{1-t}{1+r}\right\} + y^*\{(h-1)(1-t)\} - c(1-\varrho) = 0 \quad (14.5)$$

Since both t and ϱ are < 1 there will always be one negative and one positive root, but only the positive root is relevant. When $t = 1$, the margin is indeterminate. Notice that g does not affect the value of y^*.

The value of y^* can be obtained from (14.5), given values of u, h, ϱ, r, c and t. However, t is endogenous as it depends on the proportion of people who receive education, which in turn depends on y^*. This relationship may be called the 'educational choice schedule'; an example is shown in Figure 14.1. Increasing the value of ϱ directly reduces the costs to individuals of investing in higher education so the schedule shifts to the left, and when $\varrho = 1$ the tax rate has no effect on educational choice. This result can be seen by substituting for $\varrho = 1$ in equation (14.5), giving:

$$y^* = (1 - h)(1 + r)/u \quad (14.6)$$

which is independent of t. At values of ϱ less than unity the tax has a greater effect at the higher ranges of t because the cost of education, c, has to be met out of post-tax income. If the private returns to education rise, caused by a rise in u, the educational choice schedule shifts to the left.

Deficit Neutrality

It is next necessary to obtain the tax rate required to finance education. This depends on the proportion, p, of individuals who receive education, which in turn is equal to the proportion of people with $y_i > y^*$. Let $F(y)$ denote the distribution function of y; that is, $F(y)$ measures the proportion of individuals with

Figure 14.1   Educational choice and deficit neutrality schedules

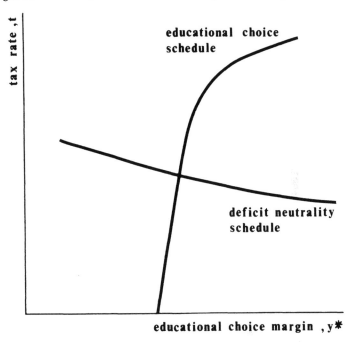

educational choice schedule

deficit neutrality schedule

tax rate ,t

educational choice margin ,y*

endowment less than or equal to y. Hence the proportion who receive education is given by:

$$p = 1 - F(y^*) \qquad (14.7)$$

The cost of financing education, per member of the cohort, is equal to pc, or $\{1 - F(y^*)\}c$, of which a proportion, ϱ, is financed by general taxation. But additional government expenditure must also be financed from income taxation. Suppose that the revenue per person required to finance non-education expenditure is equal to the fixed amount R. Hence taxation must raise an amount per person equal to R_t, given by:

$$R_t = \varrho c \{1 - F(y^*)\} + R \qquad (14.8)$$

In view of the proportionality of the tax system, it is only necessary to derive the tax base in each period. If N is the number of individuals in the cohort, the total income in the first period is equal to:

$$N\int_0^{y^*} y\,dF(y) + N\int_{y^*}^{\infty} hy\,dF(y) \qquad (14.9)$$

The first term in (14.9) is the income of the uneducated while the second term is the income of those with higher education. In the second period, the total income of those not receiving education is the same as that obtained in the first period, with the addition of the general growth in incomes resulting from the public good nature of education. It is therefore the first term in (14.9) multiplied by $(1 + g)$. The total income of those who do receive education is given by:

$$N\int_{y^*}(1 + uy + g)y\,dF(y) \qquad (14.10)$$

$$= N(1 + g)\int_{y^*} y\,dF(y) + Nu\int_{y^*} y^2\,dF(y) \qquad (14.11)$$

More convenient expressions for total income in the two periods can be obtained using the incomplete moment distribution of y. The jth moment distribution of $F(y)$ is written as $F_j(y)$ and defined by:

$$F_j(y) = \frac{\displaystyle\int_0^y v^j\,dF(v)}{\displaystyle\int_0^{\infty} v^j\,dF(v)} \qquad (14.12)$$

Income in the first period then becomes:

$$N\bar{y}\{h + (1 - h)F_1(y^*)\} \qquad (14.13)$$

The derivation of income in the second period is a little more tedious and is given in the notes to this chapter, where it is shown to be N multiplied by:

$$\bar{y}[(1 + g) + u\bar{y}(\eta_y^2 + 1)\{1 - F_2(y^*)\}] \qquad (14.14)$$

where $\bar{y}$ is the arithmetic mean of y and η_y is the coefficient of variation. The 'deficit neutrality' condition can now be established. Total expenditure of N multiplied by R_t must be equal to the present value of tax payments, since a single cohort is being considered in isolation. Rewrite (14.14) as $\bar{y}\psi$, where ψ is the term in square brackets in (14.14). The deficit neutrality condition then gives the required tax rate as:

$$t = \frac{R + \varrho c\{1 - F(y^*)\}}{\bar{y}\{h + (1 - h)F_1(y^*) + \psi/(1 + r)\}} \qquad (14.15)$$

This may be rewritten as:

$$t = \frac{R_t}{\bar{y}}\left(\frac{1}{\xi}\right) \qquad (14.16)$$

where $\xi = h + (1 - h)F_1(y^*) + \psi/(1 + r)$. In a more usual context of a proportional tax system and a single period, the obvious revenue requirement is that $R_t = t\bar{y}$. Equation (14.16) differs from this because of the two-period nature of the model and the fact that the cohort has to be divided into two groups in determining the second period's tax base. Equation (14.16) therefore allows t to be determined, given the values of R, ϱ, c, r, y^* and the form of the distribution of y, along with the relationship between g and p. The latter relationship must now be specified explicitly.

The Growth Rate

A convenient form of $g(p)$ which depends on only one parameter is:

$$g = \delta\left(\frac{p}{1 + p}\right) \qquad (14.17)$$

Thus g increases from zero, when $p = 0$, to $\delta/2$ when everyone is educated. Since $dg/dp = \delta/(1 + p)^2$ the rate of increase in g decreases as p increases. Unfortunately, there are few empirical studies which link the proportion educated directly to the growth rate, but there has been much work on estimating the social return to education. The large literature on growth accounting may be used to shed some light on the growth component of the present model.

In Denison (1984), the proportion of growth in net national income not explained by increases in the productivity of land and capital is attributed to increases in labour productivity and miscellaneous causes. Of this, a proportion is attributed to education, of which a further proportion is attributed to higher education. Denison separates the data into two periods: 1948–73 and 1973–81. For the first period he takes the total annual percentage growth rate of 3.59 and attributes 1.6 to advances in land and capital, with the remaining 1.99 to advances in knowledge and miscellaneous determinants. He finds that advancement in knowledge forms 71 per cent of this residual and therefore 40 per cent of total growth. Results are similar for the latter period. On the argument that tertiary education contributes to approximately one-quarter of this, Denison's results suggest that tertiary education adds roughly one-third of a percentage point to the growth rate per year. Others have obtained comparable results, including Schultz (1963, 1981), Psacharopoulos (1973), Jorgenson (1984), Kendrick (1983) and McMahon (1984). The growth contribution used below, bearing in mind the two-period nature of the model, falls within the range suggested by the empirical studies.

However, there has been criticism of this approach, particularly the assumption that a correlation between education and growth is proof of causation, and the attribution of such a large proportion of knowledge advancement to education. Chinloy (1980) argues that the contribution of education cannot be considered in isolation since much of this would not have come about without concomitant changes in other social and economic variables. However, Psacharopoulos (1984) suggests that in part these concomitant changes are caused by education, so that they should be counted, and that earlier studies do not account for the increasing labour force which requires greater educational expense just to maintain standards. Thus Psacharopoulos gives a figure much higher than that of Denison.

It must be recognized that all of the studies have a degree of arbitrariness in determining the exact magnitude of growth effects and even more arbitrariness is introduced when calculating the contribution of a particular component of education, as in the tertiary contribution relevant here. In view of this difficulty, sensitivity analyses are reported below.

Distributional Assumptions

The relationship between t and y^*, for given values of the other parameters of the model, may be called the 'deficit neutrality schedule'. But before it is possible to solve equation (16.16), the form of the distribution function $F(y)$ must be specified. The above expressions could be evaluated using any form of $F(y)$ that has convenient first and second moment distributions. Suppose that y is lognormally distributed as $\Lambda(y|\mu, \sigma^2)$ where μ and σ^2 are respectively the mean and variance of the logarithms of y. The jth moment distribution of the lognormal, Λ_j, is given by:

$$\Lambda_j(y|\mu, \sigma^2) = \Lambda(y|\mu + j\sigma^2, \sigma^2) \qquad (14.18)$$

and the lognormal has the property that $\bar{y} = \exp(\mu + \sigma^2/2)$, with $\eta_y^2 = \exp(\sigma^2) - 1$ and a median of $\exp(\mu)$.

In considering numerical values, the cost of education and the amount of non-education government expenditure per capita have to be set in relation to average income; the absolute values chosen are rather arbitrary. It was decided to obtain results for a distribution of y having a median value of 10. The coefficient of variation was set at 0.5, which is a reasonable approximation for industrialized countries. This implies that the lognormal distribution has a variance of logarithms of 0.223 with an arithmetic mean of 11.1795.

Deficit Neutrality Schedules

An example of the deficit neutrality schedule is shown in Figure 14.1. An increase in ϱ has two conflicting effects on this schedule. First, the 'costs effect' is simply the increase in government revenue required. This increase arises from the need to fund a greater proportion of the costs of students already investing in education, combined with the effect of the higher number educated as a result of the lower choice margin. Secondly, there is a 'tax base effect' caused by the increase in incomes of the extra individuals who become educated, plus the general increase in incomes arising from higher growth. This raises the tax base and provides more revenue at a given rate of tax. The direction of movement in the revenue neutrality schedule as ϱ increases therefore depends on the relative size of these effects. The 'costs' effect typically outweighs the 'tax base' effect, thus rendering educational investment a cost from the government's perspective; this is true except where the choice margin is very high.

Raising the private return raises the tax base and shifts the function downwards. Increasing the cost of education shifts the schedule upwards, with a greater effect for lower choice margins. This is because the lower margin implies a greater proportion educated and therefore a greater 'cost effect'.

14.2   MAJORITY VOTING

The previous section has modelled the investment decision from the perspective both of individuals and the government. Individuals are assumed to maximize net lifetime income while the state aims to achieve a balanced Budget. Assume that the government's decision rule is to finance, through the tax system, that proportion of the costs of education per person which is preferred by a simple majority of the cohort. For a given set of values of u, h, ϱ, c and r, the educational choice schedule, giving the educational choice margin for alternative tax rates, can be determined using equation (14.5). For a specified distribution of y and values of δ and R, the deficit neutrality schedule can be determined from equation (14.16). As seen in Figure 14.1 the deficit neutrality schedule is very flat while the educational choice schedule is very steep. Despite the non-linearity of the schedules there is a single point of intersection giving the solution to the model. This gives the combination of the choice margin and the tax rate where, given individual choices, the required revenue is raised. This implies consistency between all individuals' investment decisions and the investment decision of the state. In other words, the tax rate which individuals take as given, and which determines the choice margin, is equivalent to the tax rate which raises precisely the amount of revenue needed to pay the state's proportion of each person's education costs.

An important property of the model is that *all* of those who do not invest in higher education share a common interest. This is because they share equally in the general growth of earnings that results from the education of a minority of individuals and because the tax system is proportional. Hence there is a consensus among all of the non-educated concerning their preferred value of ϱ. The first-order condition for maximizing net income is independent of y_i. Since only a minority of any cohort invests in higher education, a stable majority exists and the possibility of cyclical voting may be ruled out. Furthermore, it is only necessary to examine the preferences of a representative non-educated individual; in the following analysis the person with the median value of y is selected, as this person is also the median voter.

Some Numerical Results

A two-step iterative method was adopted in order to solve for t and y^*. The procedure converges rapidly to a unique tax rate and choice margin. A solution is found for a given value of ϱ. The educational 'status' of the median voter can then easily be determined and the net lifetime income obtained using either equation (14.1) or (14.2). By comparing the values of net lifetime income for alternative values of ϱ, it is possible to find the median voter's preferred value of ϱ for given values of the other parameters.

Some results are shown in Table 14.1 for values of r and δ of 0.6 and 1.0 respectively. The table presents the value of ϱ chosen by the median voter along with the resulting proportion educated and the proportional tax rate, under a variety of conditions. For example the median voter's preferred value of ϱ is 0.8 when $u = 0.08$, $c = 3$, $h = 0.1$ and $R = 4$. The table also shows the corresponding values of p and t for zero state funding. The parameter values have been chosen to indicate the implications for relatively high and low values of each variable.

Table 14.2 shows the effect of increasing δ to 1.25. Comparison of the two tables shows the high degree of sensitivity of the majority choice of ϱ to the value of δ. As soon as p is greater than 0.5 then the median voter prefers full funding by the state ($\varrho = 1$), but the results also indicate a wide range of situations where $\varrho = 1$ but p is less than 0.5. From each table it can be seen that as the cost of education, c, increases the majority choice of ϱ

Table 14.1　Values of ϱ, p and t for alternative parameter values: majority choice and zero state funding ($\delta = 1.00$; $r = 0.6$)

			u = 0.08				u = 0.12			
			c = 3		c = 6		c = 3		c = 6	
h = 0.1	R = 4	ϱ	0.80	0	0.40	0	0.15	0	0.05	0
		p	0.090	0.052	0.046	0.030	0.202	0.187	0.120	0.115
		t	0.2161	0.208	0.215	0.211	0.185	0.182	0.190	0.188
	R = 8	ϱ	1.0	0	0.70	0	0.60	0	0.50	0
		p	0.106	0.042	0.058	0.021	0.245	0.160	0.157	0.089
		t	0.424	0.419	0.428	0.426	0.377	0.368	0.390	0.384
h = 0.3	R = 4	ϱ	0.75	0	0.40	0	1.0	0	0.025	0
		p	0.185	0.103	0.089	0.056	0.558	0.287	0.177	0.174
		t	0.213	0.199	0.211	0.205	0.227	0.169	0.178	0.177
	R = 8	ϱ	0.95	0	0.70	0	1.0	0	0.4	0
		p	0.221	0.083	0.117	0.039	0.558	0.250	0.213	0.136
		t	0.413	0.402	0.420	0.415	0.386	0.342	0.370	0.363

decreases. This is not surprising, but it is of interest to consider the comparative statics further. First, for any given value of ϱ, the educational choice schedule shifts to the right as c increases, while the deficit neutrality schedule shifts upwards as the higher cost increases the tax rate for a given choice margin. In view of the flatness of the deficit neutrality schedule, the new point of equilibrium implies a higher tax rate and higher choice margin for a given value of ϱ.

In ascertaining the median voter's likely response, in terms of preference for ϱ, it is necessary to consider the effect of changing ϱ on the marginal cost and benefit in terms of net lifetime income. Before the increase in c the marginal cost and marginal benefit were equal. To the median voter the marginal cost of increasing ϱ is the extra tax incurred, while the marginal benefit arises from the growth of second period income. The growth rate is an increasing but marginally diminishing function of the proportion educated. Therefore a rise in c which, *ceteris paribus*, leads to fewer educated means that the marginal effect on the growth rate of raising ϱ is greater. So the marginal benefit from funding

Table 14.2   Values of ϱ, p and t for alternative parameter values: majority choice and zero state funding ($\delta = 1.25$; $r = 0.6$)

			u = 0.08				u = 0.12			
			c = 3		c = 6		c = 3		c = 6	
h = 0.1	R = 4	ϱ	1.0	0	0.65	0	0.55	0	0.30	0
		p	0.107	0.052	0.063	0.030	0.256	0.187	0.151	0.116
		t	0.218	0.207	0.219	0.211	0.194	0.180	0.195	0.187
	R = 8	ϱ	1.0	0	0.90	0	0.85	0	0.65	0
		p	0.107	0.042	0.085	0.021	0.303	0.162	0.193	0.090
		t	0.420	0.417	0.431	0.424	0.379	0.364	0.392	0.381
h = 0.3	R = 4	ϱ	1.0	0	0.65	0	1.0	0	0.25	0
		p	0.238	0.104	0.127	0.056	0.558	0.288	0.218	0.174
		t	0.221	0.198	0.219	0.204	0.221	0.166	0.185	0.175
	R = 8	ϱ	1.0	0	0.80	0	1.0	0	0.55	0
		p	0.238	0.083	0.144	0.039	0.558	0.251	0.260	0.135
		t	0.409	0.400	0.421	0.413	0.377	0.337	0.372	0.359

education rises. However, the marginal cost will rise by much more than the benefit. First, as argued above, the tax rate is higher as a result of the increase in c; secondly the tax base declines as the educational choice margin rises; hence obtaining a given change in ϱ will be more expensive. The effect on the marginal cost far outweighs the increase in the marginal benefit for a given change in p. Hence the majority choice of ϱ decreases as the cost of education increases.

Increasing the private returns to education, u, lowers ϱ unless the median voter is educated. From each table it can be seen that when u is raised from 0.08 to 0.12 the majority choice of funding falls as long as p is less than 0.5. The effect of increasing u can be more clearly understood by considering its effects on the educational choice and deficit neutrality schedules. Increasing u makes education attractive from an individual's perspective and therefore shifts the educational choice schedule to the left. With higher private returns the tax base will be larger, so for given ϱ and p, the tax rate will be lower. This shifts the deficit neutrality schedule downwards. The net outcome of these two shifts is that for a given ρ the choice margin is unambiguously lower whereas the tax rate may vary either way. However, a reduction in the tax rate is the most likely outcome.

Consider the choice of ρ by the median voter, at a higher value of u. Before the rise in u the median voter preferred that level of ρ at which the marginal benefit from an increase in ρ is equal to the marginal cost. The marginal benefit to the median voter of increasing ρ comprises the increase in g along with an increase in the tax base which places downward pressure on the tax rate. The marginal cost of raising ρ arises from the increase in the amount of revenue the state must raise and the consequent increase in the tax rate. To ascertain the median voter's response to the change, it is necessary to investigate its effect on these marginal values.

When u increases, more individuals choose to become educated, so for a given level of ρ, p is higher. With the marginal effect of p on the growth rate diminishing as p increases, the marginal benefit to the median voter from an increase in ρ is now lower. So the marginal benefit from funding has fallen. At the higher level of u, increasing ρ raises the tax rate by less than before because the tax base is greater. In view of the positive skewness of the distribution of y, the number responding to the extra funding will not be as great. Therefore the marginal cost to the median voter has fallen. As both the marginal cost and the marginal benefit have fallen it is impossible to predict, *a priori*, the direction of the median voter's response to an increase in u. However, a strong result is that under all conditions examined the median voter supported a reduction in funding in response to the u increase.

Increasing h has the same qualitative effects as an increase in u; it makes education more attractive and lowers the tax rate required to achieve deficit neutrality at a given choice margin. Its effect on the median voter's preferred level of ρ cannot therefore be predicted *a priori*. However, in all situations increasing h lowers the preferred ρ for the median voter as long as p is less than 0.5.

An interesting result is that increasing R, the government revenue per person not devoted to education, always has the effect of increasing the median voter's preferred value of ρ and of increasing the proportion educated. To explain this, consider again the effects on the two schedules. The choice margin is unaltered directly by any changes in R. However, the deficit neutrality schedule shifts upwards. The new intersection implies that for a given ϱ there is a higher tax rate and a higher choice margin. In order to understand the median voter's preference it is again necessary to compare the marginal effect of changes in ϱ both before and after the increase in R. With R higher, both taxes and the choice margin are higher for a given ϱ, so p is smaller. The effect of diminishing marginal returns is now opposite to that which occurs when u increases; the effect is that the marginal benefit from an increase in ϱ is higher. On the cost side, increasing ϱ raises the tax rate but with a higher R, the tax rate rises by proportionately less. This is because those who become educated in response to the high ϱ contribute more to the tax base than before, as the externality effect is higher. Combined with the fact that tax rates are higher, the increase in the tax base contributes proportionately more to total revenue. Therefore the marginal cost of increasing ϱ falls. With the fall in the marginal cost and the rise in the marginal benefit, it is clearly in the interests of the median voter to vote for a higher value of ϱ. In considering this result it must, however, be recognized that no allowance has been made for the effects on individuals of the expenditure resulting from the revenue of R per person. A more complete model would have higher education as just one component of government expenditure and would need to consider the distributional implications of the other components. But this would by no means be a trivial extension of the present analysis.

NOTES AND FURTHER READING

Total income in the first period, given in equation (14.9), can be simplified to:

$$N\bar{y}\{h + (1 - h)F_1(y^*)\} \tag{14.19}$$

This uses the 'first moment distribution' $F_1(y)$ obtained by substituting $j = 1$ in the general form given in (14.12). In examining income in the second period, the first term in (14.14) is also simplified using the first moment distribution and is equal to $N(1 + g)(\{1 - F_1(y^*)\}$. But the second term requires the second incomplete moment distribution, $F_2(y)$. If $V(y)$ denotes the variance of y, then by definition:

$$V(y) = \int (y - \bar{y})^2 dF(y) = \int y^2 dF(y) - \bar{y}^2 \tag{14.20}$$

Hence F_2 can be written in terms of the mean and variance of y as $V(y) + \bar{y}^2$, or $\bar{y}^2(\eta_y^2 + 1)$, where η_y denotes the coefficient of variation of y. The expression in (14.11) is thus simplified to:

$$N(1 + g)\bar{y}\{1 - F_1(y^*)\} + Nu\bar{y}^2(\eta_y^2 + 1)\{1 - F_2(y^*)\} \quad (14.21)$$

It is perhaps more realistic to assume that as p rises the average cost of education falls, because of the existence of high fixed costs. The cost may be specified by the following function:

$$c = d_1(p + \theta)^{-d_2} \quad (14.22)$$

This implies that increasing d_2 and reducing θ raises the variability in costs for given changes in p while d_1 changes only the absolute size of the costs without changing their variability. The major implication for the mechanics of the model is that the 'educational choice schedule' is rather more complex and the numerical procedure for solving the model has to be modified accordingly. However, convergence is easily achieved, and calculations show that when ϱ is low the proportion educated is generally lower than in comparable cases with fixed costs. This is primarily due to the existence of a very high average cost at low values of p, which for low ϱ are borne entirely by the students. However as funding increases p rises rapidly so that at the median voter's preferred value of ϱ the proportions educated are similar to those found in the constant cost case.

The most interesting result concerns the effect on the median voter's choice of ϱ of the extent to which c varies with p. By varying the shift parameter, d_1, in order to maintain values of c for the relevant range of p at similar levels, the parameters θ and d_2 can be varied in order to isolate effects of changes in the variability of the cost with p. By comparing the values of the preferred ϱ, it was found that the median voter is prepared to support a higher level of funding as the variability increases. Results show that increasing the rate of decline in cost, even if the absolute cost is higher for a given p, often leads to the median voter's support for a higher value of ϱ.

Bibliography

Aitchison, J. and Brown, J.A.C. (1957), *The Lognormal Distribution*, Cambridge: Cambridge University Press.

Alter, G.C. and Becker, W.E. (1985), 'Estimating Lost Future Earnings Using the New Worklife Tables', *Monthly Labor Review*, **108**, 39–42.

Atiyah, P.S. (1984), *Accidents, Compensation and the Law*, London: Weidenfeld and Nicolson.

Atkinson, A.B. (1971), 'On the Measurement of Inequality', *Journal of Economic Theory*, **2**, 244–63.

Atkinson, A.B. (1983), 'Intergenerational Earnings Mobility in Britain', in W. Schmähl (ed.), *Ansätze der Lebenseinkommenanalyse*, pp. 56–72, Tübingen: J.C.B. Mohr.

Atkinson, A.B. and Jenkins, S.P. (1984), 'The Steady-State Assumption and the Estimation of Distributional and Related Models', *Journal of Human Resources*, **19**, (3), 358–76.

Atkinson, A.B., Maynard, A.K. and Trinder, C.G. (1983), *Parents and Children: Incomes in Two Generations*, London: Heinemann.

Atoda, N. and Tachibinaki, T. (1980), 'Earnings Distribution and Inequality over Time' (*Kyoto Institute of Economic Research Discussion Papers, 144*).

Australian Bureau of Statistics (1984), *Household Expenditure Survey*, Canberra.

Australian Bureau of Statistics (1988), *Income Distribution Survey*, Canberra.

Beach, C., with Cardi, D.E. and Flatters, F. (1981), *The Distribution of Income and Wealth in Ontario: Theory and Evidence*, Toronto: University of Toronto Press.

Benus, J. and Morgan, J.N. (1974), 'Time Period, Unit of Analysis and Income Concept in the Analysis of Income Distribution', in J.D. Smith (ed.), *The Personal Distribution of Income and Wealth*, pp. 209–29, New York: National Bureau of Economic Research.

Berger, M. (1985), 'The Effect of Cohort Size on Earnings Growth: a Reconsideration of the Evidence', *Journal of Political Economy*, **93**, 561–73.

Blanchflower, D.G. and Oswald, A.J. (1987), 'Internal and External Influences upon Pay Settlements: New Survey Evidence', mimeo.

Blaug, M. (1976), 'The Empirical Status of Human Capital Theory: A Slightly Jaundiced Survey', *Journal of Economic Literature*, **14**, 352–65.

Blinder, A.S. (1974), *Towards an Economic Theory of Income Distribution*, Cambridge, Mass.: MIT University Press.

Blinder, A.S. (1975), 'Distribution Effects and the Aggregate Consumption Function', *Journal of Political Economy*, **83**, 447–75.

Blomquist, N.S. (1981a), 'A Comparison of Distributions of Annual and Lifetime Income: Sweden around 1970', *Review of Income and Wealth*, **27**, 243–64.

Blomquist, N.S. (1981b), 'The Distribution of Lifetime Income: a Case Study of Sweden', in N.A. Klevmarken and J.A. Lybeck (eds), *The Statics and Dynamics of Income*, pp. 105–33, Bristol: Tieto.

Borjas, G.J. (1981), 'Job Mobility and Earnings over the Life-cycle', *Industrial and Labour Relations Review*, **34**, 365–76.

Bös, D. (1980), 'The Democratic Decision on Fees versus Taxes', *Kyklos*, **33**, 76–99.

Bowley, A.L. (1915), *The Measurement of Social Phenomena*, London: P.S. King and Son.

Bowley, A.L. (1935), 'The Occupations of Fathers and Their Children', *Economica*, **2**, (N.S. 8), 400–7.

Buchanan, J. (1967), *Public Finance in Democratic Process*, Chapel Hill: University of North Carolina Press.

Buchanan, J. and Forte, F. (1964), 'Fiscal Choice through Time: a Case for Indirect Taxation', *National Tax Journal*, **17**, 144–57.

Burkhauser, R.V. and Wilkinson, J.T. (1983), 'The Effect of Retirement on Income Distribution: a Comprehensive Income Approach', *Review of Economics and Statistics*, **65**, 653–8.

Burkhauser, R.V., Butler, J.S. and Wilkinson, J.T. (1986), 'Estimating Changes in Well-being across Life: a Realised vs. Comprehensive Income Approach', in M. David and T. Smeeding (eds), *Horizontal Equity, Uncertainty and*

Economic Well-Being, pp. 69–90, Chicago: University of Chicago Press for National Bureau of Economic Research.

Carlton, D.W. and Hall, R.E. (1978), 'The Distribution of Permanent Income', in Z. Griliches, W. Krelle, H.J. Krupp and O. Kyn (eds), *Income Distribution and Economic Inequality*, pp. 103–12, New York: Halsted Press.

Carpenter, M.D., Lange, D.R., Shannon, D.S. and Stevens, W.T. (1986), 'Methodologies for Valuing Lost Earnings: a Review, a Criticism and a Recommendation', *Journal of Risk and Insurance*, **53**, 104–18.

Chinloy (1980), 'Sources of Quality Change in Labour Input', *American Economic Review*, **70**, 108–19.

Coe, R.D. (1976), 'The Sensitivity of the Incidence of Poverty to Different Measures of Income: School-aged Children and Families', in G.J. Duncan and J.N. Morgan (eds), *Five Thousand American Families*, IV, pp. 357–409, Ann Arbor: Institute for Social Research.

Cohen, A.I., Parnes, H.S. and Shea, J.R. (1974), 'Income Instability among Young and Middle-aged Men', in J.D. Smith (ed.), *The Personal Distribution of Income and Wealth*, pp. 151–218, New York: National Bureau of Economic Research.

Cole, R.E. (1979), *Work, Mobility and Participation*, Berkeley: University of California Press.

Connolly, R. (1986), 'A Framework of Analyzing the Impact of Cohort Size on Education and Labour Earnings', *Journal of Human Resources*, **21**, 543–62.

Cowell, F.A. (1975), 'On the Estimation of a Lifetime Income – a Correction', *Journal of the American Statistical Association*, **70**, 588–9.

Cowell, F.A. (1979), 'The Definition of Lifetime Income' (*University of Wisconsin, Institute for Research in Poverty, Discussion Paper, 566*).

Cowell, F.A. (1984), 'The Structure of American Income Inequality', *Review of Income and Wealth*, **30**, 351–75.

Creedy, J. (1974), 'Earnings in Chemistry: Past and Present', *Chemistry in Britain*, **10**, 50–3.

Creedy, J. (1985), *Dynamics of Income Distribution*, Oxford: Basil Blackwell.

Creedy, J. and Disney, R. (1985), *Social Insurance in Transition: An Economic Analysis*, Oxford: Oxford University Press.

Creedy, J. and Disney, R. (1989a), 'Can We Afford to Grow Older? Population Ageing and Social Security', *European Economic Review*, **33**, 367–76.

Creedy, J. and Disney, R. (1989b), 'The Australian State Pension Scheme: Some Basic Analytics', *Economic Record*, **65**, 357–68.

Creedy, J. and Gemmell (1984), 'Income Redistribution through Taxes and Transfers in Britain', *Scottish Journal of Political Economy*, **31**, 44–59.

Creedy, J. and Hart, P.E. (1979), 'Age and the Distribution of Earnings', *Economic Journal*, **89**, 280–93.

Creedy, J. and McDonald, I.M. (1988), 'Income Tax Changes and Trade Union Wage Demands' (*University of Melbourne: Department of Economics Research Paper, 201*).

Creedy, J. and McDonald, I.M. (1992), 'Union Wage Responses to a Shift from Direct to Indirect Taxation', *Bulletin of Economic Research* (forthcoming).

Creedy, J., Hart, P.E. and Klevmarken, A. (1981a), 'Income Mobility in Great Britain and Sweden', in A. Klevmarken and J.A. Lybeck (eds), *The Statics and Dynamics of Earnings*, pp. 195–211, Bristol: Tieto.

Creedy, J., Hart, P.E., Jonsson, A. and Klevmarken, A. (1981b), 'Cohort Incomes in Sweden 1960–1973', in A. Klevmarken and J.A. Lybeck (eds), *The Statics and Dynamics of Earnings*, pp. 55–80, Bristol: Tieto.

Denison, E.F. (1984), 'Accounting for Slower Growth: An Update', in J. Kendrick (ed.), *International Comparisons of Productivity and Causes of the Slowdown*, Cambridge, Mass.: Ballinger.

Doeringer, P.B. and Piore, M.J. (1971), *Internal Labour Markets and Manpower Analysis*, Lexington: D.C. Heath.

Dooley, M. (1985), 'Changes in the Relationship among Earnings, Education and Age for Canadian Men 1971–1981' (*McMaster University, Department of Economics Working Paper, 85–17*).

Dooley, M. and Gottschalk, P. (1984), 'Earnings Inequality among US Males: Trends and the Effect of Labour Force Growth', *Journal of Political Economy*, **92**, 59–89.

Draft White Paper (1985), *Reform of the Australian Tax System*, Canberra.

Eden, B. and Pakes, A. (1981), 'On Measuring the Variance-Age Profile of Lifetime Earnings', *Review of Economics Studies*, **48**, 285–394.

Fase, M.M.G. (1971), 'On the Estimation of Lifetime Income', *Journal of the American Statistical Association*, **66**, 686–92.

Fisher, M.R. (1956), 'Explorations in Savings Behaviour', *Oxford Bulletin of Economics and Statistics*, **18**, 201–77.

Foster, C. (1988), *Towards a National Retirement Incomes Policy* (Social Security Review Issues Paper, 6), Canberra: Department of Social Security.

Friedman, M. (1957), *A Theory of the Consumption Function*, Princeton: Princeton University Press.

Friesen, P.H. (1986), 'Distortion of the Trend of Inequality by the Life-cycle Profile of Incomes', *Review of Economics and Statistics*, **68**, 170–4.

Friesen, P.H. and Miller, D. (1983), 'Annual Inequality and Lifetime Inequality', *Quarterly Journal of Economics*, **98**, 139–55.

Galton, F. (1889), *Natural Inheritance*, London: Macmillan.

Garvy, G. (1952), 'Inequality of Income: Causes and Measurement', in *Conference on Research in Income and Wealth*, pp. 25–47, New York: National Bureau of Economic Research.

Glenn, N.D. (1977), *Cohort Analysis*, Beverley Hills: Sage Publications.

Grosse, S. and Morgan, J.N. (1981), 'Intertemporal variability in income and the interpersonal distribution of economic welfare', in G.J. Duncan and J.N. Morgan (eds), *Five Thousand American Families*, XI, pp. 297–315, Ann Arbor: Institute for Social Research.

Gruen, F.H. (1985), 'Australian Government Policy on Retirement Incomes', *Economic Record*, **61**, 213–21.

Hamermesh, D.S. (1985), 'Expectations, Life Expectancy and Economic Behaviour', *Quarterly Journal of Economics*, **100**, 398–408.

Hancock, K. and Richardson, S. (1985), 'Discount Rates and the Distribution of Lifetime Earnings', *Journal of Human Resources*, **20**, 346–60.

Hanna, F.A. (1948), 'The Accounting Period and the Distribution of Income', in F.A. Hana, J.A. Pechman and S.M. Lerner (eds), *Analysis of Wisconsin Income*, New York: National Bureau of Economic Research.

Harbury, C. and McMahon (1973), 'Inheritance and the Characteristics of Top Wealth Leavers in Britain', *Economic Journal*, **83** (September), 810–33.

Hare, P.G. and Ulph, D.T. (1982), 'Imperfect Capital Markets and the Public Provision of Education', in M.J. Bowman (ed.), *Collective Choice in Education*, pp. 103–30, The Hague: Martinus Nijhoff.

Harris, W.G. (1977), 'Selecting Income Growth and Discount Rates in Wrongful Death and Injury Cases: Comment', *Journal of Risk and Insurance*, **44**, 117–32.

Heckman, J.J. and Robb, R. (1983), 'Using Longitudinal Data to Estimate Age, Period, and Cohort Effects in Earnings Equations', in S. Feinberg and W. Mason (eds), *Analysing Longitudinal Data for Age, Period and Cohort Effects*, New York: Academic Press.

Heien, D.M. (1972), 'Demographic Effects and the Multiperiod Consumption Period', *Journal of Political Economy*, **80**, 125–38.

Heller, P.S., Hemming, R. and Kohnert, P.W. (1986), *Ageing and Social Expenditure in the Major Industrial Countries 1980–2025* (Occasional paper 47), Washington, DC: International Monetary Fund.

Henman, B. (1978), 'Remuneration for Responsibility', *Chemistry in Britain*, **14**, (4), 157–9.

Hersoug, T. (1984), 'Union Wage Response to Tax Changes', *Oxford Economic Papers*, **36**, 37–51.

Hoffman, S. and Podder, N. (1976), 'Income Inequality', in G.J. Duncan and J.N. Morgan (eds), *Five Thousand American Families*, IV, pp. 319–41, Ann Arbor: Institute for Social Research.

Hunter, L.C. and Reid, G.L. (1968), *Urban Working Mobility*, Paris: Organization for Economic Cooperation and Development.

Irvine, I.J. (1980), 'The Distribution of Income and Wealth in Canada in a Lifetime Framework', *Canadian Journal of Economics*, **13**, 455–74.

Irvine, I.J. (1981), 'The Use of Cross-section Microdata in Life Cycle Models: an Application to Inequality Theory in

Nonstationary Economies', *Quarterly Journal of Economics*, **96**, 301–16.

Jaques, E. (1956), *Measurement of Responsibility*, London: Tavistock.

Jaques, E. (1961), *Equitable Payment*, London: Heinemann.

Jenkins, S.P. (1982), 'Tools for the Analysis of Distributional Models', *Manchester School*, **50**, (2), 139–50.

Jenkins, S.P. (1986), 'Snapshots versus Movies: "Lifecycle Biases" and the Estimation of Intergenerational Earnings Inheritance', *European Economic Review*, **31**, 1149–58.

Johnson, G.E. (1984), 'Subsidies for Higher Education', *Journal of Labour Economics*, **2**, (3), 303–18.

Johnson, W.R. (1977), 'The Measurement and Trend of Inequality: Comment', *American Economic Review*, **67**, 42–53.

Jorgenson, D.W. (1984), 'The Contribution of Education to US Economic Growth, 1948–1973', in E. Dean (ed.), *Education and Economic Productivity*, Cambridge, Mass.: Ballinger.

Kay, J.A. and Morris, C.N. (1979), 'Direct and Indirect Taxes; Some Effects of the 1979 Budget', *Fiscal Studies*, **1**, 1–10.

Kendrick, J.W. (1983), *Inter-industry Differences in Productivity Growth*, Washington, DC: American Enterprise Institute.

Klevmarken, A. and Quigley, J.M. (1976), 'Age, Experience, Earnings and Investment in Human Capital', *Journal of Political Economy*, **84**, 47–72.

Kravis, I. (1962), *The Structure of Income*, Pennsylvania: University of Pennsylvania Press.

Kurien, C.J. (1977), 'The Measurement and Trend of Inequality: A Comment', *American Economic Review*, **67**, 517–19.

Kuznets, S. (1950), *Shares of Upper Income Groups in Income and Savings*, New York: National Bureau of Economic Research.

Lansberger, M. (1970), 'The Life Cycle Hypothesis: A Reinterpretation and Empirical Test', *American Economic Review*, **60**, 175–84.

Larsen, N.L. and Martin, G.D. (1981), 'Income Growth Factors: Error Introduced through the Application of Cohort Data', *Journal of Risk and Insurance*, **48**, 143–8.

Layard, R. (1977), 'On Measuring the Redistribution of Lifetime Income', in M.S. Feldstein and R.P. Inman (eds), *The Economics of Public Services*, pp. 45–72, London: Macmillan.

Le Grand, J. (1987), 'Three Essays on Equity' (*Suntory Toyota International Centre for Economics and Related Disciplines, WSP/23*).

Lillard, L.A. (1977), 'Inequality: Earnings vs. Human Wealth', *American Economic Review*, **67**, 42–53.

Lindbeck, A. and Snower, D. (1986), 'Wage-setting, Unemployment and Insider–Outsider Relations', *American Economic Review, Papers and Proceedings*, **76**, 235–9.

Luntz, H. (1990), *Assessment of Damages for Personal Injury and Death*, London: Butterworths.

Lydall, H. (1968), *The Structure of Earnings*, Oxford: Oxford University Press.

Majumdar, T. (1983), *Investment in Education and Social Choice*, Cambridge: Cambridge University Press.

McDonald, I.M. and Solow, R.M. (1981), 'Wage Bargaining and Employment', *American Economic Review*, **71**, 896–908.

McMahon, W.W. (1984), 'The Relation of Education and R&D to Productivity Growth', *Economics of Education Review*, **3**, (4), 299–313.

Minarik, J.J. (1977), 'The Measurement and Trend of Inequality: Comment', *American Economic Review*, **67**, 513–16.

Modigliani, F. (1986), 'Life Cycle, Individual Thrift and the Wealth of Nations', *American Economic Review*, **76**, 297–313.

Modigliani, F. and Ando, A. (1957), 'Tests of the Life Cycle Hypothesis of Savings: Comments and Suggestions', *Oxford Bulletin of Economics and Statistics*, **19**, 99–124.

Mookherjee, D. and Shorrocks, A.F. (1982), 'A Decomposition Analysis of the Trend in UK Income Inequality', *Economic Journal*, **92**, 886–902.

Moon, M. (1977), *The Measurement of Economic Welfare: Its Application to the Aged Poor*, New York: Academic Press.

Mukatis, W.A. and Widicus, W. (1986), 'Towards Just Compensation: A Statistical Comparison of the Total Offset Method of Valuing Lost Future Earnings Awards and United States Supreme Court Methods', *Temple Law Quarterly*, **59**, 1131–58.

Murray, J. (1964), 'Potential Income from Assets: Findings of the 1963 Survey of the Aged', *Social Security Bulletin*, December, 3–11.

Nagatani, K. (1972), 'Life Cycle Saving: Theory and Fact', *American Economic Review*, **62**, 344–53.

Nelson, E.R. (1977), 'The Measurement and Trend of Inequality: A Comment', *American Economic Review*, **67**, 497–501.

Nieswiadomy, M. and Slottje, D.J. (1987a), 'Estimating Lost Wage and Pension Income Using the Worklife Tables' (*SMU Working Paper, 8528*).

Nieswiadomy, M. and Slottje, D.J. (1987b), *A Comment on Using Alter and Becker's Method for Estimating Lost Future Earnings* (SMU Working Paper, 8527).

Nordhaus, W. (1973), 'The Effects of Inflation on the Distribution of Economic Welfare', *Journal of Money, Credit and Banking*, **5**, 465–508.

OECD (1988), *Ageing Populations: The Social Policy Implications*, Paris: OECD.

Okun, A.M. (1981), *Prices and Quantities: A Macroeconomic Analysis*, Oxford: Basil Blackwell.

Oswald, A.J. (1982), 'The Microeconomics Theory of the Trade Union', *Economic Journal*, **92**, 576–95.

Oswald, A.J. (1986), 'The Economic Theory of Trade Unions: an Introductory Survey', *Scandinavian Journal of Economics*, **87**, 160–93.

Paglin, M. (1975), 'The Measurement and Trend of Inequality: A Basic Revision', *American Economic Review*, **65**, 598–609.

Pissarides, C.A. (1978), 'Liquidity Considerations in the Theory of Consumption', *Quarterly Journal of Economics*, **92**, 279–96.

Prais, S.J. (1977), *Evaluating the Importance of Inheritance – a Diagrammatic Approach* (National Institute of Economic and Social Research, mimeo).

Prest, A.R. (1970), 'Some Redistributional Aspects of the National Superannuation Scheme', *Three Banks Review*, **86**, 3–22.

Prest, A.R. and Stark, T. (1967), *Some Aspects of Income Distribution in the UK since World War II*, Manchester: Manchester Statistical Society.

Psacharopoulos, G. (1973), *Returns to Education*, New York: American Elsevier.

Psacharopoulos, G. (1984), 'The Contribution of Education to Economic Growth', in J.W. Kendrick (ed.), *International*

Comparisons of Productivity and Causes of the Slowdown, Cambridge, Mass.: Ballinger.

Royal Commission on the Distribution of Income and Wealth (1975), *Report No. 1 Initial Report for the Standing Reference*, London: HMSO (Cmnd. 6171).

Royal Society of Chemistry (1983), *Remuneration Survey 1983*, London: RSC.

Sampson, A.A. (1986), 'The Shift to Indirect Taxation in a Unionised Economy', *Bulletin of Economic Research*, **38**, 87–91.

Schultz, T.W. (1963), *The Economic Value of Education*, New York: Columbia University Press.

Schultz, T.W. (1981), *Investing in People*, Los Angeles: University of California Press.

Shorrocks, A.F. (1978), 'Income Inequality and Income Mobility', *Journal of Economic Theory*, **19**, 376–93.

Simon, H. (1957), 'The Compensation of Executives', *Sociometry*, **20**, (1), 32–45.

Solow, R.M. (1985), 'Insiders and Outsiders in Wage Determination', *Scandinavian Journal of Economics*, **87**, 411–28.

Soltow, L. (1965), *Towards Income Equality in Norway*, Madison, Wisc.: University of Wisconsin Press.

Steinberg, E. (1977), 'Measuring Income Inequality with Extended Earnings Periods', *Monthly Labour Review*, June.

Stoikow, V. (1975), 'How Misleading are Income Distributions?', *Review of Income and Wealth*, **21**, 239–50.

Strotz, R.H. (1956), 'Myopia and Inconsistency in Dynamic Utility Maximisation', *Review of Economic Studies*, **23**, 165–80.

Summers, L.H. (1981), 'Capital Taxation and Consumption in a Life Cycle Growth Model', *American Economic Review*, **17**, 533–44.

Taussig, M.K. (1973), *Alternative Measures of the Distribution of Economics Welfare* (Research Report 116), Princeton University Press.

Thurow, L.C. (1969), 'The Optimal Lifetime Distribution of Consumption Expenditures', *American Economic Review*, **59**, 324–30.

Thurow, L.C. (1983), *Dangerous Currents: The State of Economics*, Oxford: Oxford University Press.

Tuck, R.H. (1954), *An Essay on the Economic Theory of Rank*, Oxford: Basil Blackwell.

Ulph, A.M. and Ulph, D.T. (1988), 'Union Bargaining – a Survey of Recent Work' (*University of Southampton Department of Economics Discussion Papers*).

Vandome, P. (1958), 'Aspects of the Dynamics of Consumer Behaviour', *Oxford Bulletin of Economics and Statistics*, **20**, 65–105.

Warren, N. (1990), 'Indirect Taxes, Tax Mix and Tax Equity', in J.G. Head and R. Krever (eds), *Flattening the Tax Rate Scale*, pp. 363–86, Melbourne: Longman.

Weber, W. (1970), 'The Effect of Interest Rates on Aggregate Consumption', *American Economic Review*, **60**, 591–600.

Weisbrod, B. and Hansen, W. (1968), 'An Income Net-worth Approach to Measuring Economic Welfare', *American Economic Review*, **58**, 1315–29.

Weiss, Y. and Lillard, L.A. (1978), 'Experience, Vintage and Time Effects in the Growth of Earnings', *Journal of Political Economy*, **86**, 427–47.

Weizsäcker, C.C. von (1978), 'Annual Income, Lifetime Income and Other Income Concepts in Measuring Income Distribution', in W.H. Kelle and A.F. Shorrocks (eds), *Personal Income Distribution*, pp. 101–5, Amsterdam: North Holland.

Welch, F. (1979), 'Effects of Cohort Size on Earnings: The Baby Boom Babies' Financial Bust', *Journal of Political Economy*, **87**, 565–97.

Wertz, K.L. (1979), 'The Measurement of Inequality: Comment', *American Economic Review*, **69**, 670–2.

White, B.B. (1978), 'Empirical Tests of the Life Cycle Hypothesis', *American Economic Review*, **68**, 547–60.

Whitfield, K. (1983), 'Occupational Labour Market Structures', DPhil. thesis, Oxford University.

Wolfson, M.C. (1979), 'Wealth and the Distribution of Income, Canada 1969–70', *The Review of Income and Wealth*, **25**, 129–40.

Yaari, M.E. (1964), 'On the Consumer's Lifetime Allocation Process', *International Economic Review*, **5**, 304–17.

Index